St. Teresa of Avila

The Way of Perfection

A Study Edition

St. Teresa of Avila

The Way of Perfection

Translated by Kieran Kavanaugh, O.C.D.
and Otilio Rodriguez, O.C.D.

A Study Edition
Prepared by Kieran Kavanaugh, O.C.D.

ICS Publications
Institute of Carmelite Studies
Washington, D.C.
2000

ICS Publications
2131 Lincoln Road NE
Washington, DC 20002–1199
800-832-8489
www.icspublications.org

Typeset by Stephen Tiano Graphic Design/Editing Services

Cover design by Nancy Gurganus of Grey Coat Graphics

Typeset and produced in the U.S.A.

Library of Congress Cataloging-in-Publication Data

Teresa of Avila, Saint, 1515–1582.
   [Camino de perfección. English]
   The way of perfection / St. Teresa of Avila; translated by
Kieran Kavanaugh and Otilio Rodriguez.—Study ed. /
prepared by Kieran Kavanaugh.
     p. cm.
   Includes bibliographical references and index.
   ISBN: 0–935216–70–7 (pbk.)
   1. Perfection—Religious aspects—Catholic Church. 2. God—
Worship and love. I. Kavanaugh, Kieran, 1928- II. Rodriguez,
Otilio. III. Title.
BX2179.T4 C313   2000
248.8'943—dc21   00–022378
                                         CIP

Table of Contents

Preface to the Study Edition
of *The Way of Perfection*

THE WAY OF PERFECTION is a title that would attract few people today. We prefer that old adage, "No one's perfect." If this book after four centuries enjoys such popularity, the title must have little to do with it. Teresa herself did not give her book a name. She thought of it as a book of counsels and advice about prayer, and the life of prayer, presented in a familiar tone and destined for the few nuns who had embraced the form of Carmelite life established by her in Avila. It gave the nuns the spirituality that lay behind their constitutions and rule. It was Teresa's handbook for initial and ongoing spiritual formation.

Despite the limited number of destinees envisioned by Teresa, the book over the centuries has become a classic on prayer, the appeal of which stretches far beyond the walls of the Carmelite monastery. More and more *The Way of Perfection* is speaking to those interested in prayer, in need of education for contemplation, and provides them with basic teaching on what they are about in prayer and how to avoid potential pitfalls. As the readership and interest grow, so does the need for some helps in working with the text.

The principles and teachings in Teresa's work, presented within limited horizons, lend themselves easily enough to broader applications and can work well in all walks of life. In this study edition, I have tried to provide the kind of information I think will assist readers to mine the spiritual riches contained in the text.

Following each chapter is a *chapter review* in which the reader can run through the general thrust of the text just finished and note summarily the progress of Teresa's thought and its principal ideas. Each chapter will be placed in the context of the entire work, with the result also that the numerous digressions will less likely cause one to lose the thread of the whole.

The *interpretive notes* are the kind I would make for myself in preparing a conference on a particular chapter. What interests us first is any light that Teresa herself might shed on the text in her other writings, which also contain doctrine and experience. In certain matters Teresa has her own lexicon; her terms call for clarification. The historical and social situations in which she found herself are often essential factors in coming to any, or at least a better, understanding of her words. Sometimes the notes and deletions of her censors have influenced the text, and it can be helpful to know what was going on behind the scenes here. Since Teresa had strong desires that her writings be in harmony with Scripture, I have pointed out some traditional scriptural texts that stand behind or support various ideas. In addition, present-day teachings of the church can show the correctness of Teresa's basic notions, but also advise us how to apply such principles in our times.

Neither the chapter review nor the interpretive notes can substitute for Teresa's written word. If they have a value, it will lie in their leading us back to the text with more understanding. The *questions for discussion* will force us to go back to the text—to reflect on it, find inspiration in it, and apply it to our lives. Although an individual reader may want to work alone with the questions, they presuppose a group studying and discussing the book together. Sometimes the questions will have definite answers that can be found in the text, sometimes they will do no more than promote an exchange of ideas and perspectives, and sometimes they will encourage mutual sharing and support for the life of prayer. But a group need not bind itself to the questions. It often happens that discussions lead off in their own way to different concerns and insights that respond more appropriately to the needs and interests of the group. The questions are not a straitjacket.

The introduction I wrote for this book contains important background information. For the most part in the present interpretive notes I have avoided repetition of what I wrote there. Worth mentioning again, though, is that there are two redactions or drafts of this work. The first draft written by Teresa is called *Escorial* and the second, *Valladolid.* The text used in this edition is *Valladolid.* The passages appearing in brackets are passages from *Escorial* omitted by Teresa in *Valladolid* for various reasons.

I thank Marc Foley, O.C.D., particularly for reading my manuscript and helping me see places where more needed to be said or statements needed further clarification. I am also grateful to Michael Dodd, O.C.D., for proofreading, to Regis Jordan, O.C.D., for preparing the index, and to Stephen Tiano, for the page design and layout. Especially valuable in the preparation of this guide were the "Lecturas teresianas: "Camino de Perfección" by Tomás Alvarez, O.C.D., that appeared in issues of *Teresa de Jesús* from 1984 to 1993.

KIERAN KAVANAUGH, O.C.D.
Carmelite Monastery
Washington, D.C.

Abbreviations

The following abbreviations will be used in references to Teresa's works:

IC=*The Interior Castle*
F=*The Book of Her Foundations*
L=*The Book of Her Life*
M=*Meditations on the Song of Songs*
S=*Soliloquies*
ST=*Spiritual Testimonies*
W=*The Way of Perfection*

Principal divisions, such as chapters and numbers, are separated by a period; references to several parts within the same major division (e.g., several numbers within the same chapter) are separated by a comma. An initial Roman numeral is used to indicate the "dwelling places" in references to *The Interior Castle*. Thus "IC VI.7.8, 9" refers to *The Interior Castle*, sixth "dwelling places," seventh chapter, numbers 8 and 9, while "W 1.2" refers to the second number in the first chapter of *The Way of Perfection*.

Unless otherwise noted, all quotations from St. Teresa of Avila are taken from *The Collected Works of St. Teresa of Avila*, trans. Kieran Kavanaugh, O.C.D., and Otilio Rodriguez, O.C.D., 3 vols. (Washington, D.C.: ICS Publications, 1976–1985).

Introduction

Origins

IN THE LAST FIVE CHAPTERS of her *Life*, St. Teresa describes the unusual events that surrounded her first foundation of a monastery for nuns. These chapters were added in her revision of this work and were written when she was already living in the new monastery called St. Joseph's.[1] Her confessor at the time was the Dominican theologian Domingo Báñez, who was a professor of theology at St. Thomas College in Avila. But it was another Dominican friar, García de Toledo, for whom she wrote her *Life*. Because he was anxious to have it, she sent her final version to him without taking time to read it over.[2] This account of her life dealing with so many personal matters and such unusual and sublime mystical experiences passed, a few months later, into the hands of Báñez. Though the work contained excellent doctrine about contemplative prayer, he nonetheless shunned the thought of allowing it to be circulated among nuns or others interested in the subject.

Having got word of this work written by their Mother Foundress, the nuns at St. Joseph's were understandably curious and eager to read it. Teresa herself did not share her confessor's misgivings and thought the book could be read profitably by those who were favored with passive prayer.[3] But since Báñez refused to hear of this and even threatened to throw the manuscript into the fire, the nuns pressed Teresa to write another work just for them about prayer. The learned Dominican was more receptive to this idea, and he allowed Teresa to "write some things about prayer."[4] The nuns themselves, in addition to Báñez's general permission, made their own specific requests about the subject matter. Some of them were eager to learn about contemplation and even perfect contemplation. Others, apparently frightened by the thought of such elevated topics, asked for simpler themes such as how to recite vocal prayer.[5] In any event, Teresa wrote *The Way of Perfection* for her nuns and with their requests and needs in mind; and she therefore dialogues with them throughout the work.

In Teresa's view, her response to the Sisters' urgings was like an act of obedience; "I have decided to obey them,"[6] she says. And when at different times she begins to sense the lack of order in the way she is proceeding, she comforts herself with the thought that she is writing for her Sisters, in obedience to them, and that they will not mind. At one point in the middle of her work, she moans in complete dissatisfaction over the jumbled way the material is being treated: "But what disorder in the way I write! Really, it's as though the work were done by one who doesn't know what she's doing. The fault is yours, Sisters, because you are the ones who ordered me to write this. Read it as best you can, for I am writing it as best I can. And if you find that it is all wrong, burn it—Time is necessary to do the work well, and I have so little as you see, for eight days must have gone by in which I haven't written anything. So I forget what I have said and also what I was going to say."[7]

When she comes to the conclusion of her work, Teresa summarizes briefly the subject matter she dealt with: "how one reaches this fount of living water, what the soul feels there, how God satisfies it,"[8] and so on. She then implies that she has thought of this book as an introduction to her *Life* by asserting that those who have reached the fount of living water will find her *Life* very beneficial and receive much light from it.[9]

At the outset, Teresa tells of her intention to submit her work to a theologian for censorship before turning it over to any of her nuns to read. For reasons we do not know, the censor was not Báñez, the person she mentions,[10] but García de Toledo. Less severe as a censor than his Dominican confrere would probably have been, García de Toledo nonetheless performed his task diligently, making in all about fifty corrections. Some of them concerned trifles, but others were more extensive and amounted to canceling entire pages. He obviously had a clear grasp of the polemics underlying a number of the topics that were discussed. Though posterity can be grateful to him for not having consigned the book to the flames, as Teresa suggested he might if it did not meet with his approval, the number of corrections did call for a cautious revision of the whole work.

Leaving the prologue almost intact, including the reference to Báñez as the possible censor, Teresa amended the problematical passages and conformed them to the censor's opinion. In addition, she elaborated on some doctrinal matters and toned down many of the more spontaneous and confidential assertions and some of the subtle irony that flowed from her pen. Her second version also manifests a decided effort to write more legibly, as though the censor might have complained of difficulty in reading the text.

Teresa probably wrote her first redaction of *The Way of Perfection* in 1566, the year after she had completed her *Life*. Although some have thought the work was composed between 1562 and 1564, it seems from internal evidence, such as her references to Báñez and to her *Life*, that the date would more likely be 1566.[11]

The year in which she actually composed her second version of *The Way of Perfection* is also a matter for debate. Almost unanimously, historians of the past set 1569 as the date of composition. They established their opinion on the testimony given by a young novice from the monastery of Toledo. The worth of this testimony has been recently challenged, and the date suggested is 1566.[12] Thus Teresa would have undertaken the task as soon as the censored manuscript had been returned to her. This opinion is based on her failure to allude to any new Carmels founded by her or to the missionary spirit she received from the enthusiastic Franciscan missionary Fr. Alonso Maldonado in the autumn of 1566 after his return from the Indies.

This second version of *The Way of Perfection* was censored again by García de Toledo as well as by another censor whose identity is unknown. Neither of them made cancellations or observations that required any major change in the book this time. One passage of the second redaction Teresa herself later modified. It is in chapter 16. In answer to the question whether God might give mystical graces to imperfect souls, Teresa thinks that he would, so as to free them from their imperfections. But she categorically denies that contemplation would ever be granted to someone in mortal sin. In her altered view she simply says: "I want to say, then, that there are times when God will want to grant some great favor to persons who are in a bad state so as to draw them by this means out of the hands of the devil." [13]

The Autographs

Happily the two autographs of *The Way of Perfection* censored by García de Toledo are still conserved. The first is on display in the royal library of the Escorial and the second is kept in the monastery of the Carmelite nuns in Valladolid, one of Teresa's own foundations. The first manuscript, referred to as "Escorial," begins with a prologue and continues without any division into chapters, although Teresa did indicate where she desired that a chapter begin. There are seventy-two chapters and the headings of these are written in the back of the book in Teresa's hand.

Since the length of some of the chapters in the Valladolid manuscript was increased, there are, in all, only forty-two chapters. Knowing now that this work would be read by others besides her Sisters at St. Joseph's, and also, as was said, in response to the remarks of the censors, Teresa suppressed some of the material. But in other areas she enlarged upon the matter being discussed and developed her ideas further; for example, this is seen in the important matter of the prayer of recollection and quiet.

The autograph of Valladolid is the work approved by the Dominican censor, and the text that was circulated in the new Carmels. The copies made of Valladolid, however, were not always carefully done. Two of the copies, which were reviewed, corrected, and annotated by Teresa herself, are conserved today in the monasteries of the Carmelite nuns in Salamanca and Madrid.

Historical Context

In sixteenth-century Spain, political events were closely tied to religious ideas. What was happening in the world at large, particularly in Spain and in other parts of Europe, left its traces on Teresa's works. What was happening in the little world of the monastery of the Incarnation also left its mark on Teresa and her writings. An understanding of some of these events enlivens many of the pages of her treatises on prayer.

Reflecting on the final experiences of which Teresa writes in her *Life*, the reader is left with the notion that the Castilian Saint was living more among the church triumphant of heaven than the church of this earth. She beholds the glorious risen Christ, the Blessed Virgin Mary, the saints, and the angels. In an extraordinary vision of the angels, she experiences the glory of heaven within herself, though she does not see the Divinity clearly."[14] How much she was living in heaven is reflected in her following thoughts: "These revelations helped me very much, I think, in coming to know our true country and realizing that we are pilgrims here below.... It happens to me sometimes that those who I know live there are my companions and the ones in whom I find comfort; it seems to me that they are the ones who are truly alive and that those who live here on earth are so dead that not even the whole world, I think, affords me company, especially when I experience those impulses."[15] All of this in addition to the painful longings of love that she felt caused her to surmise that she would soon die.[16]

The first chapter of *The Way of Perfection*, however, reveals a Teresa very much back on earth, keenly distraught over the afflicted church. "At that time news reached me of the harm being done in France and of the havoc the Lutherans had caused and how much this miserable sect was growing. The news distressed me greatly, and, as though I could do something or were something, I wept with the Lord and begged him that I might remedy so much evil."[17] What had occurred is that some harsh rumors had reached Teresa, but her remarks show that her knowledge of the facts was vague. It must be remembered that her references to the Lutherans in France represent her hazy way of speaking of Protestantism and demonstrate neither historical nor geographical precision. The unhappy news that had spread even to the enclosure of St. Joseph's concerned the religious war between the Catholics and the Huguenots. Teresa's stereotyped remarks reflect the way the ordinary people in Spain probably commented on the news. "Churches were being destroyed, the Blessed Sacrament taken away, many priests were being lost."[18]

In Teresa's mind the church and Christianity were identical. The attack of "those Lutherans" was an attack against Christianity, she thought. Nowhere in this work does she use the qualifier "Catholic" to designate the members of the church or the church itself. Moreover the relationship between her mystical life and the church, both in its ministry and its sufferings, was inseparable. Curiously enough, despite all her locutions, visions, and communications from God, Teresa never received revelations destined for the church as did other saints, such as Bridget of Sweden, Catherine of Siena, and Margaret Mary Alacoque. Her mystical life, rather, consisted of an inner experience of the content of Revelation. While it issued from within the faith, it also brought what was contained in that faith into sharper focus resulting for her in a convinced and powerful awareness of faith's mysteries. Understandably a love of the faith accompanied her experiences and, in addition, moved her to look to the church and Scripture for guidance. In this respect she writes: "And with this love of the faith, which God then infuses and which is strong living faith, it always strives to proceed in conformity with what the church holds, asking of this one and that, as one who has already made a firm assent to these truths." [19] And further on she adds: "For from what I see and know through experience, a locution bears the credentials of being from God if it is in conformity with Sacred Scripture." [20] In her mind, the faith was what the church holds, the truths of Sacred Scripture.

Consequently, in consulting learned men and giving them an account of her spiritual life, Teresa was most of all concerned with whether or not her life and experiences were in agreement with the truths of the Sacred Scriptures. In a general manifestation of her soul, written in 1563 for García de Toledo, she explains with reference to Domingo Báñez: "He was a very spiritual man and a theologian with whom I discussed everything about my soul. And he discussed these matters with other learned men, among whom was Father Mancio. They found that none of my experiences was lacking in conformity with Sacred Scripture. This puts me very much at peace now, although I understand that as long as God leads me by this path I must not trust myself in anything. So I have always consulted others, even though I find it difficult."[21] The learned man, the theologian, is envisioned by Teresa as the spokesman for "what the church holds," a master in "the truths of Sacred Scripture."

Not for the mere sake of fulfilling a formality, then, did Teresa submit her writings. Thus, at the beginning and end of *The Way of Perfection*, she mentions Fr. Báñez as the one who she thinks will take on the task of being her censor; and on two occasions in the course of her work she states her adherence to the faith professed by the church.[22] An interesting aside is that only later, sometime around 1578, when reviewing her text in preparation for its publication, she added the qualifier "Roman." The attestation of faith at the beginning was also inserted at this time. Similar changes were introduced into the *Interior Castle* and the *Book of Foundations*. These factors, it would seem, point to little more than her eagerness for orthodoxy. In her simple view, she finds in "Holy Mother Church" the truths of Revelation, the sacraments, and a family of Christians.

"Don't allow any more harm to come to Christianity, Lord."[23] It was easy to speak of the church as Christianity; just as easily did Teresa feel that what was done against the church was done against Christ, "who is so roughly treated."[24] What might Teresa do to prevent this harm, these "great evils"? She has no use for any recourse to violence. "Human forces are not sufficient to stop the spread of this fire caused by these heretics, even though people have tried to see if with the force of arms they could remedy all the evil that is making such progress. It has seemed to me that what is necessary is a different approach.... For as I have said, it is the ecclesiastical, not the secular, arm that will save us."[25] Now the "ecclesiastical arm" consisted of preachers and theologians; and on the plane of knowledge, they were the ones who must through their learning and words defend the church. This excluded

Teresa. "I realized I was a woman and wretched and incapable of doing any of the useful things I desired to do in the service of the Lord."[26] The result of these reflections, though, was not a surrender to apathy but the resolve "to do the little that was in my power."[27]

This "little" developed into the Teresian ideal: a small group of Christians (in the beginning only eleven or twelve, later increased to fifteen and then to twenty-one), who would be good friends of the Lord by striving to follow the evangelical counsels as closely as possible and living a life of prayer for preachers and theologians, the defenders of the church; thus a life in service of the church, in service of Christ.

But a group of women dedicating themselves to a life of prayer and contemplation in that age and in those circumstances was destined to be looked upon, if not with complete distrust, then at least with caution.[28] The Spanish people in general were officially taught to follow the "level" and "safe" paths of both the ascetical life and vocal prayer and to shun the extraordinary ways of mysticism, especially its accessory phenomena of locutions, visions, and revelations.

In the case of women, the teaching was put forward with greater urgency. And the examples of false women mystics became material for small talk and subtle threat. Moreover, there were the interpretations of genetic laws which claimed that women were a mistake of nature, a kind of unfinished man. The shocking extent to which antifeminism could reach is evident in a passage from a writing by Francisco de Osuna: "Since you see your wife going about visiting many churches, practicing many devotions, and pretending to be a saint, lock the door; and if that isn't sufficient, break her leg if she is young, for she can go to heaven lame from her own house without going around in search of these suspect forms of holiness. It is enough for a woman to hear a sermon and then put it into practice. If she desires more, let a book be read to her while she spins, seated at her husband's side."[29] More than mere jest was involved in a saying of the time that a woman should be allowed to leave the house on only three occasions: once for her baptism, another in order to go to the house of the man she marries, and a third for her burial.

The scholastic theologians themselves were influenced by Aristotle's reasoning that women were guided by their passions rather than by stable judgments. In the processes for Teresa's canonization, Báñez acknowledged his unwillingness to let the writings of women be circulated.[30] And in his official judgment of Teresa's *Life*, he praises her virtues but warns against the many revelations and visions "which are always to be greatly feared, especially in women, who are more inclined to believe that these are from God and to make sanctity consist of them."[31]

The deleterious effects these attitudes may have had on women can be imagined; and as a woman Teresa indeed did feel incapable of much. Nonetheless, her defense of women was so clear and forceful in her first writing of *The Way of Perfection* that the censor intervened, and she felt obliged to omit a large portion in her revision. After pointing out that the Lord found as much love in women as in men, and more faith, while he was on this earth and that the world has so intimidated women that they do not dare do anything worthwhile in public for him or "dare speak some truths that we lament over in secret," she concludes sharply: "Since the world's judges are sons of Adam and all of them men, there is no virtue in women that they do not hold suspect. Yes, indeed, the day will come, my King, when all will be known for what they are. I do not speak for myself, because the world already knows my wickedness and I have rejoiced that this wickedness is known publicly—but because I see that these are times in which it would be wrong to undervalue virtuous and strong souls, even though they are women."[32]

Teresa's small group of women were to become good friends of the Lord, developing this friendship through a life of unceasing prayer as the Carmelite rule prescribed. But over and above their being women, the notion that they were to practice mental prayer also created problems. For both the followers of Erasmus and the *Alumbrados* went to such extremes in urging the practice of mental prayer that they manifested a certain contempt for vocal prayer, including liturgical prayer and other ceremonies and rituals. Whether or not such contempt was indeed a part of the teaching of many of the groups classified as *Alumbrados* is a matter for further research. Archbishop Carranza intimates the possibility of false accusations when he speaks of a person who was accused of being an *Alumbrado* merely for praying before a crucifix.[33] In his defense of mental prayer, Carranza holds that such prayer is more excellent than vocal prayer, but he does not condemn the latter.

Nonetheless, conservative theologians feared that in the practice of mental prayer lay the seeds of Protestantism, which was as dreaded as the plague by both the civil and the ecclesiastical rulers of Spain in the golden age. The Dominican friar Melchior Cano, a theologian at the Council of Trent and consultant to Philip II and to the Inquisition, attacked his fellow Dominican, Archbishop Carranza, and Luis de Granada for promoting the practice of mental prayer among the common people. Fernando Valdés, the Inquisitor General, complained that Luis de Granada was trying to write things about contemplation for mere carpenter's wives.[34] It was Valdés who published in 1559 an Index of forbidden books which included almost all those dealing with prayer.[35] The ordinary people were to be busy maintaining their households. For such people, Mass and vocal prayer were sufficient. Another theologian in this camp, Domingo Soto, confessed that he did not understand how those who were on their knees before the tabernacle for two hours could be thinking of God since God is invisible.[36] And Mancio de Corpus Christi, another theologian at Trent, criticized Carranza for speaking of prayer as though it were a sharing between friends.

This was the skeptical environment in which Teresa founded a monastery of women who would dedicate themselves to a life of prayer, of intimate friendship with God, of living faith and love, the most perfect exemplar of which was, for her, the Blessed Mother, a carpenter's wife. All this mistrust of women is clearly enough implied in Teresa's words: "You will hear some persons frequently making objections: there are dangers; so-and-so went astray by such means; this other one was deceived; another who prayed a great deal fell away; it's harmful to virtue; it's not for women, for they will be susceptible to illusions; it's better they stick to their sewing; they don't need these delicacies; the Our Father and the Hail Mary are sufficient."[37]

With the last statement, however, Teresa was in full agreement. If the Our Father is to be prayed in an authentic manner, it must be joined by mental prayer. Almost as if she were a mother scolding her child, she points accusingly to the senselessness of what was being urged: "Well, what is this, Christians, that you say mental prayer isn't necessary? Do you understand yourselves? Indeed, I don't think you do, and so you desire that we all be misled. You don't know what mental prayer is, or how vocal prayer should be recited, or what contemplation is, for if you did you wouldn't on the one hand condemn what on the other hand you praise."[38] Teresa, here, offers a strong defense of mental prayer, but she exalts vocal prayer, joining it to mental prayer and observing that it may lead one into perfect contemplation.

While insisting that if there is any danger that danger lies in the neglect of mental prayer, she exclaims with enthusiasm: "Hold fast, daughters, for they cannot take from you the Our Father and the Hail Mary."[39] Here the censor, quick to catch the point, intervened and, going a step further from his usual method of simply crossing out a passage, wrote in the margin: "It seems she is reprimanding the Inquisitors for prohibiting books on prayer."[40]

That prayer is a work of the church and particularly efficacious in the case of God's close friends, Teresa is convinced, even though it may be women's prayer. "I trust, my Lord, in these your servants who live here, and I know they desire and strive for nothing else than to please you. For you they renounced the little they had—and would have wanted to have more so as to serve you with it. Since you, my Creator, are not ungrateful, I think you will not fail to do what they beg of you. Nor did you, Lord, when you walked in the world despise women; rather, you always, with great compassion, helped them."[41] The petitions of these souls closely united to Christ, she further observes, are in conformity with him and his Spirit and are granted through his own merits.[42]

This community of women that had come together to live a life of prayer could find support also in the spirit of the Carmelite rule. The hermits of the past who had spent their days in rugged solitude and contemplation on Mount Carmel were to be the group's inspiration.[43] Despite the fact that Teresa did not seem to know about the earlier Carmelite rule written for hermits and approved by Honorius III in 1226, there was for her enough of the eremitical spirit in the rule for Carmelite mendicants approved in 1247 by Innocent IV to lead her to emphasize the practice of solitude through an enclosure and withdrawal from the world greater than that which existed at the Incarnation.[44] Because of the large numbers living in the Incarnation and the penury of the community, the nuns were obliged to spend more time in the company of benefactors both in the monastery and outside in private homes. For similar reasons, in times of sickness they often had to leave their monastery and seek assistance outside. There were other motives as well for which they could easily enough obtain permission to leave the enclosure. Some nuns at the Incarnation desired a stricter observance of enclosure so as to comply with the mandate of the Council of Trent in this regard. But Teresa's appeal was to the eremitical spirit: "For the style of life we aim to follow is not just that of nuns but of hermits."[45] Solitude was important for her small community dedicated to prayer. Thus work in a common room was to be avoided; "silence is better observed when each nun is by herself; and to get used to solitude is a great help for prayer."[46]

Though there is much evidence to attest to the fact that the community of the Incarnation was a devout and fervent one, there did exist a class structure with its varying lifestyles according to whether one was of wealthy or poor background. Individuals were able to obtain permission to keep money, from whatever source they may have received it, and some were even allowed to have an income. Thus we find references to the custom of buying and selling rooms, the better rooms, of course, going to the richer nuns. And the nuns who were poor didn't have rooms at all but slept in dormitories. The difference between the rich and the poor was indicated also in the religious garb by means of such things as pleats, colors, buckles, and so on. Some wore rings, and others owned pet dogs. There were those who, like Teresa, kept the title *doña* and had ample private quarters where members of their families could visit or stay. Some had servants or slaves. There were those who in virtue of their family rank took the first places in the choir. It might be added as well that in those times it was not unusual for many to enter a monastery as the solution to a social problem rather than in response to a religious vocation.[47]

Upon all these practices and ways of looking at religious life, Teresa turned her back. The poverty of spirit of the gospels, like a powerful magnet, drew her. "But the one who is from nobler lineage should be the one to speak least about her father. All the Sisters must be equal."[48] Poverty was to be the insignia of Teresa's nuns: "in houses, clothing, words, and most of all in thought."[49] And closely linked with detachment from money is detachment from honor because "honor and money always go together; anyone who wants honor doesn't despise money, and anyone who despises money doesn't care much about honor."[50] This life of equality and humility was meant, as Teresa envisioned it, to blossom into a life of authentic sisterly love, the love Christ insisted upon for his followers. As she puts it, "in this house where there are no more than thirteen—nor must there be any more—all must be friends, all must be loved, all must be held dear, all must be helped."[51]

The Central Theme

When Teresa revised *The Way of Perfection* after Fr. García de Toledo had examined the work, she wrote somewhat formally on the opening page: "This book deals with the advice and counsel Teresa of Jesus gives to her religious Sisters and daughters." Only later was a title given to this book of "advice and counsel," and the title was not composed by Teresa. However she knew of it and approved. The title appears in her manuscript on the opposite side of the opening page: "The book called *The Way of Perfection* written by Teresa of Jesus, a nun of the Order of Our Lady of Mount Carmel." *The Way of Perfection* is therefore a practical book of advice and counsel destined to initiate the Carmelite nun into the life of prayer. Thus, Teresa is a teacher throughout the work, demonstrating how, pointing to the pitfalls, and explaining the right way from the wrong.

The Foundation of Prayer

In beginning her work, she first established the reasons behind this new manner of contemplative life. Because of her keen desire that the Lord's friends be good ones, she wanted the little community to follow Christ's counsels as perfectly as possible.[52] This implies careful observance of the rule, and for Teresa the essential element of the Carmelite rule is unceasing prayer.[53] Peace is necessary for a life of prayer. Thus Teresa avoids placing burdens on her nuns. She dwells mainly on only three practices because these will help them to possess both inwardly and outwardly the peace the Lord recommends to them and will dispose them to a life of prayer.[54] What are these three practices? Love of neighbor, detachment, and humility. Together they form a foundation for prayer. Since they touch upon the ties that are felt in one's relationship to others, to the world, and to oneself, they free the spirit.

Though admittedly there is an underlying structure and a logic in her works, Teresa makes little effort to present her ideas according to a well-ordered plan. In her characteristically simple manner, she confesses at the outset: "Since I don't know what I am about to say, I cannot say it in an orderly way."[55] It is not only in the first part of her work that she speaks of these practices that serve as a foundation for prayer, but the subjects of charity, detachment, and humility provide material for discussion again later as effects of prayer. Her digressions, too, for which she is well known, may cause readers some frustration in their efforts to follow her thought; hardly does she begin her work when she goes off into a lengthy digression (the entire second chapter) that would fit better elsewhere. Consequently, subjects treated in one section of the book will frequently be complemented by what is said on the matter in other places.

Taking up the first practice, love of neighbor, Teresa devotes four chapters to an analysis of love. Dividing love into that which is purely spiritual and that which is mixed with sensuality, she met with particular difficulty in explaining the latter. After rewriting the entire part in her revision, she then tore out the page and tried a third time.[56]

With regard to the whole subject of love, she complains that the term "love" is applied to much that has nothing to do with true and perfect love. She acknowledges the importance of friendships and of how they must grow into this perfect love and are enriched by it; but for her nuns living close together and only few in number she encourages them all to be friends. Furthermore, with her great capacity for friendship, Teresa observed that too much restraint could frighten people away from the service of God. "Our nature is such that this constraint is frightening and oppressive to others, and they flee from following the road that you are taking, even though they know clearly it is the more virtuous path."[57] Her own spontaneity and freedom from excessive constraint are noticeable in many passages of her first redaction that were censored or omitted in her revision. For example, in warning her nuns against magnificent buildings, she concluded: "And if I can say this in good conscience, may such a building fall to the ground the day you construct one." But the words used in her first writing are much stronger: "...may such a building fall to the ground and kill you all the day you desire one."[58]

However sublime the spirituality of which she speaks, Teresa would never want her daughters or any of her readers to lose the compassion that goes with charity. "For at times it happens that some trifle will cause as much suffering to one as a great trial will to another; little things can bring much distress to persons who have sensitive natures. If you are not like them, do not fail to be compassionate."[59]

The subject of detachment includes all that Teresa has to say through such expressions as poverty of spirit, mortification, and surrender to the will of God. What she observed in the human condition that most influenced her thinking about detachment was "how quickly all things come to an end."[60] Nor is the practice of detachment exclusively for nuns, no more than is that of charity or humility. Though Teresa wrote *The Way of Perfection* for her nuns, and it is, in a sense, a commentary on the constitutions she drafted for them, the treatise has become a popular book of spirituality since much of her advice is applicable to whoever is reading it. Remarkably, Teresa avoids any claim that nuns have a greater occasion for the practice of detachment or that their life is harder; rather, at times, she observes that married people are forced to practice greater self-discipline because of their obligations and that people living in the world have difficult trials from which the nuns are freed.[61] She states: "I do not call 'giving up every-thing' entering religious life, and the perfect soul can be de-tached and humble anywhere."[62]

The happy result of detachment is inner freedom, free-dom from worry about bodily comfort, honor, and wealth. Con-sidering the times in which she lived, the role Teresa gives to spartan fasts and penances is a small one. "But I am speaking about persons who by temperament like to be esteemed and honored and who look at the faults of others and never at their own, and other similar things that truly arise from lack of humility."[63]

Detachment and humility: so closely joined that Teresa could not speak of the one without the other; these two vir-tues "it seems always go together."[64] For humility implies de-tachment from oneself, from worry about esteem and honor. Then, just as the Virgin by humility drew the King of heaven to earth, so the soul by humility draws Love into itself. "I can-not understand how there could be humility without love or love without humility; nor are these two virtues possible with-out detachment from all creatures."[65]

There is that lack of self-esteem which has nothing to do with humility and is discernible through the agitation it causes. "Humility does not disturb or disquiet," Teresa writes, "how-ever great it may be; it comes with peace, delight, and calm.... This humility expands it [the soul] and enables it to serve God more."[66]

In humility one is touched with the conviction that every good thing comes from God. If she felt great detachment from all things one day, Teresa knew through experience that on another such detachment could be taken from her; and she therefore concludes: "Now since this is true, who will be able to say of themselves that they are virtuous or rich? For at the very moment when there is need of virtue one finds oneself poor."[67]

A Method of Prayer

A question often proposed is whether Teresa had a method of prayer which she taught. A popular method of prayer in her day was that of discursive meditation. And in turning her attention to the subject of prayer in the second part of her work in which she writes a commentary on the Our Father, she begins by referring to the many books of meditations. One of the most famous was the Dominican friar Luis de Granada's *Book of Prayer and Meditation*, published in 1554, a work she recommends in her constitutions. While praising these books, Teresa adds a significant qualification: "There are so many good books written by able persons for those who have methodical minds and for souls that are experienced and can concentrate within themselves that it would be a mistake if you pay attention to what I say about prayer." [68] She, indeed, does not intend to write for those who possess these qualities. Her method is for those whose minds, similar to hers, are like "wild horses." [69] "I pity these souls greatly, for they seem to be like very thirsty persons who see water in the distance, but when they want to go there, they meet someone who prevents their passing from the beginning through the middle to the end." [70]

To these persons and to all others who cannot follow the path of discursive meditation, Teresa offers her method. In doing so, she turns to the Our Father, the prayer Christ taught us; for vocal prayer does not impede contemplation. But the recitation of this prayer must be informed by Teresa's method, which she calls the prayer of recollection. She calls it "recollection" because "the soul collects its faculties together and enters within itself to be with its God." [71] What is necessary along with this centering of attention is the realization that God is very close. She insists on the nearness of God to each one. "All the harm comes from not truly understanding that he is near." [72]

Not only is he near, but he "never takes his eyes off you." And she asks: "Who can keep you from turning the eyes of your soul toward this Lord?"[73]

Her method is one of presence, of being fully present to God in our prayer, for he is fully present to us at all times. "What I'm trying to point out is that we should see and be present to the One with whom we speak without turning our back on him."[74] Centering the attention within, being fully present, looking at, gazing upon; these are the expressions that fit her method. "I'm not asking you now that you think about him or that you draw out a lot of concepts or make long and subtle reflections with your intellect—I'm not asking you to do anything more than look at him."[75]

It is sufficient that one make the effort, and for that reason Teresa calls this prayer of recollection a method.[76] Understandably, the degrees of this recollection may vary, and Teresa predicts that in the beginning it may be a little difficult, but soon "the gain will be clearly seen."[77]

This prayer of recollection, accompanied by vocal prayer, proved to be an excellent method, Teresa discovered, of disposing one for contemplative prayer. "And its divine Master comes more quickly to teach it and give it the prayer of quiet than he would through any other method it might use."[78] She claims she "never knew what it was to pray with satisfaction until the Lord taught me this method."[79] And concludes: "Therefore, Sisters, out of love for the Lord, get used to praying the Our Father with this recollection, and you will see the benefit before long. This is a manner of praying that the soul gets so quickly used to that it doesn't go astray, nor do the faculties become restless, as time will tell."[80]

Strict adherence to any one formula never became a part of Teresa's teaching. Her own spontaneity in prayer is displayed on almost every page and includes petitions, praise, adoration, offering, thanksgiving—all the forms of prayer. The opening words of the Our Father lead her into flights of her own unpremeditated prayer, and she teaches us to pray by praying herself. But the Our Father is always there to return to. In addition to this freedom from restriction, she values variety in the mode of being present to Christ: in joy, to be with him as risen; in trial and sadness, to be with him in his Passion. Presence to Christ within as he is shown to us in the different gospel accounts can be a further important aid, then, to the practice of recollection and of centering one's attention on him. Although risen, he still influences us through his earthly mysteries by which he draws close to us in a more tangible way.[81]

At times during this prayer, the soul will feel a passive quieting and be drawn gradually to a greater silence. "I know there are many persons who while praying vocally, as has been already mentioned, are raised by God to sublime contemplation."[82] From this method of recollection, then, Teresa goes on to describe the prayer of quiet, the initial stage of contemplation which, in her terminology, is always passive prayer and unattainable through any human efforts. This initial stage of contemplation, in which there is not yet a complete silencing of the faculties, is followed by the prayer of union in which all the faculties come to rest in the inner silence. As contemplation begins, the recollection takes deeper hold; the words become fewer, one word uttered from time to time being sufficient. But one's own efforts are of no avail in either producing or holding on to mystical prayer. "The best way to hold on to this favor is to understand clearly that we can neither bring it about nor remove it; we can only receive it with gratitude, as most unworthy of it; and this not with many words."[83] Contemplation is like living water drunk from the fount; yet it is different from earthly water in that, while satisfying the soul's thirst, at the same time it increases that thirst.

The Lord gave the Our Father in a rather obscure form, Teresa thinks, so that each petition may be made according to one's own intention. As for herself, she came to the knowledge of many deep secrets unfolded before her by the Master who teaches those who say this prayer. "Certainly, it never entered my mind that this prayer contained so many deep secrets; for now you have seen the entire spiritual way contained in it, from the beginning stages until God engulfs the soul and gives it to drink abundantly from the fount of living water, which he said was to be found at the end of the way."[84]

The end of the way cannot be reached without Teresa's indomitable determination, a *muy determinada determinacion.* "They must have a great and very resolute determination to persevere until reaching the end, come what may, happen what may, whatever work is involved, whatever criticism arises, whether they arrive or whether they die on the road, or even if they don't have courage for the trials that are met, or if the whole world collapses."[85]

Our Translation

Because of the demand and the lack of copies, Teresa thought, after a time, of having her book printed; but she felt the need of help for some careful editing. The unknown editor she commissioned entered unscrupulously into the delicate task. His polished text no longer bore many of the fascinating Teresian traits. She dutifully reviewed it, patiently canceling and rewriting some of his excessive changes; and this manuscript is now conserved in the monastery of the Carmelite nuns in Toledo. It was a copy of this text that served for the first editions of *The Way of Perfection* that appeared in Evora, 1583, in Salamanca, 1585, and in Valencia, 1587. But since those acquainted with Teresa's unlabored, conversational style were unhappy with it, Fray Luis de León in his edition of Teresa's complete works chose the autograph of Valladolid as the text. The different versions of the book, however, left the matter very confused, even into our own century, until Fr. Silverio brought clarity to the entire question in his critical editions.

Our translation is of the Valladolid autograph, the work revised by Teresa and for which she received approval from Fr. García de Toledo. A translation only of the Valladolid text, however, would bring with it certain disadvantages. The lively passages and interesting variations in the Escorial text would be lost to the English-speaking reader. Many of these omissions and variations from Escorial can be inserted into the Valladolid text without seriously damaging the flow of thought. We have indicated whatever is taken from Escorial and introduced into our main text from Valladolid by enclosing it in brackets. Where there are two versions of the same passage, yet with significant differences, we give a translation of the Escorial version in a note.

The Way of Perfection may be divided as follows:
  I. Purpose of the Teresian Carmel (chs. 1–3)
  II. Foundations of prayer:
    A. Love for one another (chs. 4–7)
    B. Detachment (chs. 8–14)
    C. Humility (chs. 15–18)
  III. Prayer in general (chs. 19–26)
  IV. Commentary on the Our Father:
    A. Christ as Master and Guide in prayer (chs. 26–27)
    B. Prayer of recollection (chs. 28–29)
    C. Prayer of quiet (chs. 30–31)
    D. Abandonment to the will of God (ch. 32)
    E. The Eucharist (chs. 33–35)
    F. Pardon of offenses and detachment from honor and esteem (chs. 36–37)
    G. Deliverance from deception and illusions (chs. 38–41)
    H. Desires for eternal life (ch. 42)

KIERAN KAVANAUGH, O.C.D.

Many deserve to receive an expression of gratitude for this translation of *The Way of Perfection*. Special thanks go to Padre Tomás de la Cruz (Alvarez) for allowing the translators to make use of his Spanish edition of the complete works of St. Teresa. His plentiful footnotes were indispensable to us in preparing our own notes. I would also like to thank the Carmel in Elysburg, Pennsylvania, for its important contribution to the index. Several other Carmels were helpful with some much-needed editorial assistance and proofreading, the Carmels of Danvers, Roxbury, and Indianapolis. Father Adrian Cooney assisted with some editorial advice, and Jean Mallon carefully typed the entire manuscript. Finally, I must express my appreciation to the many who encouraged Father Otilio and me to do a complete translation of Teresa's writings.

KIERAN KAVANAUGH, O.C.D.

The Way of Perfection

The book called *The Way of Perfection* written by Teresa of Jesus, a nun of the Order of our Lady of Mount Carmel. This book is intended for the discalced nuns who observe the primitive rule of our Lady of Mount Carmel.

JHS

This book deals with the advice and counsel Teresa of Jesus gives to her religious Sisters and daughters who live in the monasteries that, with the help of our Lord and the glorious Virgin Mother of God, our Lady, she founded. These monasteries follow the primitive rule of our Lady of Mount Carmel. She directs her counsel particularly to the Sisters at St. Joseph's monastery in Avila, which was the first foundation and the place where she was prioress when she wrote this book.[1]

In all that I say in this book I submit to what our Mother the Holy Roman Church holds.[2] If there should be anything contrary to that, it will be due to my not understanding the matter. And so I beg the learned men who will see this work to look it over carefully and to correct any mistake there may be as to what the church holds, as well as any other mistakes in other matters. If there should be anything good in this work, may it be for the honor and glory of God and the service of his most Blessed Mother, our Lady and Patroness, whose habit I wear despite my being very unworthy to do so.

JHS

Prologue

1. The Sisters in this monastery of St. Joseph have known that I received permission from the Father *Presentado*,[1] Friar Domingo Báñez, of the order of the glorious St. Dominic, who at present is my confessor,[2] to write some things about prayer. It seems I might be able to meet with success in doing this because I have discussed prayer with many spiritual and holy persons. The Sisters have urged me so persistently to tell them something about it that I have decided to obey them. I am aware that the great love they have for me will make what I say, so imperfectly and with such poor style, more acceptable than what is in some books that are very well written by those who know what they are writing about. And I trust in the Sisters' prayers that possibly through them the Lord will be pleased that I manage to say something about the mode and manner of life proper to this house. And if I should be mistaken, the Father *Presentado*, who will be the first to see this book, will either make corrections or burn it. I will not have lost anything by obeying these servants of God, and they will see what I have when left to myself and when His Majesty doesn't help me.

2. I am thinking of listing some remedies for certain common, small temptations of the devil, for since they are so common perhaps little attention is paid to them. And I shall

write of other things as the Lord inspires me or that might come to my mind; for since I don't know what I'm going to say, I cannot say it in an orderly way. I believe this lack of order is best since writing this book is a thing already so out of order for me. May the Lord have a hand in all that I do so that it may conform to his holy will; these are my desires always, even though my works are as faulty as I am.

3. I know there is no lack of love in me and of the desire to help as much as I can that the souls of my Sisters may advance in the service of the Lord. This love together with my age and the experience I have from living in some monasteries may help me in speaking of ordinary things to be more successful than learned men. Since these learned men have other more important occupations and are strong, they don't pay so much attention to things that don't seem to amount to much in themselves. But everything can be harmful to those as weak as we women are. The wiles of the devil are many for women who live a very cloistered life, for the devil sees that new weapons are needed in order to do harm. I, as wretched as I am, have known how to defend myself only poorly. So I have desired that my Sisters might take warning from my own experience. I shall say nothing about what I have not experienced myself or seen in others [or received understanding of from our Lord in prayer.]

4. Not long ago I was ordered to write a certain account of my life, in which I also dealt with some things about prayer.[3] It could be that my confessor would not want you to see this account, and so I shall put down here something of what was said there. I shall also write of other things that to me seem necessary. May the Lord's own hand be in this work, as I have begged him; and may he direct the work to his glory, amen.

COUNSELS OF LOVE ROOTED IN EXPERIENCE

Pro. 1: She has received permission from her confessor to write some things about prayer.

- The sisters have urged her to do so.
- She has decided to obey them.
- The sisters' love for her will enable them to accept her poor style.
- She will say something about the manner of life proper to St. Joseph's.
- Her confessor will make the necessary corrections or burn it.

Pro. 2–4: A. She will write about some small temptations and other things as the Lord inspires; she cannot write in an orderly way.

B. Her love for the sisters, her age, and her experience may contribute to the value of what she says.

C. She will include some things she mentioned in her *Life* about prayer.

INTERPRETIVE NOTES. 1. "The Way of Perfection" is not the title given by Teresa to her book, although she knew and approved it. She speaks of her work as practical "advice and counsel." Within a climate of intimacy, she offers her teachings as a mother to her daughters.

2. The incentive for her task lay in her awareness of her sisters' desires, of their love for her, and of her love

for them. They will make allowances for her unsophisticated style, and she will give guidance about some
of the little things that learned men judge unimpor-
tant. The dialogue is not between Teresa and her
spiritual directors, as in her *Life*, but between Teresa
and her nuns.

3. Her counsels flow from her own rich experience.
Without misgivings, she submits what she says to her
censors and the church. For Teresa, her censors were
more like advisors or mentors who would review her
manuscript and point out anything needing further
attention.

4. The censor Teresa mentions at both the beginning
and end of her work was to be Domingo Báñez. But
for whatever the reason, Báñez was not the censor.
Another Dominican, García de Toledo, the noble friar
Teresa addresses in her *Life*, who encouraged her to
enlarge on it, accepted the task of mentor for this work
also. In chapter 34 of the *Life*, she addresses him as
"my Father who is also like a son." García de Toledo
was the typical aristocrat in soul and blood. A nephew
of the count of Oropesa, he became commissary of
the Dominican order in Peru. Later in 1569, he again
went to Peru as counselor to his cousin who had been
appointed viceroy.

5. Báñez testifies in the process for Teresa's canonization that the only work of Teresa's he had read was her
Life. None of the marginal remarks in the manuscript
of *The Way of Perfection* are in Báñez's handwriting. All
of this may have been fortunate, for Báñez would pre-
sumably have been a more demanding censor than was

Teresa's friend García de Toledo. Báñez never did give permission for the nuns to read Teresa's *Life*. In writing her revision of the present work she withdrew her recommendation that the nuns read her first book.

6. Not a passage of those marked for correction or deletion by Padre García did Teresa refuse to change. If anything, she did more cutting and revising than he had asked for. Some of his marginal remarks praised the text. When he came to the part on the prayer of quiet, he wrote these words of praise: "an exquisite explanation of this prayer of quiet." Where she insists on freedom for her nuns in choosing confessors, he commented that this was good because there are confessors who for fear of making mistakes quench the Spirit.

QUESTIONS FOR DISCUSSION: 1. What prompted Teresa to write this book?

2. What gave her confidence in undertaking the task?

3. What are some of the small temptations that today are perhaps so common that little attention is paid to them?

Chapter 1

The reason I founded the monastery with such strict observance.

WHEN I BEGAN to take the first steps toward founding this monastery (for the reasons given in the book I mentioned that I wrote and also because of some great favors from the Lord through which I learned that he would be greatly served in this house), it was not my intention that there be so much external austerity or that the house have no income; on the contrary, I would have desired the possibility that nothing be lacking. In sum, my intention was the intention of the weak and wretched person that I am although I did have some good motives besides those involving my own comfort.

2. At that time news reached me of the harm being done in France and of the havoc the Lutherans had caused and how much this miserable sect was growing. The news distressed me greatly, and, as though I could do something or were something, I wept with the Lord and begged him that I might remedy so much evil. It seemed to me that I would have given a thousand lives to save one soul out of the many that were being lost there. I realized I was a woman and wretched and incapable of doing any of the useful things I desired to do in the service of the Lord. All my longing was and still is that since he has so many enemies and so few friends that these few friends be good ones. As a result I resolved to do the little that

was in my power; that is, to follow the evangelical counsels as perfectly as I could and strive that these few persons who live here do the same. I did this trusting in the great goodness of God, who never fails to help anyone whois determined to give up everything for him. My trust was that if these Sisters matched the ideal my desires had set for them, my faults would not have much strength in the midst of so many virtues; and I could thereby please the Lord in some way. Since we would all be occupied in prayer for those who are the defenders of the church and for preachers and for learned men who protect her from attack, we could help as much as possible this Lord of mine who is so roughly treated by those for whom he has done so much good; it seems these traitors would want him to be crucified again and that he have no place to lay his head.

3. O my Redeemer, my heart cannot bear these thoughts without becoming terribly grieved. What is the matter with Christians nowadays? Must it always be those who owe you the most who afflict you? Those for whom you performed the greatest works, those you have chosen for your friends, with whom you walk and commune by means of your sacraments? Aren't they satisfied with the torments you have suffered for them?

4. Indeed, my Lord, one who withdraws from the world nowadays is not doing anything. Since the world so little appreciates you, what do we expect? Do we perhaps deserve to be treated better? Have we perhaps done better toward those in the world that they would keep us in their friendship? What is this? What do we now expect, those of us who through the goodness of the Lord are freed of that contagious, scabby sore, that sect whose followers already belong to the devil? Indeed, they have won punishment with their own hands and have easily earned eternal fire with their pleasures. That's their worry! Still, my heart breaks to see how many souls are lost. Though I can't grieve so much over the evil already done — that is irreparable — would not want to see more of them lost each day.

5. O my Sisters in Christ, help me beg these things of the Lord. This is why he has gathered you together here. This is your vocation. These must be the business matters you're engaged in. These must be the things you desire, the things you weep about; these must be the objects of your petitions — not, my Sisters, the business matters of the world. For I laugh at and am even distressed about the things they come here to ask us to pray for: to ask His Majesty for wealth and money — and this is done by persons who I wish would ask him for the grace to trample everything underfoot. They are well intentioned, and in the end we pray for their intentions because of their devotion — although for myself I don't think the Lord ever hears me when I pray for these things. The world is all in flames; they want to sentence Christ again, so to speak, since they raise a thousand false witnesses against him; they want to ravage his church — and are we to waste time asking for things that if God were to give them we'd have one soul less in heaven? No, my Sisters, this is not the time to be discussing with God matters that have little importance.

6. Indeed, were I not to consider the human weakness that is consoled by receiving help in time of need (and it is good that we help in so far as we can), I'd be happy only if people understood that these are not the things they should be begging God for with so much care.

PURPOSE OF THE TERESIAN CARMEL

Before responding to her sisters' desires for counsels on prayer, Teresa, in a conversational tone characteristic of her entire work, speaks of the reason they have come together in community.

1.1–2: Why are we here?

- The community arose out of her experience of the tribulations within the church.

- Her distress over the situation prompted her to gather a community of those who would be good friends of the Lord by striving to live the evangelical counsels as perfectly as possible.

1.3–4: She interrupts her conversation with her daughters and friends to enter into conversation with her Lord and Friend whom the Christians of her day treated so poorly.

1.5–6: She takes up again her conversation with her sisters, begging them to help her pray for the church and for humanity.

INTERPRETIVE NOTES. 1. Prayer is not isolated from what takes place in the Body of Christ. In *The Interior Castle* Teresa says that in the fifth dwelling place a soul begins to experience a "deep pain at seeing both that God is offended and little esteemed in this world and that many souls are lost, heretics as well as Moors; although those that grieve it most are Christians." This suffering is mystical and purifying (IC V.2.10; cf. also

L 30.8; ST 3.7–8). It reverberates in the words of the present chapter. This "deep pain at seeing God offended" will also make one more aware of those small temptations, referred to in the prologue, to which people tend to pay little attention.

2. Everyone can benefit from Teresa's reflections about living her particular vocation as well as she could because Jesus' counsels, his call (vocation) to discipleship, are not meant only for priests and religious. After the Lord's resurrection the meaning of discipleship became clearer. It includes the following of Christ in his passage from death to life. The way of Jesus means taking up our cross and following him, having even a willingness to give up our own life. Thus discipleship in the New Testament entails a personal following of Jesus that will touch every area of our life. It shapes our attitudes toward money and property, affects our human relationships, gives a new meaning to love, changes the way we understand success, and leads us to embrace God's will (cf. Mk 8:34–38; Jn 15:13; Rom 6:3–5; Phil 3:8–11).

3. Teresa believed that by living their lives as perfectly as they could, and thereby becoming authentic friends of the Lord, the nuns would receive an answer to their prayers for the church. She linked the efficacy of prayer to intimate friendship with Christ. Her conviction has some words from Scripture as its basis: "If you remain in me and my words remain in you, ask for whatever you want and it will be done for you" (Jn 15:7); "Beloved, if our hearts do not condemn us, we have confidence

in God and receive from him whatever we ask, because we keep his commandments and do what pleases him" (1 Jn 3:21–22).

QUESTIONS FOR DISCUSSION. 1. After Teresa's example, what "little that is in our power" can we do to become good friends of the Lord?

2. Why does Teresa suffer such affliction?

3. What kinds of things did she find it difficult to pray for?

Chapter 2

Treats of how one should not worry about bodily needs and of the blessing there is in poverty.

D ON'T THINK, my Sisters, that because you do not strive to please those who are in the world you will lack food. I assure you that such will not be the case. Never seek sustenance through human schemes, for you will die of hunger — and rightly so. Your eyes on your Spouse! He will sustain you. Once he is pleased, those least devoted to you will give you food even though they may not want to, as you have seen through experience. If in following this advice you should die of hunger, blessed be the nuns of St. Joseph's! For the love of the Lord, do not forget this. Since you have given up an income, give up worry about food. If you don't, everything will be lost. God wants some to have an income, and in their case it's all right for them to worry about their income since that goes with their vocation; but for us to worry, Sisters, would be absurd.

2. Worry about the financial resources of others, it seems to me, would amount to thinking about what others are enjoying. Indeed, your worrying won't make others change their thinking, nor will it inspire them with the idea to give alms. Leave this worrying to the One who can move all, for he is the Lord of money and of those who earn money. By his command we came here. His words are true; they cannot fail; rather, heaven and earth will fail.[1] Let us not fail him; do not fear that he will

fail you. And if some time he should fail you, it will be for a greater good. The lives of the saints failed when they were killed because of the Lord, but this happened so that through martyrdom their glory would be increased. It would be a good exchange to give up everything for the enjoyment of everlasting abundance.

3. Sisters, what I am saying is so important that I want you to remember it after my death — and that's why I'm leaving it for you in writing — for while I live I will remind you of it. I have seen by experience the great gain that comes from not worrying about such things. The less there is the more carefree I become. The Lord knows that, in my opinion, it distresses me more when we have a large surplus than when we are in need. I don't know if this is because I've experienced that the Lord immediately gives what we need. For us to worry about money would amount to deceiving the world, making ourselves poor in an exterior way but not being poor in spirit. I would feel scrupulous, so to speak, and it would seem to me as though a rich person were begging alms. Please God such may not be the case, for where there are too many cares about whether others will give us alms, sooner or later these cares will become habitual; or it could happen that we would go asking for what we have no need of, perhaps from someone more needy than we ourselves. Although those who give to us cannot lose anything but only gain, we would be losing. No, please God, my daughters! If you should start worrying like this, I would prefer that you have an income.

4. I beg you for the love of God and as an alms to me, in no way let your thoughts be taken up with these cares. If at any time such cares should be present in this house, let the youngest Sister cry out to His Majesty and bring the matter to the attention of the prioress. She may humbly tell the prioress that the latter is mistaken, and so mistaken that little by little true poverty will be lost. I hope in the Lord that this will

never happen and that he will not abandon his servants. May this book you have asked me to write, even if it do no more, serve to awaken you in these matters.

5. Believe me, my daughters, that for your good the Lord has given me a little understanding of the blessings that lie in holy poverty. Those who experience them will understand, though perhaps not as much as I. For not only had I failed to be poor in spirit, even though I professed it, but I was foolish in spirit. Poverty of spirit is a good that includes within itself all the good things of the world. [And I believe it has many of the good things contained in all the virtues. I am not saying this for certain, because I don't know the worth of each virtue. I will not speak about what in my opinion I do not understand well. But, for myself, I hold that poverty of spirit embraces many of the virtues.] In it lies great dominion. I say that it gives once again to one who doesn't care about the world's good things dominion over them all. What do kings and lords matter to me if I don't want their riches, or don't care to please them if in order to do so I would have to displease God in even the smallest thing? Nor what do I care about their honors if I have understood that the greatest honor of a poor person lies in being truly poor?

6. In my opinion honor and money almost always go together; anyone who wants honor doesn't despise money, and anyone who despises money doesn't care much about honor. Let this be clearly understood, for it seems to me that the desire for honor always brings with it some interest in money or income. It would be a wonder if any poor person were honored in the world; on the contrary, even though worthy of honor, someone who is poor is little esteemed.[2] True poverty brings with it overwhelming honor. Poverty that is chosen for God alone has no need of pleasing anyone but him. It is certain that in having need of no one a person has many friends. I have become clearly aware of this through experience.

7. So much is written about this virtue that I wouldn't know how to understand it all or still less speak of it. And so in order not to do an injustice to this virtue by trying to praise it, I will say no more. I have only spoken of what I have seen through experience, and I confess that until now I have been so absorbed in speaking of these things that I did not realize I was doing so. But since I have written this, for the love of the Lord, keep in mind that holy poverty is our insignia and a virtue which at the beginning, when our order was founded, was so esteemed and well kept by our holy fathers. For I have been told, by someone who knows, that they did not keep anything for the next day. If exteriorly we do not carry out this practice so perfectly, let us strive to do so interiorly. Life lasts but a couple of hours; exceedingly great will be the reward. If we should do nothing else but what the Lord counseled us to do, the pay of just being able in some way to imitate him would be great.

8. These are the insignia that must be on our coat of arms, for we must desire to observe poverty in every way: in houses, clothing, words, and most of all in thought. As long as you do this, have no fear that the religious life in this house will fail; God will help. As St. Clare said, great walls are those of poverty. She said that it was with walls like these, and those of humility, that she wanted to enclose her monasteries.[3] Surely, if poverty is truly observed, recollection and all the other virtues will be much better fortified than with very sumptuous buildings. Be careful of buildings like these; I beg you for the love of God and by his precious blood. And if I can say this in good conscience, may such a building fall to the ground the day you construct one.[4]

9. It looks very bad, my daughters, if large houses are built with money from the poor. May God not allow it. The houses must be poor and small in every way. Let us in some manner

resemble our King, who had no house but the stable in Bethlehem where he was born and the cross where he died. These were houses where there was little room for recreation. Those who build large ones know what they are doing; they have other holy intentions. But for thirteen poor little women, any corner should be enough.[5] If it is necessary because of the extremely secluded life you live to have a stretch of land (and this even helps prayer and devotion) with some hermitages where you can withdraw to pray, well and good. But no buildings, or large and ornate house. God deliver us from them! Always remember that everything will come tumbling down on the day of judgment. Who knows whether this will come soon?

10. Now it would not be right for the house of thirteen poor little women to make a loud crash when it falls; the truly poor must make no noise. They must be noiseless people so that others will take pity on them. And how they will rejoice when they see someone freed from hell because of giving them an alms! That's all possible because they are much obliged to pray continually for the souls of their benefactors, since their food comes from them. The Lord also desires that, even though it comes from him, we show gratitude to those persons through whose means he gives this food to us. Do not be negligent about showing gratitude.

11. I don't know what I began to say, for I have wandered off the subject. I believe the Lord wanted me to do so, for I never thought about saying what I have said here. May His Majesty always help us so that we never fail in the practice of poverty, amen.

POVERTY AND FREEDOM FROM WORRY

The fact that benefactors asked the nuns to pray for their intentions for wealth and money led Teresa into this digression on poverty.

2.1–5: Since the nuns have willingly foregone an income (i.e., endowment with a benefice), they should also be careful not to worry about food, shelter, and clothing.

- Eyes on the Lord! Do not fear that he will fail you!

- Exterior poverty must always be accompanied by poverty of spirit.

- In poverty of spirit lies great dominion over all the world's goods.

2.6: Honor and money almost always go together. Poverty chosen for God alone has no need of pleasing anyone but him.

2.7–9: The appropriateness of poverty for Carmelites: imitating the early Carmelites on Mt. Carmel, if not exteriorly, at least interiorly.

- Specifications about buildings, dress, words, and thoughts. St. Clare: enclose monasteries with the great walls of poverty and humility.

- Look at the poverty of Christ in the stable and on the cross.

2.10: On praying for benefactors and showing gratitude.

2.11: "I have wandered off the subject." She had never thought about saying what she said.

INTERPRETIVE NOTES. 1. In her *Foundations*, Teresa writes of an experience of desperate poverty: "For some days we had no more than the [two] straw mattresses and the blanket, and even that day we didn't have so much as a stick of wood to make a fire to cook a sardine.... The experience was very good for us; the interior consolation and happiness we felt were so great that I often think about what the Lord keeps stored up within the virtues. It seems to me this lack we experienced was the cause of a sweet contemplation" (15.13–14).

2. At the end of her life, Teresa grew resigned to the fact that in none of her monasteries was her ideal of living without an income practicable, an ideal she had so struggled for in her first foundation (cf. L 35). In a letter to Gracián (21 February 1581), she suggested that the prescription in her constitutions about not having an income be deleted.

3. Poverty can be a condition in which people go hungry, are without housing and clothing, lack education, medical care, and job opportunities. Seen from this perspective poverty is an evil in which the poor suffer exploitation and oppression.

4. "It seems I have much more compassion for the poor than I used to. I feel such great pity and desire to find relief for them that if it were up to me I would give them the clothes off my back. I feel no repugnance

whatsoever toward them, toward speaking to or touching them. This I now see is a gift given by God. For even though I used to give alms for love of him, I didn't have the natural compassion. I feel a very noticeable improvement in this matter" (ST 2.3).

5. Jesus was born into a people of faith who had experienced the poverty of the Exodus and the Exile. He sympathized with the afflicted and those seeking divine deliverance from their plight, knowing that God was their source of refuge (Ps 22:24; 35:9–10; 109:30–31). Jesus was himself poor. Bethlehem (Lk 2:7), Nazareth (Mt 13:55), the public life (Mt 8:20), the cross (Mt 27:35) are so many varied forms of poverty espoused by Jesus, to the point of total destitution.

6. In Matthew's Gospel, Jesus teaches "Blessed are the poor in spirit" (5:3) and he demanded that his followers have interior detachment regarding temporal goods whether they possessed these goods or not, so that they might be capable of desiring and receiving the true riches of the kingdom (6:24, 33; 13:22); and he tells them not to "worry about your life, what you will eat or drink, or about your body, what you will wear" (Mt 6:25–34).

7. Teresa's initial way of embracing poverty did not remain feasible. Throughout history, followers of Christ have shown ingenuity through a variety of ways of adopting poverty as a positive value; they continue to do so. They may renounce the lifestyles of power, status, or prestige that accompany wealth. They may live a life of simplicity based on the invitation to sell all one's possessions, give to the poor, and follow Jesus.

They may cultivate a reverence for the material cosmos and the goods of earth as God's creations and resist the loud demands of the advertising industry to keep the endless cycle of consumption turning. They can be found living in solidarity with the poor, bonding with them, living among them, and struggling with them. Their way of dealing with the evil of poverty may be to serve the poor directly and become advocates for them.

QUESTIONS FOR DISCUSSION. 1. What does Teresa recommend to those who tend to worry about their material necessities?

2. What is necessary in order to give material poverty a value?

3. How does poverty of spirit give us dominion over all the world's goods?

4. In my daily life, does my concern about what other people think of me enslave me to the pursuit of the goods of this world?

Chapter 3

Continues the subject she began to discuss in the first chapter; she urges her Sisters to busy themselves begging God to help those who labor for the church. The chapter ends with an earnest plea.

TO RETURN TO THE MAIN REASON the Lord brought us together in this house and why I have greatly desired that we live so as to please His Majesty, I want to speak of helping to remedy the great evils I have seen. Human forces are not sufficient to stop the spread of this fire caused by these heretics, even though people have tried to see if with the force of arms they could remedy all the evil that is making such progress. It has seemed to me that what is necessary is a different approach, the approach of a lord when in time of war his land is overrun with enemies and he finds himself restricted on all sides. He withdraws to a city that he has well fortified and from there sometimes strikes his foe. Those who are in the city, being chosen people, are such that they can do more by themselves than many cowardly soldiers can. And often victory is won in this way. At least, even though victory is not won, these chosen people are not conquered. For since they have no traitor, they cannot be conquered — unless through starvation. In this example the starvation cannot be such as to force them to surrender — to die, yes; but not to surrender.

2. But why have I said this? So that you understand, my Sisters, that what we must ask God is that in this little castle where there are already good Christians not one of us will go

53

over to the enemy and that God will make the captains of this castle or city, who are the preachers and theologians, very advanced in the way of the Lord. Since most of them belong to religious orders, ask God that they advance very far in the perfection of religious life and their vocation; this is most necessary. For as I have said, it is the ecclesiastical, not the secular, arm that will save us. Since in neither the ecclesiastical nor the secular arm can we be of any help to our King, let us strive to be the kind of persons whose prayers can be useful in helping those servants of God who through much toil have strengthened themselves with learning and a good life and have labored so as now to help the Lord.

3. You may perhaps ask why I am stressing this so much, and saying that we must help those who are better than we ourselves are. I will tell you why: it is because I don't think that as yet you understand well how much you owe the Lord for bringing you here where you are so removed from business affairs, occasions of sin, and worldly occupations. Indeed, it is a very great mercy. As for those persons I mentioned, who are not free in this way, it is good that they are not free; more so in these times than in the past. They are the persons who must strengthen people who are weak, and encourage the little ones. A fine state things would be in — soldiers without captains! These persons must live among men, deal with men, live in palaces, and even sometimes outwardly behave as such men do. Do you think, my daughters, that little is required for them to deal with the world, live in the world, engage in its business, and, as I said, resemble it in its conversation, while interiorly remaining its strangers, its enemies; in sum, not being men but angels? For if they do not live in this way, they do not deserve to be called captains; nor may the Lord allow them to leave their cells, for they will do more harm than good. This is not the time for seeing imperfections in those who must teach.

4. And if they are not interiorly fortified through an understanding of the importance of trampling everything underfoot, of detachment from things that come to an end, and of attachment to eternal things, they will show some sign of this lack no matter how much they try to conceal it. Is it not the world they have to deal with? Have no fear that the world will forgive this deficiency; nor is there any imperfection it fails to recognize. It will overlook many good things and perhaps not even consider them good; but have no fear that it will overlook any evil or imperfect things. Now I wonder who it is that teaches people in the world about perfection, not so much that these people might seek perfection (for it doesn't seem to them they have any obligation to do this, but they think they are doing enough if they keep the commandments reasonably well), but that they might condemn others. And at times what is virtuous seems to them luxury. So, then, do not think that little help from God is necessary for this great battle these preachers and theologians are fighting; a very great deal is necessary.

5. I beg you to strive to be such that we might merit from God two things: First, that among the numerous learned men and religious there be many who will meet these requirements I mentioned that are necessary for this battle, and that the Lord may prepare those who do not meet them; one who is perfect will do much more than many who are not. Second, that after being placed in this combat, which, as I say, is not easy, they may receive protection from the Lord so as to remain free of the many perils there are in the world, and stop their ears in order not to hear the siren's song on this dangerous sea. If we can obtain some answers from God to these requests, we shall be fighting for him even though we are very cloistered. And if some of our requests are answered, I would consider well worthwhile the trials I have suffered in order to found this little corner, where I have also sought that this rule

of our Lady and Empress be observed with the perfection with which it was observed when initiated.

6. Do not think it is useless to have these petitions[1] continually in your heart, for with some persons it seems a difficult thing for them not to be praying a great deal for their own soul. But what better prayer is there than these petitions I mentioned? If you are uneasy because you think your sufferings in purgatory will not be shortened, know that by this prayer they will be; and if you must still pay some debts, so be it. What would it matter were I to remain in purgatory until judgment day if through my prayer I could save even one soul? How much less would it matter if my prayer is to the advantage of many and for the honor of the Lord. Pay no attention to sufferings that come to an end if through them some greater service is rendered to him who endured so many for us. Always try to be informed about what is more perfect [for as I will ask you later, and will give my reasons, you must always communicate with learned men].

So, then, I beg you for the love of the Lord to ask His Majesty to hear us in this matter. Miserable though I am, I ask His Majesty this since it is for his glory and the good of the church; this glory and good is the object of my desires.

7. It seems bold that I think I could play some role in obtaining an answer to these petitions. I trust, my Lord, in these your servants who live here, and I know they desire and strive for nothing else than to please you. For you they renounced the little they had and would have wanted to have more so as to serve you with it. Since you, my Creator, are not ungrateful, I think you will not fail to do what they beg of you. Nor did you, Lord, when you walked in the world, despise women; rather, you always, with great compassion, helped them. [And you found as much love and more faith in them than you did in men.

Among them was your most blessed Mother, and through her merits and because we wear her habit we merit what, because of our offenses, we do not deserve. Is it not enough, Lord, that the world has intimidated us ... so that we may not do anything worthwhile for you in public or dare speak some truths that we lament over in secret, without your also failing to hear so just a petition? I do not believe, Lord, that this could be true of your goodness and justice, for you are a just judge and not like those of the world. Since the world's judges are sons of Adam and all of them men, there is no virtue in women that they do not hold suspect. Yes, indeed, the day will come, my King, when all will be known for what they are. I do not speak for myself, because the world already knows my wickedness — and I have rejoiced that this wickedness is known publicly — but because I see that these are times in which it would be wrong to undervalue virtuous and strong souls, even though they are women.][2] When we ask you for honors, income, money, or worldly things, do not hear us. But when we ask you for the honor of your Son, why wouldn't you hear us, eternal Father, for the sake of him who lost a thousand honors and a thousand lives for you? Not for us, Lord, for we don't deserve it, but for the blood of your Son and his merits.

8. O eternal Father, see to it that so many lashes and injuries and such heavy torments are not forgotten! How then, my Creator, can a heart as loving as yours allow that the deeds done by your Son with such ardent love and so as to make us more pleasing to you (for you commanded that he love us) be esteemed so little? For nowadays these heretics have so little regard for the Blessed Sacrament that they take away its dwelling places by destroying churches. Was something still to be done to please you? But he did everything. Wasn't it enough, eternal Father, that while he lived he did not have a place to lay his head — [3] and always in the midst of so many trials? But

now they are taking away the places he has at present to which
he can invite his friends, for he realizes that we are weak and
knows that the laborers must be nourished with such food.
Hasn't he already paid far more than enough for the sin of
Adam? Whenever we sin again must this loving Lamb pay?
Don't allow this, my Emperor! Let your Majesty be at once
appeased! Do not look at our sins but behold that your most
blessed Son redeemed us, and behold his merits and those of
his glorious Mother and of so many saints and martyrs who
died for you!

9. Ay, what a pity, Lord, and who has dared to make this
petition on behalf of all of us? What a bad intermediary, my
daughters, is she who seeks to be heard and to make such a
petition for you! Indeed, this sovereign Judge should become
more indignant — and rightly and justly so — at seeing me so
bold! But behold, my Lord, that you are a God of mercy; have
mercy on this little sinner, this little worm that is so bold with
you. Behold, my God, my desires and the tears with which I
beg this of you; forget my deeds because of who you are; have
pity on so many souls that are being lost, and help your
church. Don't allow any more harm to come to Christianity,
Lord. Give light now to these darknesses.

10. I ask you, my Sisters, for the love of the Lord, to recommend to His Majesty this poor little thing, and beg him to
give her humility. Do this as something you are obliged to do.
I am not requesting you to pray in particular for kings and prelates in the church, especially our bishop.[4] I see you now so
careful about doing so that it doesn't seem necessary for me
to insist. Let those who are to come realize that if the bishop
is holy the subjects will be so too; and as something very important always ask this of the Lord in your prayers. And when
your prayers, desires, disciplines, and fasts are not directed

toward obtaining these things I mentioned, reflect on how
you are not accomplishing or fulfilling the purpose for which
the Lord brought you here together. [And may the Lord because of who His Majesty is never allow you to forget this.]

PURPOSE OF THE TERESIAN CARMEL
(CONTINUED)

Teresa returns to her theme. How can this little community of nuns help stop the fire that is ravaging the church? She introduces a symbol to explain her ideal.

3.1–2: The need for a fortified city in time of war. Those in the city are chosen ones, Christians faithful to the gospel.

- Within this city, looking like a castle, is another little castle, the community of St. Joseph's.

- Good Christians do not try to put out the fire with the arms of war; they must struggle in a different way (through spiritual combat).

- Preachers and theologians are the captains, strengthened through learning and a good life.

- The little contemplative community of St. Joseph's must strive to be of the kind whose prayer will be useful in the battle.

3.3: The hardships and demands made on the captains.

3.4: People in the world learn about perfection so as to condemn others. The preachers and theologians living in the world need much help.

3.5–6: The nuns must pray, with these petitions habitually in their hearts, that the captains be detached and not seduced by the world's allurements.

3.7–9: Teresa, now practicing what she advises, begins to pray.

- She prays to Christ for her little community of women who are undervalued. The blood of Christ along with their virtuous lives give power to their petitions.

- She prays to the Father, with her eyes on Christ suffering in his church; recognizing her boldness, she prays for mercy for herself, for the church, and for souls being lost.

3.10: She returns to address her sisters.

- Asks them to pray for her and for bishops and rulers.

- Your prayers, desires, disciplines, and fasts must be directed toward obtaining these things.

INTERPRETIVE NOTES: 1. Teresa knew that the religious wars in France and elsewhere in Europe were stirring King Philip II to the use of arms to "stop the spread of this fire." Her allusion to these plans was censored in her first redaction. She appeared to be criticizing the king. Recognizing the need for a completely different approach than the use of human force and man-made arms, she urged the study of Scripture, preaching the Word, virtuous living, and prayer and fasting.

2. Another passage that caught a censor's eyes was her defense of women. The entire section in brackets of

no. 7 was crossed out with bold strokes and omitted in the second redaction. Four hundred years later, in our times, the Second Vatican Council has made a plea that we recognize and foster the talents and skills of women:

"Every effort should be made to provide for those who are capable of it the opportunity to pursue higher studies so that as far as possible they may engage in the functions and services, and play the role in society, most in keeping with their talents and the skills they acquire.... At present women are involved in nearly all spheres of life: they ought to be permitted to play their part fully according to their own particular nature. It is up to everyone to see to it that woman's specific and necessary participation in cultural life be acknowledged and fostered" (*Gaudium et Spes*, no. 60).

3. At a time when St. Ignatius of Loyola established the apostolic form of religious life, in which everything was ordered to the salvation of souls, Teresa, in a similar vein, gave an apostolic thrust to her communities of contemplative nuns. Their life of prayer was to serve the church and humanity, not to be only a means to contemplative union with God.

4. The Second Vatican Council has these words in support of the contemplative way of life:

"There are institutes that are entirely ordered toward contemplation in such wise that their members give themselves over to God alone in solitude and silence, in constant prayer and willing penance. These will always have an honored place in the mystical Body of Christ, in which 'all the members do not have the same function' (Rom 12:4), no matter how pressing may be the needs of the active ministry. For they offer to God an exceptional sacrifice of praise, they lend luster to God's people with abundant fruits of holiness, they sway them by their example, and they enlarge the church by their hidden apostolic fruitfulness. They are thus an ornament to the Church and a fount of heavenly graces" (*Perfectae Caritatis,* no. 7).

5. Along with chapter 1, this chapter shows Teresa's experience of connectedness with the Body of Christ. The connection that Jesus' disciples have with him links them also with one another in a new kind of friendship: "We, though many, are one body in Christ, and individually parts of one another" (Rom 12:5). The differences in gifts are real but complementary (1 Cor 12:27–30). The Body of Christ is not only a metaphor; it is a physical reality, a new being brought into existence among the disciples of Jesus in the resurrection of Jesus Christ. Christians are baptized into this new being. Teresa knows experientially the correlation between the Body of Christ as Eucharist and the Body of Christ as community. She brings together the body of Jesus in life, the Body of the risen Christ, the Body of Christ that Christians are, and the Body of Christ in the Eucharist. All these belong together in the Body of Christ's total meaning. "Wasn't it enough, eternal Father, that while he lived he did not have a place to lay his head — and always in the midst of so many trials? But now they are taking away the places he has at

present to which he can invite his friends, for he realizes that we are weak and knows that the laborers must be nourished with such food.... Behold that your most blessed Son redeemed us, and behold his merits and those of his glorious Mother and of so many saints and martyrs who died for you" (8).

6. Some other words from Vatican II are pertinent here: "In this one and only Church of God from its very beginnings there arose certain rifts, which the Apostle strongly censures as damnable. But in subsequent centuries much more serious dissensions appeared and large communities became separated from full communion with the Catholic Church — for which, often enough, men of both sides were to blame. However, one cannot charge with the sin of the separation those who at present are born into these communities and in them are brought up in the faith of Christ, and the Catholic Church accepts them with respect and affection as brothers" (*Unitatis Redintegratio*, no. 3).

QUESTIONS FOR DISCUSSION. 1. How can our prayer become more fruitful for the church and the world?

2. What was Teresa's attitude toward the religious wars of her time?

3. What do Teresa's words tell us about the way women were treated by men in her day?

4. Why are prayer and virtue important to the church as Mystical Body of Christ?

Chapter 4

Urges the observance of the rule and discusses three things that are important for the spiritual life. Explains the first of these, which is love of neighbor, and how particular friendships do harm.[1]

NOW, DAUGHTERS, you have seen the great task we have undertaken [for the prelate and bishop who is your superior and for the order, already included in what was mentioned, since all is for the good of the church; and to pray for the church is an obligation]. What do you think we must be like if we are not to be considered very bold by God and the world? Clearly, we must work hard, and it helps a great deal to have lofty thoughts so that we will exert ourselves and make our deeds comply with our thoughts. For if we strive to observe our rule and constitutions very carefully, I hope in the Lord that our prayers will be heard. I am not beseeching you to do something new, my daughters, but only that we observe what we profess; to observe this is our vocation and obligation — although there are many degrees of observance.

2. Our primitive rule states that we must pray without ceasing.[2] If we do this with all the care possible — for unceasing prayer is the most important aspect of the rule — the fasts, the disciplines, and the silence the order commands will not be wanting. For you already know that if prayer is to be genuine, it must be helped by these other things; prayer and comfortable living are incompatible.

3. It is about prayer that you asked me to say something, and I beg you that in recompense for what I am going to say you eagerly do what I have said up until now, and read it often. Before I say anything about interior matters, that is, about prayer, I shall mention some things that are necessary for those who seek to follow the way of prayer; so necessary that even if these persons are not very contemplative, they can be far advanced in the service of the Lord if they possess these things. And if they do not possess them, it is impossible for them to be very contemplative. And if they think they are, they are being highly deceived. May the Lord help me speak of these things, and may he teach me what I am about to say so that it may be for his glory, amen.

4. Do not think, my friends and daughters, that I shall burden you with many things; please God, we shall do what our holy fathers established and observed, for by walking this path they themselves established they merited this title we give them. It would be wrong to seek another way or try to learn about this path from anyone else. I shall enlarge on only three things, which are from our own constitutions, for it is very important that we understand how much the practice of these three things helps us to possess inwardly and outwardly the peace our Lord recommended so highly to us. The first of these is love for one another; the second is detachment from all created things; the third is true humility, which, even though I speak of it last, is the main practice and embraces all the others.

5. About the first, love for one another, it is most important that we have this, for there is nothing annoying that is not suffered easily by those who love one another — a thing would have to be extremely annoying before causing any displeasure. And if this commandment were observed in the world as it should be, I think such love would be very helpful for the observance of the other commandments. But, because

of either excess or defect, we never reach the point of observing this commandment perfectly.

It may seem that having excessive love among ourselves could not be evil, but such excess carries with it so much evil and so many imperfections that I don't think anyone will believe this save the one who has been an eyewitness. The devil lays many snares here, for this excess is hardly noticed by persons having consciences that deal only roughly with pleasing God, and the excess even seems to them virtuous; but those who are interested in perfection have a deep understanding of this excessive love, because little by little it takes away the strength of will to be totally occupied in loving God.

6. I believe this excessive love must be found among women even more than among men; and the harm it does in the community is well known. It gives rise to the following: failing to love equally all the others; feeling sorry about any affront to the friend; desiring possessions so as to give her gifts; looking for time to speak with her, and often so as to tell her that you hold her dear and other trifling things rather than about your love for God. For these great friendships are seldom directed toward helping one love God more. On the contrary, I think the devil gets them started so as to promote factions in religious orders. For when love is in the service of His Majesty, the will does not proceed with passion but proceeds by seeking help to conquer other passions.

7. I should like that there be many of these friendships where there is a large community, but in this house where there are no more than thirteen — nor must there be any more[3] — all must be friends, all must be loved, all must be held dear, all must be helped. Watch out for these friendships, for love of the Lord, however holy they may be; even among brothers they can be poisonous. I see no benefit in them. And if the friends are relatives, the situation is much worse — it's a pestilence![4] And

believe me, daughters, even though this kind of talk seems extreme, great perfection and great peace lie in keeping my advice; and many occasions are removed from those who are not strong. But if the will should be inclined to one more than to another (this cannot be helped, for it is natural and we are often drawn to love the worst one if that person is endowed with more natural graces), let us be careful not to allow ourselves to be dominated by that affection. Let us love the virtues and interior good, and always studiously avoid paying attention to this exterior element.

8. Let us not condescend, oh daughters, to allow our wills to be slaves to anyone, save to the One who bought it with his blood.[5] Be aware that, without understanding how, you will find yourselves so attached that you will be unable to manage the attachment. Oh, God help me, the silly things that come from such attachment are too numerous to be counted. And because these things are so minute that only the one who sees such friendship will understand and believe what is said about them, there's no reason to say any more here — except that such a friendship is bad when found in anyone; but when found in the prioress it's a pestilence.

9. To break away from these friendships involving a particular fondness, great care is necessary at the outset of the friendship. This breaking away should be done delicately and lovingly rather than harshly. In providing a remedy it is important that the friends avoid being together and speaking to each other save at the designated hours. This would be in conformity with the custom we now follow, which is that we are not to be together but each one alone in her own cell, as the rule commands.[6] At St. Joseph's the nuns should be excused from having a common workroom, for although having one is a laudable custom, silence is better observed when each nun is by herself; and to get used to solitude is a great help for prayer.

Since prayer must be the foundation of this house, it is necessary that we strive to dedicate ourselves to what most helps us
in prayer.

10. Returning to the subject of our loving one another,
it seems pointless to be recommending this love. For are
there persons who can be so like brutes that they will not love
each other even though they must always deal with and be in
the company of one another and have no dealings and no
recreation with persons outside the house and believe that
God loves them and they him, since for his sake they have left
everything? I say this especially since virtue always inspires
love, and I hope in His Majesty that those living in this house
will with the help of God always be virtuous. So, in my opinion, I don't have to recommend this love a great deal.

11. What I would like to say a little about now is how this
love for one another must be practiced. I would like to speak
also of the nature of this virtuous love — which is the love I
want practiced here — and how we know if we have this love;
for our Lord recommended it so highly and so urgently to his
apostles.[7] What I say will be in conformity with my dullness of
mind; and if in other books you find a detailed explanation
don't take anything from me, for perhaps I don't know what
I'm talking about.

12. Two kinds of love are what I'm dealing with: One kind
is spiritual, because it in no way seems to stir sensuality or affect the tenderness of our nature so as to take away purity.
The other is spiritual mixed with our sensuality and weakness
or good love, for it seems to be licit, as is love for our relatives
and friends. I have already said something about it.[8]

13. I want to speak now about the love that is spiritual,
that which is not affected by any passion; where passion is
present the good order is thrown into complete disorder.

And if we deal with virtuous persons discreetly and moderately, especially confessors, we will benefit. But if you should become aware that the confessor is turning toward some vanity, be suspicious about everything and in no way carry on conversations with him even though they may seem to be good, but make your confession briefly and bring it to a conclusion. And it would be best to tell the prioress that your soul doesn't get on well with him and change confessors. That would be the most proper thing to do — if you can do it without hurting his reputation.

14. In similar cases and others as well, in which the devil could ensnare one in many difficulties and in which one does not know what counsel to take, the best thing to do is try to speak with some learned person; when necessary there should be the freedom to do this. Make your confession to him and do what he tells you to do about the matter; for since one must provide some remedy, one could fall into great error. How many mistakes have been made in the world by doing things without counsel, especially in matters that could be harmful to someone! Failing to provide a remedy cannot be allowed; for unless the devil is quickly cut short, the effect will not be something of minor importance when he begins to interfere. Thus what I have said about trying to speak with another confessor is what is best to do, provided that there be an opportunity; and I hope in the Lord there will be.

15. Keep in mind that this is a very important point, for such friendship is dangerous, harmful, and a hell for all the Sisters. I say that you must not wait until you recognize that serious evil is present, but you should in the beginning cut the relationship short by every possible and knowable means. In good conscience you can do so. But I hope in the Lord that he will not permit that persons who must always be engaged in prayer

will be able to love anyone who is not the Lord's great servant. That they ought not is very certain — or else they have neither the prayer nor the perfection that is in conformity with our goal here. For if they see that a person doesn't understand their language and doesn't love to speak of God, they will not be able to love him, because he will not be like them. If he is like them, since the opportunities for these servants of God to engage in such friendship are so few, he will not want to disturb them; or he will be a simpleton.

16. Now I have begun to speak about this matter because, as I have said,[9] the harm the devil can here cause is great, and only very slowly is it recognized; thus perfection can be gradually vitiated without one's knowing why. For if this confessor wants to allow room for vanity, because he himself is vain, he makes little of it even in others. May God, because of who he is, deliver us from such things. A situation like this would be enough to disturb all the nuns because their consciences tell them the opposite of what their confessor does. And if they are restricted to only one confessor, they don't know what to do or how to be at peace. For the one who should be calming them and providing a remedy is the one who is causing the harm. There must be a lot of these kinds of affliction in some places. It makes me feel great pity, and so you shouldn't be surprised if I have tried to explain this danger to you.

vitiate v
1) to reduce the value or impair the quality of
2) to corrupt morally
3) to invalidate

vitiation n

FOUNDATIONS FOR A LIFE OF PRAYER

Teresa takes up the question of what we must do that our prayers be heard. Her immediate interest is not prayer itself and its development, but the one who prays, the kind of life that must accompany prayer.

4.1: We must observe what we profess.

4.2–3: A. Unceasing prayer is the most important aspect of the Carmelite rule.

B. Before speaking of prayer, however, she will deal with some virtues necessary for those who follow the way of prayer.

4.4: She reduces them to three: love, detachment, and humility. They are sources of the inward and outward peace so favorable to prayer.

4.5: Teresa begins her analysis of the first: love for one another.

- Where there is love, annoyances from one another are suffered easily.

- Love fails through "excess" or defect. She immediately begins to speak of "excessive love."

4.6–9: Friendships formed with this kind of love are seldom directed toward helping one love God more.

- The excess lies in the attraction based on self-interest, which results in enslavement.

- Gives advice on breaking away from these attachments.

4.10: As for the defect in love: to live together without love is to live like brutes. Virtue inspires love.

4.11–13: She now directs her attention to virtuous love, which is of two kinds: 1) spiritual; 2) spiritual mixed with sensuality.

* The spiritual love is not affected by any passion

* Hardly does Teresa begin speaking of spiritual love, when she is led into a lengthy digression about confessors.

* Advice about what to do if the confessor turns toward "some vanity."

4.13–16: Continues with her advice. Consult with some learned person.

* How many mistakes have been made in the world by doing things without counsel.

* If those who live here see that someone doesn't love to speak of God, they will not be able to love him.

* The sisters don't know how to be at peace because the one who should be helping and calming them is the one who causes the harm.

INTERPRETIVE NOTES. 1. The inward and outward peace that ought to accompany the contemplative life streams from the three virtues that Teresa promises to speak about. But we mortals can be fooled by a false peace that results from a steadily growing blindness.

In her *Meditations on the Song of Songs,* Teresa discusses false kinds of peace that come from the devil, the flesh, and the world: "When such persons of the world remain quiet, while going about in serious sin, and so tranquil about their vices, for their consciences don't feel remorseful about anything, their peace, you have read, is a sign that they and the devil are friends" (M 2.1).

2. Spiritual warfare is a favor from the Lord. She is suspicious of the prayer of those who live in peace without struggle (cf. M 2.2–4). The peace that Christ offers, and is so necessary for unceasing prayer, comes through a complete remaking of those who pray: in their relationships with others (love-charity); in their attitude toward possessions (detachment-hope); and in their attitude toward self (humility-faith). In St. Paul's words: "you should put away the old self of your former way of life, corrupted through deceitful desires, and be renewed in the spirit of your minds, and put on the new self, created in God's way" (Eph 4:22–24; cf. Rom 6:5–6; Col 3:9–10).

3. At the summit of her spiritual journey of prayer, Teresa felt St. Paul's words could well be her own: "*For me to live is Christ, and to die is gain* [Phil 1:21].... And that its life is Christ is understood better, with the passing of time, by the effects this life has. Through some secret aspirations the soul understands clearly that it is God who gives life to our soul.... It is understood clearly that there is Someone in the interior depths who shoots these arrows and gives life to this life, and

that there is a Sun in the interior of the soul from which a brilliant light proceeds and is sent to the faculties. The soul, as I have said, does not move from that center nor is its peace lost; for the very One who gave peace to the apostles when they were together can give it to the soul" (IC VII.2.5–6).

4. Unceasing prayer (1 Thes 5:17), to which the nuns were called also by their Carmelite rule, could not be produced through mere human efforts. Teresa felt it more and more as a gift along with Christ's peace. The exact words of the Carmelite rule are: "Each of you is to stay in your own cell or nearby, *pondering the Lord's law day and night* and *keeping watch at your prayers* unless attending to some other duty" (*Rule of St. Albert*, no 8).

5. We can do our part to prepare for contemplation. So before she begins to deal with prayer and contemplation, Teresa has many things to say about the preparation for contemplation. Even when she is as far along as chapter 20, she marvels: "But how many things come to mind in beginning to discuss this path.... Would that I had many hands with which to write so that while putting down some of these things I wouldn't forget the others" (20.6).

6. In the previous chapter, Teresa spoke in favor of women, and the censor objected. Here she admits frankly to a defect she thinks is found more in women of her time (6) than in men. Of course, here the censor did not object. A fault Teresa observed in the men of her time was their tendency to turn prayer into an exercise for the composition of syllogisms (L 13.11); they

smother the fire with the heavy wood of their erudition (L 15.7); they must learn to delight in the presence of Christ and that the important thing is not to think much but to love much (IC IV.1.7).

QUESTIONS FOR DISCUSSION. 1. How can we find peace in life?

2. Have I had any experiences in which acts of charity, humility, or detachment have brought me greater peace?

3. What does St. Teresa mean by unceasing prayer? Is it a possibility in our lives?

4. What are some of the negative factors in the "excessive love" about which Teresa speaks?

Chapter 5

Continues on the subject of confessors. Speaks of the importance of their being learned.

MAY THE LORD, because of who he is, not allow anyone in this house to undergo the trial that has been mentioned; that is, to find oneself in this affliction of body and soul. Nor may he allow a situation in which if the prioress gets along well with the confessor no one dares to speak either to him about her or to her about him. The result of this state of affairs will be the temptation to omit the confession of very serious sins for fear of being disturbed. O God help me, what harm the devil can cause here, and how dearly the nuns will pay for this restriction and concern about honor! For while they think that by dealing with no more than one confessor they are doing something great for religious life and the reputation of the monastery, the devil manages in this way to catch souls, since he cannot in any other. If they ask to go to another confessor, it immediately seems as if the peace and harmony of religious life will be lost. Or if the desired confessor is not from the same order, merely speaking with him, even though he may be a saint [Jerome], is taken as an affront by the others. [Praise God very much, daughters, for this freedom that you have, since you are able here to speak to others — though not too many others — besides your ordinary confessors, and these will give you light about everything.][1]

2. I ask, for the love of the Lord, that this holy freedom be allowed by the one who is superior. May she always ask permission from the bishop or the provincial that, besides speaking with the ordinary confessors, she and all the others might sometimes speak and discuss their souls with learned persons, especially if the confessors, however good, may not be learned.[2] Learning is a great help for shedding light upon every matter. It will be possible to find both learning and goodness in some persons. And the more the Lord favors you in prayer, the more necessary it will be that your prayer and good works have a good foundation.

3. You already know that the cornerstone must be a good conscience and that with all your strength you must strive to free yourselves even from venial sins and seek what is the most perfect. It will seem to you that any confessor knows this, but that is misleading. It happened to me that I spoke about matters of conscience with a confessor who had gone through the whole course of theology, and he did me a great deal of harm by telling me that some matters didn't amount to anything. I know that he didn't intend to misinform me and had no reason to, but he simply didn't know any more. And the same thing happened to me with two or three others, besides the one I mentioned.[3]

4. Having true light at our disposal for the sake of keeping the law of God with perfection is all our good; prayer is well founded on such light. Without this strong foundation and if the Sisters are not given freedom to confess and discuss their souls with persons like those I have mentioned, the whole building will be wobbly. [Thus they must speak to spiritual and learned persons. If the appointed confessor is not spiritual and learned, they should at times seek out others. And if, perhaps, they receive orders not to confess to others, they can speak outside of confession to the kind of person I mentioned.] And I dare say more, that even if the confessor has all the

qualities I mentioned, it is good sometimes to consult others because it is still possible for him to be mistaken; and it is important that not all be misled by him. One should seek always that there be nothing contrary to obedience, for there are ways and means for everything. And so it is good that in all possible ways one seek such counsel that is so valuable to souls.

5. All this that I have said should be of concern to the prioress. So I beg her again that, since no other consolation is sought here than the soul's, she should seek the soul's consolation by doing what I said. For there are different paths along which God leads souls, and one confessor perhaps will not know them all. I assure you there will not be lacking holy persons who will want to speak to you about your souls and bring you comfort if your souls are what they should be — even though you may be poor. He who sustains your bodies will awaken someone and give him the desire to enlighten your souls and bring a remedy to this evil that I fear. For even if the devil tempts a confessor so as to deceive him about some doctrine, he will be careful and consider with caution everything he does when he knows that you speak to others.

Once this entrance has been taken away from the devil, I hope in God he will not find another one in this house. So I beg the bishop, whoever he may be, for love of the Lord, to allow the Sisters this freedom and not take it away from them when the persons they consult possess learning and goodness, a fact they can easily get to know in a city as small as this.[4]

6. I have seen and understood what I have mentioned here, and discussed it with learned and holy persons who have considered what was most suitable for this house so that there would be progress along the path of perfection. Among dangers, which are always present as long as we live, we find that this one is a lesser one. The vicar[5] should never have a free hand to come and go, nor should the confessor have this

freedom. Rather, they should be protecting the recollection and decorum of the house and its progress, both interior and exterior, and should tell the bishop when there is some fault; but neither the vicar nor the confessor should be the superior.[6]

7. This is our practice at present — but not merely because of my opinion. The bishop we now have, under whose obedience we are (for many reasons obedience was not given to the order),[7] is a person fond of religious life and holiness and is a great servant of God. (His name is Don Alvaro de Mendoza; he is of high nobility and lineage and very fond of favoring this house in every way.) He gathered persons of learning, spirituality, and experience together in order to deal with this point; and freedom was decided upon. It is only right that the superiors who follow should hold to this opinion; it was decided upon by such good persons and sought from God with many prayers for enlightenment about the best thing to do. And from what has been known up until the present, this practice certainly is the best thing. May the Lord be pleased to preserve it always since it is for his greater glory, amen.

THE NEED FOR LEARNING

Still working with her material, now in a digression about confessors, Teresa allows herself to get drawn into another digression, on the need for consulting learned men. Here she does not call for restrictions but cries out in favor of a "holy freedom."

5.1–4: There is no reason for considering it a praiseworthy practice that a monastery of nuns be restricted to one confessor.

- The prioress and all the other nuns should sometimes consult persons of learning.

- "Learning is a great help for shedding light on every matter."

- Knowledge is necessary in order to form a good conscience so as to be free even from venial sin and keep the law of God with perfection.

- Prayer is well founded on such light.

5.5: A. Begs the prioress to allow the nuns to seek counsel from others besides the confessor.

B. Begs the bishop to allow the nuns this freedom.

5.6–7: A. She wants teachers from outside and a group of women eager for light and doctrine, the former on the condition that they do not interfere in the internal life of the community.

B. She appeals to the authoritative opinion of the bishop who had consulted persons of learning and decided that this freedom would be a beneficial practice.

INTERPRETIVE NOTES. 1. "Through loyalty to conscience, Christians are joined to others in the search for truth and for the right solution to so many moral problems which arise both in the life of individuals and from social relationships. Hence the more a correct conscience prevails, the more do persons and groups turn aside from blind choice and try to be guided by the objective standards of moral conduct. Yet it often happens that conscience goes astray through ignorance which it is unable to avoid, without thereby losing its dignity. This cannot be said of the one who takes little trouble to find out what is true and good, or when conscience is by degrees almost blinded through the habit of committing sin" (Vatican II, *Gaudium et Spes*, no. 16). Teresa is a moving example of willingness to consult others when making choices and endeavoring to stay the course.

2. Her own experience with confessors as described in her *Life* is worth quoting in full:

"Half-learned confessors have done my soul great harm when I have been unable to find a confessor with as much learning as I like. I have come to see by experience that it is better, if they are virtuous and observant of holy customs, that they have little learning. For then they do not trust themselves without asking someone who knows, nor do I trust them; and a truly learned man has never misguided me. Those others certainly could not have wanted to mislead me, but they didn't know any better. I thought that they really knew and that I was obliged to no more than to believe them, especially since what they told me was liberal and permissive. If it had been rigid, I am so wretched that I would have sought out others. What was venial sin they said was no sin at all, and what was serious mortal sin they said was venial. This did me so much harm that it should not surprise anyone that I speak of it here in order to warn others against so great an evil. I see clearly that in God's eyes there is no excuse for me, for that the things by their nature were wrong should have been enough for me to have been on guard against them. It was on account of my sins, I believe, that God permitted these confessors to be mistaken themselves and to misguide me. And I misled many others by telling them what these confessors told me.

"I went on in this blindness for I believe more than seventeen years until a Dominican father, a very learned man, enlightened me about many things. And the Jesuit fathers made me fear everything so much by showing me how wrong those theories were, as I shall tell later" (L 5.3).

3. Teresa's love for learning was not encouraged everywhere: The Dominican Melchior Cano, counselor of Philip II, maintained that divulging the mysteries of the faith, of theology, and of the spiritual life in the Castilian language for women was "something injurious to the public good."

The Franciscans who had initiated reforms at that time tended to be suspicious of learning. Thus the reformer Pedro de Villacreces once announced: "St. Francis often asserted that knowledge would be the downfall of the order. And I learned more in my cell weeping in darkness than studying by candlelight at Salamanca, Toulouse, or Paris."

QUESTIONS FOR DISCUSSION. 1. In what ways might we receive bad counsel from the world around us?

2. Sin — personal, social, original — is a reality in our lives; what steps might we take to acquire the light needed for our moral and spiritual lives?

Chapter 6

Returns to the subject already begun, that of perfect love.

I HAVE DIGRESSED ENOUGH, but what was said is so important that anyone who understands it will not blame me. Let us return now to the love that it is good for us to have, that which I say is purely spiritual.[1] I don't know if I know what I am saying. At least I don't think it's necessary to speak much about this love, because few have it. Let the one to whom the Lord has given it praise him very much because such a person must have reached the highest perfection. Anyway, I want to say a little about this love. Doing so will perhaps be of some benefit; for when virtue is placed before our eyes, the one who desires it grows fond of it and seeks to gain it.

2. May it please God that I understand this love; and even more, that I know how to speak of it. For I don't think I know which love is spiritual, or when sensual love is mixed with spiritual love, nor do I know why I want to speak about this spiritual love. My situation is like that of one who hears others speaking in the distance but doesn't understand what they are saying. So it is that sometimes I don't think I understand what I'm saying, but the Lord wills that it be well said. If at other times what I say is nonsense, that is what is most natural to me — not being correct in anything.

3. Now it seems to me that those whom God brings to a certain clear knowledge love very differently than do those who have not reached it. This clear knowledge is about the nature of the world, that there is another world, about the difference between the one and the other, that the one is eternal and the other a dream; or about the nature of loving the Creator and loving the creature (and this seen through experience, which is entirely different from merely thinking about it or believing it); or this knowledge comes from seeing and feeling what is gained by the one love and lost by the other, and what the Creator is and what the creature is, and from many other things that the Lord teaches to anyone who wants to be taught by him in prayer, or whom His Majesty desires to teach.

4. It may be, Sisters, that you will think it useless for me to speak of this love and that you will say everybody already knows these things I have mentioned. May it please the Lord that this be so, that you know them in such a way that they be important to you and impressed deep within your being. For if you have this knowledge, you will see that I do not lie in saying that whoever the Lord brings to the state of perfection has this love. The persons the Lord brings to this state are generous souls, majestic souls. They are not content with loving something as wretched as these bodies, however beautiful they may be, however attractive. Yes, it pleases them to see such bodies, and they praise the Creator; but, no, they do not stop there. I mean stop in such a way that they love these things. It would seem to them that they were loving something of no substance, loving a shadow. They would feel chagrin, and they wouldn't have the courage, without great shame, to tell God they love him.

5. You will tell me that such perfect persons do not know how to love or repay the love others have for them — at least, they care little about being loved. At times nature suddenly rejoices at being loved, but then when these persons return to themselves they see that this is foolish, unless the souls of the

others will benefit either by doctrine or by prayer. All other affection wearies these persons, for they understand that no benefit comes from it and that it could be harmful. But this does not make these persons ungrateful or unwilling to repay the love of others by recommending them to God. They entrust to the Lord the care of those who love them, for they understand that the love comes from him. It doesn't seem there is anything within themselves to love, and they immediately think they are loved because these others love God. They leave it to His Majesty to repay those who love them, and they beg him to do so. In this way they remain free, for it seems to them that repaying the love is not their business. And, in fact, I think at times that if love does not come from those persons who can help us gain the blessings of the perfect, there would be great blindness in this desire to be loved.

6. Now, note well that when we desire love from some person, there is always a kind of seeking our own benefit or satisfaction, and these perfect persons have already trampled underfoot all the good things and comforts the world has to offer them. Their consolations are of a kind that even though they may desire them, so to speak, they cannot tolerate having them apart from God or from speaking of him. For what benefit can come to them from being loved?

7. Since this truth is made known to them, they laugh at themselves because of the affliction they once suffered as to whether or not their love was repaid. Although our affection is good, the desire that it be repaid is very natural. But once we receive the payment, we realize that the pay is all straw; it's all air and without substance so that the wind carries it away. No matter how much we have been loved, what is there that remains for us? As a result, you shouldn't care whether you are loved or not, unless the love is for your spiritual benefit as in the case of those perfect souls I mentioned, for they realize that our nature is such that if we are not loved we soon grow weary.

It will seem to you that such persons do not love or know anyone but God. I say, yes they do love, with a much greater and more genuine love, and with passion, and with a more beneficial love; in short, it is love. And these souls are more inclined to give than to receive. Even with respect to the Creator himself they want to give more than to receive. I say that this attitude is what merits the name "love," for these other base attachments have usurped the name "love."

8. You will also wonder what they have affection for if they do not love because of the things they see. It is true that what they see they love and what they hear they become attached to; but the things that they see are stable. As soon as these persons love, they go beyond the bodies and turn their eyes to the soul and look to see if there is something to love in the soul. And if there isn't anything lovable, but they see some beginning and readiness so that if they love this soul and dig in this mine they will find gold, their labor causes them no pain. Nothing could be presented to them that they wouldn't eagerly do for the good of this soul, for they desire to continue loving it; but they know that if it does not love God very much and have his blessings, their loving it is impossible. And I say that this is impossible, no matter how much they are obligated to it; and even if it dies with love for them and does all the good works it can for them and possesses all natural graces combined, their wills will not have the strength to love it or make this love last. These persons with perfect love already have experience and know what everything is; they will not be deceived. They see that they are not at one with the other and that it is impossible for the two to continue loving each other. For it is a love that must end when they die if the other is not keeping the law of God, and these persons understand that the other does not love God and that the two must then go to their different destinies.

9. And one of these persons to whom the Lord has given true wisdom cannot esteem this love, which lasts only here on earth, for more than what it is worth, or even for less. Those who like to find their pleasure in the things of the world, in its delights, honors, and riches will attribute some value to whether the other is rich or has the means to provide for diversion and recreation. But whoever has already come to abhor all of this cares little or nothing about such things.

Well now in the case of perfect love, if a person loves there is the passion to make the other soul worthy of being loved, for, as I say, this person knows that otherwise this love for the other will not continue. It is a love that costs dearly. This person does everything possible for the other's benefit, would lose a thousand lives that a little good might come to the other soul. O precious love that imitates the Commander-in-chief of love, Jesus, our Good!

SPIRITUAL LOVE IN THEORY

After two digressions, Teresa returns to the subject she began to speak of, which seems to have been fending her off: the subject of spiritual or perfect love. Underlying her teaching is her own personal story. This entire chapter was written in the form of a dialogue in which Teresa answers the questions and doubts of the nuns.

6.1: Few have this love, but when virtue is placed before our eyes, the one who desires it grows fond of it.

6.2: Doubts whether she herself understands or is capable of speaking of this love.

6.3: God gives some a "certain clear knowledge."

- They thus love differently from those without it.

- They have an experiential knowledge:

  - of two worlds: the one eternal; the other a dream.

  - of two loves: one for the Creator; the other for the creature.

  - of what is gained by the one love, and lost by the other.

6.4–9: A. An imagined dialogue with the sisters:

Srs: Everybody knows the above things.

T: May you have them impressed deep within you. This love is characteristic of the state of perfection:

It is not drawn by attractive bodies.
When pleased by them, it praises the Creator.
Otherwise, its object would be a shadow.

Srs: Persons with such perfect love don't know
how to repay the love of others.

T: They entrust to the Lord the care of those
who love them. It doesn't seem there is
within themselves anything to love. So, they
think they are loved because these others
love God. They cannot tolerate having anything apart from God. They no longer
worry about whether or not their love is
repaid. The pay is all straw.

Srs: Such persons do not love or know anyone
but God.

T: Yes they do love — with passion. They want
to give more than receive. Base attachments have usurped the name of love.

Srs: What do they have affection for if they do
not love what they see?

T: The things they see are stable. They look to
see if there is something to love in the soul.
Sometimes they must dig to find the gold
in another. There is nothing they wouldn't
do for the good of a soul. But if that soul
does not love God, they cannot love it; the
two must go their separate ways.

B. True wisdom cannot esteem the love that lasts only
here on earth.

C. A person with perfect love does everything possible to make the other worthy of being loved. It is a love that costs dearly.

INTERPRETIVE NOTES. 1. Taking up the subject of pure spiritual love, Teresa has to rely on her own long experience with love (cf. L 7.6–19; 24.5–8; 37.4–5). Love has as its basis knowledge of reality. The ultimate reality engendering love is God. God was not for Teresa a mental recourse for facilitating an activity that is annoying and arduous. God is definitively the living presence that works in the deep regions of our being. God is the greatest good of our neighbor. For Teresa, pure spiritual love finds its foundation in an understanding of Truth. In her *Life* she explains the effects flowing from her mystical vision of Truth:

"From this divine Truth, which showed itself to me, there was engraved upon me, without my knowing how or what, a truth that gives me a new reverence toward God; for it gives knowledge of his majesty and power in an indescribable way.... I think that without my understanding how, the Lord gave me very much with this favor. I felt no suspicion that it was an illusion. I didn't see anything, but I understood the great blessing there is in not paying attention to what doesn't bring us closer to God. Thus I understood that the Lord gave me understanding of what Truth itself is" (L 40.3).

2. The New Testament portrays God's love, made visible in Jesus, as the source and substance of a new, compassionate, and selfless love offered by Christians to all

people. Jesus adroitly describes this love through his unforgettable story of the Good Samaritan (Lk 10:30–37).

3. St. Paul delineates all God's activities as well as a rule for human behavior in a song of love: "Love is patient, love is kind. It is not jealous, love is not pompous, it is not inflated, it is not rude, it does not rejoice over wrongdoing but rejoices with the truth. It bears all things, believes all things, hopes all things, endures all things" (1 Cor 13:4–7).

QUESTIONS FOR DISCUSSION. 1. What are some of the traits of pure, or perfect, love given by Teresa?

2. Can we think of any others?

Chapter 7

Treats of the same subject, spiritual love, and gives some advice on how to obtain it.

IT'S STRANGE HOW IMPASSIONED THIS LOVE IS, the tears it costs, the penances and prayer; what concern to ask prayers for the one loved from all who it thinks can help that person toward God; what constant desire that others recommend that person to God. It is not happy unless it sees the loved one make progress. If, on the other hand, it sees that person improving and then turning back somewhat, there doesn't seem to be any pleasure for it in life. It neither eats nor sleeps without this care about the other. It is always fearful lest the soul it loves so much be lost and the two be separated forever. Death here below matters nothing to it, for it doesn't want to become attached to anything that in a mere moment escapes from one's hand and cannot be grasped again. It is, as I said,[1] a love with no self-interest at all. All that it desires or wants is to see the other soul rich with heavenly blessings.

2. This is what love is, and not these other miserable earthly affections — although I don't mean evil ones, for God deliver us from them. We must never tire of condemning anything that leads to hell, for the slightest evil of hell cannot be exaggerated. We shouldn't let our mouths utter even a word about this sinful love, Sisters, nor should we think that it exists in the world. We shouldn't listen to anything said about

it, whether this be done in jest or in truth. Do not allow that this type of love be spoken of or discussed in your presence. Such love has nothing good in it, and even hearing about it can be harmful. You may speak about the licit love I mentioned, which we have for one another or for relatives and friends and in which our care is that our loved ones don't die; or, if the other's head aches our souls seem to ache too, and if they suffer trials, it seems that we lose our patience; and other things like that.

3. Spiritual love is not like this. Even though some grief is at first felt through natural weakness, reason immediately considers whether the trial is good for the one loved, whether there is an enrichment in virtue and how that soul bears the suffering; it asks God to give the other patience and merit in the trials. If this love sees that the other person has patience, no distress is felt; rather it rejoices and is consoled. This love would much rather suffer the trial itself than see the other suffer it if the merit and gain that lies in suffering could be given to the other entirely — but not because this love is disquieted and disturbed.

4. I say once again[2] that spiritual love seems to be imitating that love which the good lover Jesus had for us. Hence, these lovers advance so far because they embrace all trials, and the others, without trial, receive benefit from those who love. And believe me, either these lovers will cut off their relationship — I mean special friendship — or they will obtain from our Lord that the one loved walk along their own way toward the same goal, as did St. Monica with St. Augustine. These lovers cannot in their hearts be insincere with those they love; if they see them deviate from the path or commit some faults they immediately tell them about it. They cannot help but do so. And since they are not going to change their attitude, nor are they going to flatter or hide anything from the other, either others mend their ways or the friendship is broken. For these

lovers cannot suffer such a thing, nor should it be suffered. There is a continual war between the two attitudes these lovers have; on the one hand they go about forgetful of the whole world, taking no account of whether others serve God or not but only keeping account of themselves; on the other hand, with their friends, they have no power to do this, nor is anything covered over; they see the tiniest speck. I say that they bear a truly heavy cross. [Oh fortunate are the souls loved by such as these! Fortunate was the day they came to know them! O my Lord, would you not be doing me a favor if there were many who so loved me? Certainly, it would be more beneficial to me than if I were loved by all the kings and lords of the world; and rightly so, for these persons strive in as many ways as they can that we ourselves be lords of that very world and that all things be subject to us.

When you know some person like this, Sisters, let the Mother prioress diligently strive to have that one speak with you. Love such persons as much as you like. They must be few, but the Lord does desire that it be known when someone has reached perfection. You will be immediately told that speaking with such a one is unnecessary, that it is enough to have God. But a good means to having God is to speak with his friends, for one always gains very much from this. I know through experience. After the Lord, it is because of persons like these that I am not in hell, for I was always very attached to their praying for me, and so I strove to get them to do this. Now let us return to our subject.]

5. This spiritual love is the kind of love I would desire us to have. Even though in the beginning it is not so perfect, the Lord will gradually perfect it. Let us begin by using the suitable means, for even though the love bears with it some natural tenderness no harm will be done provided this tenderness is shown toward all. It is good and necessary sometimes in loving to show and also have affection, and to feel some of the

trials and sicknesses of the Sisters, even though these may be small. For at times it happens that some trifle will cause as much suffering to one as a great trial will to another; little things can bring much distress to persons who have sensitive natures. [And do not be surprised, for perhaps the devil employed all his energy here, more energy than what he uses when you feel great sufferings and trials.] If you are not like them, do not fail to be compassionate. And perhaps our Lord desires to exempt us from these sufferings, whereas in other matters we will suffer. And those sufferings that for us are heavy — even if in themselves they truly are — may be light for another. So in these matters let us not judge from ourselves, nor let us think that we are at a stage in which perhaps the Lord without our own effort has made us stronger, but let us think of the stage we were at when we were weaker.

6. Consider that this advice is important for knowing how to sympathize with your neighbor who is having trials, however small they may be. This is especially true in the case of those souls that were mentioned.[3] Since they desire trials they make little of everything, and it is very necessary that they take the time to remember how they themselves were once weak and that if they are not weak now, their strength doesn't come from themselves. For it could be that the devil by this means

will make charity toward one's neighbor grow cold, and make us think that what in reality is a fault belongs to perfection. It is necessary to be careful and awake in everything, for he does not sleep. This is truer in the case of those advancing in perfection. The temptations are then very deceiving, since the devil wouldn't dare anything else. It doesn't seem the harm is recognized until it is already done if, as I say, one doesn't take care. In sum, it is necessary to watch and pray always, for there is no better remedy than prayer for discovering these secret things of the devil and bringing them to light.

7. Strive also to take time for recreation with the Sisters when there is need and during the time set aside for it by

custom, even though this may not be to your pleasure, for everything done with a pure intention is perfect love. [And so it is that when I desire to speak of that other love that is not so perfect, I do not find in this house any path in which I think it would be good for us to have such love. For however good this love might be, everything must hark back to its origin, which is the perfect love I spoke of. I thought of saying much about this other love, and now that I've come to discuss its fine points, I don't think it fits our way of life. So, I want to leave the matter as it stands; I hope in God that in this house there will be no opportunity for any other kind of love than perfect love, even though our love may not be entirely perfect.] Thus, it is very good that some take pity on others in their need. Let them take care that there be no lack of discretion in things that would go against obedience. Even though within yourself the prioress's commands may seem harsh, don't show this or let anyone know about it — unless, with humility, the prioress herself — for you would cause much harm. And learn how to understand which are the things one ought to feel sorry about and take pity on with regard to the Sisters. And always grieve over any fault, if it is publicly known, that you see in a Sister. Here love shows itself, and it is practiced well when you know how to suffer the fault and not be surprised; so the others will do with respect to your faults, for you may have many more than you are aware of. Recommend the Sister to God and strive yourself to practice with great perfection the virtue opposite the fault that appears in her. Make every effort to do this so that you teach that Sister in deed what perhaps through words or punishment she might not understand or profit by; and the imitation of the virtue in which one sees another excel has a great tendency to spread. This is good advice; don't forget it.

8. Oh, how good and true will be the love of the Sister who can help others by setting aside her own advantage for their sake. She will make much progress in all the virtues and

keep her rule with great perfection. Better friendship will this be than all the tender words that can be uttered, for these are not used, nor should they be used, in this house; those like, "my life," "my soul," "my only good," and other similar expressions addressed now to one, now to another, of the Sisters. Keep these words of affection for your Spouse, for you must be with him so much and so alone that you will need to be helped by everything; His Majesty allows us to use these words with him. But if they are used a lot among ourselves, they will not be so touching when used with the Lord. And besides, there's no reason for using them. They are very womanish, and I would not want you, my daughters, to be womanish in anything, nor would I want you to be like women but like strong men. For if you do what lies in your power, the Lord will make you so strong that you will astonish men. And how easy this is for His Majesty since he made us from nothing.

9. Another very good proof of love is that you strive in household duties to relieve others of work, and also rejoice and praise the Lord very much for any increase you see in their virtues. All these things, not to mention the great good they contain in themselves, help very much to further peace and conformity between the Sisters, as we now, by God's goodness, see through experience. May it please His Majesty that this love always continue. The contrary would be a terrible thing, and very difficult to endure: that is, few in number and disunited. God forbid.[4]

10. If by chance some little word should escape, try to remedy the matter immediately and pray intensely. And if things of this sort against charity continue, such as little factions, or ambition, or concern about some little point of honor (for I think my blood freezes when I write about this and think that at some time it could happen, because I see it is the main evil in monasteries); when these things begin to take place consider yourselves lost. Think and believe that you have thrown

your Spouse out of the house and have made it necessary for him to go in search of another dwelling, since you threw him out of his own house. Cry out to His Majesty. Seek a remedy; for if you don't find one after such frequent confession and Communion, there is reason to fear a Judas among you.

11. Let the prioress for the love of God watch carefully that no place be given to such concerns, and root them out from the beginning; from whether she does this or not will stem either all the harm or all the remedy. [And if love doesn't suffice to do this, let it be done with severe punishments.] And anyone found to be the cause of such disturbance should be sent to another monastery, for God will provide her with the dowry. Get rid of this pestilence; cut off the branches as best you can, and if this is not enough pull up the roots. And if that doesn't work, do not let the one who is taken up with these things leave the prison cell. That's much better than letting so incurable a pestilence infect all the nuns. Oh, how great an evil it is! God deliver us from the monastery where it enters; I would rather that the monastery catch fire and all be burned. Because I believe I shall say something about this elsewhere — since it is something so important — I'll not enlarge on it any more here.[5]

SPIRITUAL LOVE IN PRACTICE

The previous chapter developed the teaching about spiritual love doctrinally. Now Teresa gives practical instructions about it: how this spiritual love may be lived in community.

7.1: This love is an impassioned love; it is not happy unless it sees the other make progress in the love of God; it is a love with no self-interest at all.

7.2–4: She contrasts spiritual love with another kind of love in which there is no evil affection of the type that leads to hell, but which is licit.

- Grief may be felt over another's misfortune, but in spiritual love reason immediately considers whether the trial is good for the loved one.

- Like Jesus' love it would rather suffer the trial itself than see the other suffer it.

- Like St. Monica, in spiritual love one cannot be insincere with the one loved if that one deviates from the path.

- You gain greatly from speaking with one who loves you with this love.

7.5–10: Practical instructions:

- In the beginning this love is not so perfect; if tender affections are mixed with it, the effort should be made to show the same kind of love to all.

- Little things can cause real distress to some; we should be compassionate even though to us they seem little, and think of the stage we were at when weaker.

- Take recreation with the sisters.

This I think need to be updated

- Suffer the faults of others; recommend them to God and practice the opposite virtue.

- Set aside your own advantage for your sister's sake; this is a better sign of friendship than tender words:

  – These sentimental words only confirm the stereotype in vogue that women are too sentimental.

  – Demonstrate the truth: with the Lord's help, women can be so strong as to astonish men.

- In household duties, relieve others of work.

- If some word should escape, remedy the matter immediately.

7.10–11: Deeds against charity: factions, ambition, holding grudges over points of honor. These make my blood freeze; get rid of this pestilence!

INTERPRETIVE NOTES. 1. Contrary to what we are apt to think, spiritual love does not exclude intensity. Teresa's warm letters abound with concrete expressions of her heart before all kinds of people. Each community, each friendship has its own features. We would be mistaken to think that all must be loved equally; rather, each one must be loved uniquely. Theological love does not obliterate the human personality. Some examples from Teresa's own experience can exemplify the different situations in which she manifests her love.

First, the love for one of her confessors expressed in her *Life*, who now happens to be a censor of this work:

"I've experienced this for some years: as soon as I see a person who greatly pleases me, with longings I sometimes cannot bear, I want to see him give himself totally to God. And although I desire that all serve God, the longings come with very great impulses in the case of these persons I like; so I beg the Lord very much on their behalf. With the religious I'm speaking of, it so happened to me" (L 34.7).

Second, in a letter to María Bautista who both complained that Padre Báñez didn't answer her letters and wanted to return like for like, Teresa responded:

"Had God not prevented me, I should long ago have done what you wanted to do, but the Lord would not permit me, and I know he is God's servant, and for that reason he ought to be loved, and deserves to be, like all of God's servants who live on this earth. We would be very foolish to expect to get more from them, but that is no reason why we should be like him, though we must always be grateful to him for the kindnesses he has done us. So your reverence must stop being so oversensitive, and not give up writing to him but try gradually to gain freedom of spirit. For myself, glory to God, I have plenty of this, though not as much as you say. Blessed be the Lord, who when we seek his friendship is always our true Friend" (María Bautista, 2 November 1576).

Third, María de San José had the kinds of qualities that exercised a particular attraction over Teresa: gentleness of manner, joy, affability, discretion, and good intelligence. Teresa writes to her:

"All the nuns were amazed to find how clever you are, and are very, very grateful to you, and so am I, for it is quite clear how much you love me from the way you give me pleasure in everything. I have known this all the time — and I can assure you that the love on my side is even greater, for I am amazed at my affection for you. You must not imagine I love anyone more than you, for not all the nuns appeal so much to my nature. The worst of it is that I am so wicked that I can be of little use to you, though I am most particular about commending you to God" (4 June 1578).

Fourth, when attractive qualities were lacking, Teresa's love of God could break down the walls of her natural resistance. This was clearly the case with her brother Pedro de Ahumada, who suffered from melancholia and caused his brother Lorenzo, to whom Teresa was very close, no end of trouble. In a letter to Lorenzo, she writes:

"I declare God seems to be allowing this poor man to try us so as to discover the extent of our charity. And really, brother, I have so little as far as he is concerned that it quite distresses me. For, even if he were not my brother at all, but only my neighbor, I ought to be moved by his need, and yet I feel most uncharitable towards him. I try to get over this feeling by reminding myself of what I ought to do to please God, and once His Majesty enters into it, I find I would go to any lengths to help him. Were it not for that I assure you I would not do a thing" (10 April 1580).

QUESTIONS FOR DISCUSSION. 1. In what ways is spiritual love like Jesus' love?

2. What are some of the tangible ways in which we can try to practice this spiritual love?

Chapter 8

The great good that lies in detaching oneself inwardly and outwardly from all created things.

NOW LET US TALK ABOUT the detachment we ought to have, for detachment, if it is practiced with perfection, includes everything. I say it includes everything because if we embrace the Creator and care not at all for the whole of creation, His Majesty will infuse the virtues. Doing little by little what we can, we will have hardly anything else to fight against; it is the Lord who in our defense takes up the battle against the demons and against the world.

Do you think, Sisters, it is a small blessing we receive in obtaining this grace to give ourselves to the All entirely and without reserve? And since in him are all blessings, as I say, let us praise him very much, Sisters, for having brought us together here where the only concern is to give ourselves entirely to him. Indeed, I don't know why I am saying this because every one of you here can teach me. I confess that in this matter so important I am not as perfect as I desire or understand to be fitting. And this goes for all the virtues and all that I say here, for it is much easier to write about these things than to put them into practice. And I don't even succeed in writing about them, because sometimes knowing how to speak of them requires experience; and if I do succeed, it is perhaps by writing of the opposite of what I have practiced.

2. With regard to externals, obviously we are separated here from everything. [I think the Lord wants all of us he has gathered together in this house to withdraw from everything so that His Majesty may unite us to himself here without any hindrance. O my Creator and Lord! When did I merit such honor? For it seems you went a roundabout way to bring us closer to yourself. May it please your goodness that we do not lose through our own fault this nearness to you.] O Sisters, understand, for the love of God, the great favor the Lord has granted those whom he brought here. Each of you should reflect upon this carefully, for there are only twelve here and His Majesty desired that you be one of them.[1] And how many there are who are better than I, who I know would take this place eagerly, and the Lord gave it to me who so poorly deserved it! May you be blessed, my God, and may all creatures praise you! One cannot repay you for this favor — as is likewise so for many others you have granted me — for my vocation to be a nun was a very great favor! Since I have been so miserable, you did not trust me, Lord. Instead of keeping me where there were so many living together and where my wretchedness would not have been so clearly seen during my lifetime, you have brought me to a place where, since there are so few nuns, it seems impossible for this wretchedness not to be known. That I might walk more carefully, you have removed from me all opportunities to conceal it. Now I confess there is no longer an excuse for me, Lord, and so I have greater need of your mercy that you might pardon any fault I may have.[2]

3. What I ask of you, Sisters, is that if anyone sees within herself that she is unable to follow what is customarily practiced here she say so; there are other monasteries where the Lord is also served. Do not disturb these few nuns brought here together by His Majesty. In other places there is the freedom to find relief by being with relatives; here if some relatives are

allowed to visit, it is that they might find relief by being with us. But the nun who desires to see them for her own consolation, if these relatives are not spiritual persons, should consider herself imperfect. She ought to believe that she is not detached, not healthy; she will not possess freedom of spirit; she will not possess complete peace. She needs a doctor; and I say that if this attachment is not removed and she is not cured, she is not meant for this house.

4. The best remedy I know is that she not see them until obviously she is free and obtains this freedom from the Lord through much prayer. When it is clear that she considers these visits a cross, it will be all right for her to see them, for then she will be of benefit to her relatives and not be harmed herself. [But if she loves her relatives, if she grieves a great deal over their sufferings and eagerly listens to what they tell her about their business affairs in the world, she should believe that she will bring harm to herself and no good to them.]

DETACHMENT

Teresa now turns her attention to the second virtue recognized by her as a foundation for prayer. Treating this topic in the next five chapters, she offers us a little treatise on detachment. Detachment provides the freedom neccesary to surrender one's own person to Christ.

8.1–2: Detachment if practiced with perfection includes everything.

- It enables us to give ourselves to the All in all.

- Teresa is not as perfect as she desires in this matter.

- In this house there is already a detachment from externals.

- A prayer of gratitude to God for having brought her to this little community where her wretchedness is clearly seen and she must walk more carefully.

8.3–4: Begins to speak of detachment from relatives.

INTERPRETIVE NOTES. 1. Detachment is the antonym of being attached or bound to. More important, for Teresa, detachment has as its purpose the gift of self to the Lord.

2. If detachment for Teresa has as its purpose the gift of self to the Lord, then it clearly distinguishes itself from forms of detachment found in other religions or philosophies. Mani (ca. 215 A.D.), the founder of Manichaeism, borrowing elements from Zoroastrianism,

Buddhism, Gnosticism, and Christianity, saw himself as following the Old Testament prophets, Zarathustra, Buddha, and Jesus in seeking to free the spark of light in human beings and so deliver them from matter and darkness. This spark, he taught, is a portion of the divine substance that has fallen into matter. Systems of thought like this that regard matter as evil, something the spirit must be freed from, often stress the practice of detachment in alluring ways. So also with systems that, though they may not see the world as evil, do see it as no more than a stepping stone to the world of light (Platonism), or as offering no occasion at all for the perfectibility of human beings (Gnosticism).

3. At the other end of the spectrum, Teresa's detachment must not be confused with Jansenism. Jansenism, named after Cornelius Jansen (1585–1638), was a pluriform movement difficult to reduce to a unity. Taking shape in the century following Teresa's, it certainly did not look on matter as evil. But as it grew into a movement it tended to instill servile fear, with the presupposition that God has elected only a few and that one may not be numbered among the elect. The sacraments came to be seen more as a reward for perfection than as a means to attaining it. The purity necessary before receiving them led to the promotion of penance and dominion over self. Exercises of penance and mortification could, in addition, give souls a certain persuasion of their own election.

4. Vatican Council II reaffirms the Christian belief that the material world is God's creation, preserved in being by his loving providence, and having a destiny

in which the redeemed human family will play a role. The Christian vision of matter is optimistic and positive.

"Therefore, the world which the Council has in mind is the whole human family seen in the context of everything which envelopes it: it is the world as the theater of human history, bearing the marks of its travail, its triumphs and failures, the world, which in the Christian vision has been created and is sustained by the love of its maker, which has been freed from the slavery of sin by Christ, who was crucified and rose again in order to break the stranglehold of the evil one, so that it might be fashioned anew according to God's design and brought to its fulfillment" (*Gaudium et Spes*, no. 2).

QUESTIONS FOR DISCUSSION. 1. Why does Teresa think we should be detached?

2. What attitude toward creatures does her prayer reveal?

Chapter 9

On how good it is for those who have left the world to flee from relatives and how they find truer friends.

OH, IF WE RELIGIOUS COULD understand the great harm that comes from having too much to do with relatives! How we would flee them! I don't know what consolation they give us (if in talking with them we leave out what pertains to God and deal only with what pertains to our comfort and rest), for we cannot enjoy their recreations, nor would this be lawful for us. Oh yes, we can grieve over their trials; in fact, we do cry over all their tribulations and sometimes more than they themselves do. Surely, if they give the body some comfort, the spirit pays well for it. You are removed from this here. Since everything is held in common and no one can have any special comfort, the alms they give you are given in a general way; and you are freed from trying to please them on this account, for you know that it is the Lord who provides for all in common.

2. I am astonished by the harm that is caused from dealing with relatives. I don't think anyone will believe it except the one who has experienced it for himself. And how this practice of perfection seems to be forgotten nowadays in religious orders. I don't know what it is in the world that we renounce when we say that we give up everything for God if we do not give up the main thing, namely, our relatives. The situation has reached the state in which it seems to be a lack of virtue

for religious not to love and talk a great deal with their relatives, and these religious are not afraid to say and even advance their reasons.

3. In this house, daughters, great care should be taken to recommend them to God; that is right. As for the rest, we should keep them out of our minds as much as possible, because it is a natural thing for the will to become attached to them more than to other persons.

I have been much loved by my relatives — according to what they have said — and I loved them so much that I didn't let them forget me. But I know through my own experience as well as that of others that in time of trial my relatives helped me least. It was the servants of God who helped me. By relatives I do not mean parents, for parents very seldom fail to help their children, and it is right for us to console them in their need. Let us not remain aloof from them if we see that communicating with them does no harm to our religious life. This communication can be carried on with detachment; and so, too, with brothers and sisters.

4. Believe, Sisters, that if you serve His Majesty as you ought, you will not find better relatives than those he sends you. I know that this is so. Convinced of that, as you are here, and understanding that in doing otherwise you would be failing your true Friend and Spouse, believe that in a very short time you will gain this freedom. Believe that you can trust those who love you only for his sake more than you can all your relatives, and that these former will not fail you. And you will find fathers and brothers in those about whom you had not even thought. For since these seek to be repaid by God, they do things for us. Those who seek to be repaid by us soon grow tired, since they see that we are poor and unable to help them in any way. And although this may not be universally so, it is now more usually so; for, after all, the world is the world. Do

not believe whoever tells you to do something else and that it is virtue to do so. For if I should mention all the harm that this association with relatives brings in its wake, I would have to enlarge a great deal. And because others who know what they are saying better than I do have written about this, what I have said should suffice. If I who am so imperfect have understood so much about this, I wonder what those who are perfect know?

5. All that the saints counsel us about flight from the world is clearly good. Well, believe me, our relatives are what clings to us most from the world, as I have said,[1] and the most difficult to detach ourselves from. Consequently, those who flee from their own countries do well — if it helps them, I say, for I don't think it helps to flee bodily; rather what helps is that the soul embrace the good Jesus, our Lord, with determination, for since in him everything is found, in him everything is forgotten. Yet, it is a very great help to withdraw even bodily until we have come to know this truth. For afterward it may be that the Lord will want us to have dealings with them, giving us a cross where we used to find pleasure.

DETACHMENT FROM RELATIVES

Teresa continues the topic begun toward the end of the previous chapter. From the category of relatives she rules out parents, brothers, and sisters.

9.1: The nuns at St. Joseph's are freed from the need to please relatives so as to receive alms from them.

9.2: Religious seem to have forgotten the practice of perfection in which one should renounce everything for God, including relatives.

9:3–4: She confesses to the great love she has had for her relatives and their love for her.

- But in time of trial they did not help her.
- Those who love you for God's sake will not fail you.

9.5: Relatives are what clings to us most from the world. The remedy is to embrace the good Jesus our Lord; in him everything is found, in him everything is forgotten.

INTERPRETIVE NOTES: 1. Written shortly after her experience of life in her former monastery of the Incarnation, this chapter reflects some of Teresa's worst fears. Although she was fully aware of the many good nuns who lived at the Incarnation, she was dead against adopting some of its practices in her new foundations.

2. In Spain patronage of religious institutions maintained a strong association with family and clan. Many

lay members of society's elite endowed monasteries, but they reserved for themselves and members of their families critical aspects of the monastery's administration. The foundress of the Incarnation was particularly susceptible to issues of family and inheritence. Reserving the right to appoint her successor as prioress, she chose her daughter Catalina del Aguila. The Del Aguilas ruled for 70 years. The prioress when Teresa entered bore the title, "The Magnificent Lady Doña Francisca del Aguila."

3. In their profession, the nuns at the Incarnation promised only obedience. Many of them were daughters of some of the principal families of the city. Some entered not for religious reasons but simply because no marriage partner was available from their class in society.

4. But the Incarnation was poor and as the number grew beyond 100 nuns, the possibility of feeding everyone diminished. The expenses amounted to three times the income. When things got very bad, the nuns had to be sent to the homes of their parents or relatives.

5. Those coming from families of a high social class — a good percentage of the nuns — were not obliged to give up all their possessions. In speaking of the poverty of the monastery, one is speaking only of what was held in common. Every nun on making profession acquired the right of receiving from the monastery food and clothing in virtue of the dowry that was agreed upon. Besides this, many nuns had their own patrimony which they could use for their own needs. Those who didn't tried in other ways to make money or receive alms.

Despite their religious state, the nuns could buy and sell from their own possessions. Thus a nun could have in her cell her own belongings; some had their own kitchens and food and servants. Others had no cell at all but slept in dormitories. You can easily see how a nun would be led to cultivate relatives for the sake of alms. Also, you can easily imagine how the families in the higher rungs of society would keep a hand in the internal workings of the monastery.

6. In the above context, we can understand better Teresa's call for detachment from relatives. In St. Joseph's, where the number of nuns was not to exceed 12, she wanted no financial or psychological ties to relatives, no division of nuns into social classes. "Here we are all equal." "Everything is held in common." In chapter 8 she had admitted the existence of other monasteries (including the Incarnation) with legitimate lifestyles, not as revolutionary as St. Joseph's. They would be appropriate for those who found the radical detachment practiced in her new monastery too difficult.

7. A valuable passage from the *Spiritual Testimonies* casts some light on the question of detachment from relatives:

"Since my brothers had come and I owe so much to one of them, I didn't cease being with this one and discussing what was suited to his soul and state; and this all made me weary and uneasy. While offering these actions to the Lord and thinking I was thus obliged, I recalled that our constitutions tell us we should keep away from relatives. Thinking about whether I was obliged to follow these constitutions in this matter, the Lord told me: 'No, daughter, for your institutions must be in conformity with My law.' Indeed, the intention of the constitutions is that there be no attachment to relatives"(no. 41).

QUESTIONS FOR DISCUSSION. 1. What does Teresa encourage her sisters to do with respect to relatives?

2. What will help us practice detachment?

3. Does what Teresa says about the interference of relatives apply in any way to my life? What advice might Teresa give us in this regard?

Chapter 10

How it is not enough to be detached from what was mentioned if we are not detached from ourselves, and how both this virtue of detachment and humility go together.

ONCE WE HAVE DETACHED ourselves from the world and from relatives and have enclosed ourselves here under the conditions that were mentioned, it seems that we have done all there is to do and that we don't have to struggle with anything. Oh, my Sisters, do not feel secure or let yourselves go to sleep! By feeling secure you would resemble someone who very tranquilly lies down after having locked his doors for fear of thieves while allowing the thieves to remain inside the house. And you already know that there is no worse thief than we ourselves. For if you do not walk very carefully and if each Sister is not alert in going against her own will as though doing so were more important than all else, there are many things that will take away this holy freedom of spirit by which you can fly to your Maker without being held down by clay or leaden feet.

2. A great aid to going against your will is to bear in mind continually how all is vanity and how quickly everything comes to an end. This helps to remove our attachment to trivia and center it on what will never end. Even though this practice seems to be a weak means, it will strengthen the soul greatly, and the soul will be most careful in very little things. When we begin to become attached to something, we should strive to turn our thoughts from it and bring them back to

God — and His Majesty helps. He has done us a great favor because in this house most of the work of detachment has been done — although this turning and being against ourselves is a difficult thing because we live very close together and love ourselves greatly.

3. Here true humility can enter the picture because this virtue and the virtue of detachment it seems to me always go together. They are two inseparable sisters. These are not the relatives I advise you to withdraw from; rather, you should embrace them and love them and never be seen without them. O sovereign virtues, rulers over all creation, emperors of the world, deliverers from all snares and entanglements laid by the devil, virtues so loved by our teacher Christ who never for a moment was seen without them! Those who have them can easily go out and fight with all hell together and against the whole world and all its occasions of sin. Such persons have no fear of anyone, for theirs is the kingdom of heaven. They have no one to fear because they don't care if they lose everything, nor would they consider this a loss. The only thing they fear is displeasing their God, and they beg God to sustain them in these virtues lest they lose them through their own fault.

4. It is true that these virtues have the characteristic of so hiding themselves from the persons who possess them that these persons never see them or manage to believe that they have them even though they are told they do. But they esteem them so highly that they always go about striving to obtain them, and they gradually bring these virtues to perfection within themselves. Yet, these virtues are so manifest in the ones possessing them that without their desiring it, the virtues are at once recognized by others.

But what foolishness that I should set about praising humility and mortification when they were so much praised by the King of Glory and so confirmed by his many trials. Now, my daughters, this is the work that must be done in order to escape from the land of Egypt, for in finding these virtues you will find the manna.[1] All things will taste good to you. However bad a thing may taste to those who are in the world, you will find it sweet.

5. Now, then, the first thing we must strive for is to rid ourselves of our love for our bodies, for some of us are by nature such lovers of comfort that there is no small amount of work to be done in this area. And we are so fond of our health that it is amazing what a war our bodies cause, especially with nuns and even with those who are not. But some nuns it seems, including myself, didn't come to the monastery for any other reason than to strive not to die; each one strives for this as best she can. Here, truthfully, there is little opportunity to do this in deed, but I wouldn't want there to be even the desire. Be determined, Sisters, that you came to die for Christ, not to live comfortably for Christ. The devil suggests that you indulge yourselves so that you can keep the observance of the order; and a nun will so eagerly want to strive to care for and preserve her health for the sake of keeping the observance of the order that she dies without ever having kept this observance entirely for so much as a month, nor perhaps for even a day. Well, I don't know why we have come here!

6. Do not fear; very seldom will we lack discretion in this matter, for our confessors will at once be afraid that we may kill ourselves with penances. And the lack of such discretion is so abhorred by us that I wish we'd be so discreet in everything. I know that those who do the opposite will not care that I say this, nor do I care if they say I am judging from myself, for they would be saying the truth. I find for myself that the Lord wishes that we be sickly; at least in my case he granted me a great mercy in my being sick; for since I would have looked after my comfort anyway, he desired that there be a reason for my doing so.

Now it is amusing to see these persons and the torment they put themselves through. Sometimes they feel a desire to do penances without rhyme or reason, a desire that lasts a couple of days, so to speak; subsequently the devil makes them imagine that the penances did them harm. He makes them fear penance, and after some attempts they don't even dare carry out what the order commands.[2] We don't keep some of the very ordinary things of the rule, such as silence, which isn't going to do us any harm. Hardly does our head begin to ache than we stop going to choir, which won't kill us either. [We stay away one day because our head ached, another because it was just now aching, and three more so that it won't ache again.] And we seek to invent penances in our heads with the result that we can neither do the penances nor keep the observance. And at times the illness is slight, but we think we aren't obliged to do anything since we have done our duty by asking permission.

7. You will ask why the prioress gives it. If she knew what was going on inside us, perhaps she wouldn't give it. But since you tell her about your need and there is no want of a doctor to side with you about the advisability of such permission, or a friend or relative to weep at your side, what can she do? She has a scruple that she might fail in charity. She would rather that you fail than that she herself fail. [And it doesn't seem to her right to judge badly of you. Oh, God help me, this complaining among nuns! May he forgive me, but I fear it has already become a custom. Once there was a nun who complained to me about a headache, and she complained a great deal about it. When it came time to examine her, the head didn't ache at all, but she felt an ache somewhere else.]

8. These are the things that can happen sometimes; that you might be on guard against them, I am putting them down here. For if the devil begins to frighten us about losing our health, we shall never do anything. May the Lord give us the light to be right about everything, amen.

DETACHMENT FROM SELF

Continuing on the topic of detachment Teresa now turns to detachment from self. She points out how close this detachment is to humility. With good humor, she gives a number of examples, and includes herself with the others in her facetious remarks.

10.1–2: They shouldn't feel secure in their detachment just because they live in an enclosed monastery. The worst thief is inside, namely, ourself.

- Many things can still take away this holy freedom of spirit by which you can fly to your Maker.

- A great help toward this detachment is the awareness of how all is vanity.

- When you begin to become attached to something, turn your thoughts away from it and back to God.

10.3–4: Humility is like an inseparable sister of detachment. The two virtues were much loved by Christ; they take away all fear, except of displeasing him.

- A characteristic of these two virtues is that the one possessing them fails to recognize this.

- With these two virtues you will escape from Egypt and find the Manna (all things will taste good to you).

10.5–8: She now turns to the body as a part of the self.

- You came to the monastery to die for Christ.

- Seldom will you lack discretion; so don't fear that.

- The devil suggests you indulge yourself.

- We invent penances with the result that we can neither do the penances nor keep the observance.

- We must not surrender to the fear of losing our health.

INTERPRETIVE NOTES. 1. Although the body seems to be exterior to us, it forms an essential part of the human person. "We are not angels, but we have a body," Teresa observes (L 22.10). Detachment from the body does not require a diminution of respect for the body, which is a constituent element of the human person.

2. Jesus pointed out the unimportance of the body relative to the things of heaven: "I tell you, my friends, do not be afraid of those who kill the body but after that can do no more. I shall show you whom to fear. Be afraid of the one who after killing has the power to cast into Gehenna; yes, I tell you, be afraid of that one" (Lk 12:4–5; Mt 10:28).

3. When he speaks of the body St. Paul makes a distinction between two Greek terms for body, *soma* and *sarx*. His terms have influenced the way Christian spiritual writers have expressed themselves.

Soma designates the person as a whole insofar as one has a bodily existence and is thereby incorporated into the physical world, capable of interaction, communication, and relationship. Body (*soma*) in this sense alludes to more than the physical. It is ultimately meant for God: "Do you not know that your body (*soma*) is a temple of the holy Spirit within you, whom you have from God, and that you are not your own? For you have been purchased at a price. Therefore glorify God in your body" (1 Cor 6:19–20). In this sense, then, Paul stresses the dignity of the body.

Sarx, usually translated as flesh, is in Paul's understanding what separates us from God. The body is not inherently evil, but in their fallen state human beings are weak, alienated from God, and vulnerable to sin. *Sarx* is the sphere in which the passions and sin operate. The flesh is even personified as a power of evil hostile to God: "For the concern of the flesh is hostility toward God; it does not submit to the law of God, nor can it; and those who are in the flesh cannot please God" (Rom 8:7). The flesh where sin dwells takes control of the body. So there is a sinful body (Rom 6:6). Thus the body is reduced to a lowly state full of unholy cravings (Rom 6:12).

Believers united to Christ have the capacity to conquer through the body of Christ the cravings of the flesh. But here on earth the full dignity of the body is not realized; only in the next life will the body of earthly misery be transformed from a "natural body" (*soma*) into a "spiritual body" (*soma*) (1 Cor 15:44). In the painful transition of death, we should with Paul "prefer to leave this body and go home to the Lord" (2 Cor 5:8).

QUESTIONS FOR DISCUSSION. 1. Why are detachment and humility so closely linked?

2. Why would those possessing these two virtues fail to recognize them within themselves?

3. What would be a sign of indiscreet penance?

4. What attitude does Teresa want us to have toward our bodies?

Chapter 11

Continues to discuss mortification, and speaks about what must be acquired in sickness.

IT SEEMS TO ME AN IMPERFECTION, my Sisters, to be always complaining about light illnesses. If you can tolerate them, don't complain about them. When the sickness is serious, it does the complaining itself; this is different and the sickness is immediately obvious. Consider that you are few, and if one has this habit of complaining, it wears everyone out if you have love for one another and there is charity. If someone is truly sick, she should say so and take the necessary remedy. If you have lost self-love, you will feel any self-indulgence so keenly that there is no fear you will take anything without necessity or complain needlessly. If there is some need, it would be worse not to say anything than to seek your comfort without being sick, and it would be very wrong if the others did not feel compassion for you.

2. Moreover, where there's charity, and so few nuns, concern about your getting well will surely never be lacking. But with regard to some of the weaknesses and little illnesses of women, forget about complaining of them, for sometimes the devil makes us imagine these pains. They are things that come and go. If you do not lose the habit of speaking and complaining about everything — unless you do so to God — you will never finish your lamenting. [I insist so much on this because

129

I think it's very important and a reason why monasteries have mitigated their observance.] A fault this body has is that the more comfort we try to give it the more needs it discovers. It's amazing how much comfort it wants; and since in the case of health the need presents itself under the color of some good, however small it may be, the poor soul is deceived and doesn't grow.

3. Remember how many sick people there are who are poor and have no one to complain to; now it is nonsense to think one can be poor and live in comfort. Recall as well many women who are married. I know of some who are persons of high station and who have serious illnesses and heavy trials but for fear of annoying their husbands dare not complain. Well, sinner that I am! Indeed, we have not come here to receive more comfort than they! Oh, you who are free from the great trials of the world, learn how to suffer a little for love of God without having everyone know about it! If a woman in an unhappy marriage suffers much adversity without being able to receive comfort from anyone lest her husband know that she speaks and complains about it, shouldn't we suffer just between ourselves and God some of the illnesses he gives us because of our sins? And even more so because by our complaining the sickness is not alleviated.

4. In all this that I have said I am not dealing with serious illnesses, when there is great fever — although I beg for moderation and always patience — but of little ailments, that one can bear on one's feet. But what would happen if this that I'm writing were seen outside the house? What would all the nuns say about me? How willingly I would suffer their talk if someone were to make amends! For if there is but one nun like this, the situation can reach a point that for the most part no one is believed no matter how serious her sickness may be. Let us remember our holy fathers of the past, those hermits whose lives we aim to imitate. What sufferings they endured!

What solitude, cold, and hunger, and what sun and heat, without anyone to complain to but God! Do you think they were made of steel? Well, they were as delicate as we. And believe, daughters, that when we begin to conquer these wretched little bodies, we will not be so troubled by them. There will be enough Sisters to look after what is necessary; forget about yourselves except in what concerns a definite need. If we do not determine once and for all to swallow death and the lack of health, we will never do anything. Strive not to fear them; abandon yourselves totally to God, come what may. So what if we die? If our body has mocked us so often, shouldn't we mock it at least once?

5. And believe that this determination is more important than we can realize. For little by little as we grow accustomed to this attitude we will, with the Lord's help, remain lords of our bodies. Now, then, conquering such an enemy is a very important means to enduring the battle of this life. May the Lord conquer him as he alone can. I truly believe that the benefits coming from this practice are not known except by one who already enjoys the victory. They are so great, from what I believe, that none of us would feel we were undergoing trial if we could remain in this calm and dominion.

DETACHMENT FROM SELF (FROM THE BODY)

Continuing her discussion of detachment from the body, Teresa here turns her attention to physical illness, urging the nuns to gain dominion over their bodies.

11.1–5: Gives instructions on when and when not to complain of bodily illnesses.

- If they are tolerable, don't complain.

- When serious, seek a remedy; other nuns should manifest compassion.

- A fault of the body: the more comfort we try to give it the more needs it discovers.

- Remember the poor (with no one to complain to); and married women (who fear annoying their husbands).

- We must learn to swallow sickness and death; strive not to fear them; abandon yourselves totally to God.

INTERPRETIVE NOTES. 1. From her youth until her death, Teresa was assailed by bodily illnesses; sickness waged a fierce battle against her throughout her life. What is impressive is that her bad health never interfered substantially with her capacity for intellectual and organizational work or for full spiritual growth. The stress and overwork surrounding her life as a foundress, no doubt, contributed to her illnesses. In her letters, you note that her health is a frequent topic of discussion, and she doesn't hesitate to speak about illnesses; here is one example: "I have told Antonia to write to your ladyship about all that is happening, about my poor health as well as all the rest. My head is in such a condition that only God knows how I can write this" (Luisa de la Cerda, 2 November 1568).

2. Her struggle with bodily infirmities and spiritual trials heightened in her a compassion for other suffering souls. A detachment from the body would be inauthentic were it to end up in a lack of compassion for others in their illnesses. Writing to Padre Gracián, speaking of how a person can have no better sustenance than trials, she also makes it clear that this conviction does not remove the pain of seeing others suffer: "I mean there must be a whole world of difference between suffering oneself and seeing one's neighbor suffer" (29 April 1579). She counsels that healthy nuns should be ready to deprive themselves rather than allow the sick to go without some deeds of kindness.

3. Our consumer-oriented culture of the late 20th century has come to worship perfect and youthful bodies and urge the consumption of physical pleasures. Teresa wants freedom from preoccupation with the body. But she recognizes, as well, the variety, fragility, and finitude of human bodies. The freedom of detachment has nothing to do with excessive physical penances, which could result in bodily abuse. Respect for the body and its aging process will help prevent abuse. Furthermore, the body must never become an object of mistreatment or assault manifested in domestic violence, rape, sexual sin, overindulgence, substance abuse, and bodily torture.

QUESTIONS FOR DISCUSSION. 1. What are some of the ways in which we might become preoccupied with our bodies?

2. Can we overcome the fear of sickness and death?

3. How can we gain dominion over the body?

Chapter 12

How the true lovers of God will have little regard for their own life and honor.

L ET US GO ON to other things that are also quite important, although they may seem small. Everything seems to be a heavy burden, and rightly so, because it involves a war against ourselves. But once we begin to work, God does so much in the soul and grants it so many favors that all that one can do in this life seems little. And as nuns we do the most we can; that is, we give up our freedom for the love of God, placing it in the power of another, and undergo so many trials and fasts, so much silence, enclosure, and service in choir that however much we may want to please ourselves we can only seldom do so. And in many of the monasteries that I have seen, perhaps I am the only one who pleases herself. Why should we, then, delay in practicing interior mortification? For interior mortification makes everything else more meritorious and perfect, and afterward enables us to do the other things with greater ease and repose. This interior mortification is acquired, as I have said,[1] by proceeding gradually, not giving in to our own will and appetites, even in little things, until the body is completely surrendered to the spirit.

2. I repeat[2] that the whole matter, or a great part of it, lies in losing concern about ourselves and our own satisfaction. The least that any of us who has truly begun to serve the

135

Lord can offer him is our own life. Since we have given the
Lord our will, what do we fear? It is clear that if you are a true
religious or a true person of prayer and aim to enjoy the delights of God, you must not turn your back on the desire to die
for God and suffer martyrdom. For don't you know yet, Sisters,
that the life of a good religious who desires to be one of God's
close friends is a long martyrdom? A long martyrdom because
in comparison with the martyrdom of those who are quickly
beheaded, it can be called long; but all life is short, and the life
of some extremely short. And how do we know if ours won't
be so short that at the very hour or moment we determine to
serve God completely it will come to an end? This is possible.
In sum, there is no reason to give importance to anything that
will come to an end. And who will not work hard if there is the
thought that each hour is the last? Well, believe me, thinking
this is the safest course.

3. So, let us try hard to go against our own will in everything. For if you are careful, as I said,[3] you will gradually, without knowing how, find yourselves at the summit. But how extremely rigorous, it seems, to say that we shouldn't please ourselves in anything when we do not also mention the pleasure
and delight this going against our will carries in its wake and
what is gained by it even in this life. What security! Since all
of you practice this denial here, the most is done; for you awak-
en and help one another. This is the practice in which each
one should strive to be ahead of the others.

4. Take careful note of interior stirrings, especially if they
have to do with privileges of rank. God, by his Passion, deliver us from dwelling on such words or thoughts as, "I have se-
niority," "I am older," "I have done more work," "the other is
treated better than I." If such thoughts come they should be
quickly cut off. If you dwell on them or begin to speak about
them, the result is a pestilence from which great evils arise [in
monasteries. Be careful, for I know a great deal about it!] If

you should have a prioress who consents to this kind of thing, however small, believe that God has permitted, on account of your sins, that you have her as prioress so that you will begin to go astray; and pray hard that he will provide a remedy because you are in great danger.

5. Perhaps you will say: "Why should I give so much importance to this detachment and be so rigorous about it, for God gives consolations to those who are not so detached?" I believe he does do this, for in his infinite wisdom he sees that this is fitting so as to draw them to give up everything for him. I do not call "giving up everything" entering religious life, for there can be impediments to entering religious life, and the perfect soul can be detached and humble anywhere; although this latter may involve greater trial, for being in a monastery is a big help. But believe me in one thing: if there is any vain esteem of honor or wealth (and this can be had inside monasteries as well as outside, although inside the occasions for it are more removed and the fault would be greater), you will never grow very much or come to enjoy the true fruit of prayer. And this is so even though you may have many years of experience in prayer — or, better, I should say reflection because perfect prayer in the end removes these bad habits.

6. Consider, Sisters, whether any of these things pertain to you; you are here for no other purpose. It will be due to your vain esteem of honor that you will not be honored. Moreover, you will lose the benefit you could have otherwise gained; thus dishonor and loss will be joined together here.

Let each one consider how much humility she has, and she will see what progress has been made. It doesn't seem to me the devil will tempt the truly humble person about rank even with the first stirrings. Since he is so shrewd, he fears getting battered. It is impossible for a humble person not to gain strength and progress in humility when the devil tempts in this way. Clearly, the humble will reflect on their lives and consider how they have served the Lord in comparison with how the Lord ought to be served and the wonders the Lord performed in lowering himself so as to give us an example of humility; and they will consider their sins and where they merited to be on account of them. The soul ends up with so much gain that the devil doesn't dare return another day lest he get his head crushed.

7. Take this advice from me and do not forget it; do not strive only in an interior way — for it would be a very great loss if we didn't derive some benefit from these acts of humility — but strive also in an exterior way that the Sisters draw some benefit from your temptation. If you wish to take revenge on the devil and free yourself more quickly from temptation, ask the prioress as soon as the temptation comes to give you orders to do some lowly task; or, if possible, do it on your own. And go about studying how to double your willingness to do things that go contrary to your nature — the Lord will reveal these things to you — and in this way and as a result the temptation will last only a short while.[4] God deliver us from persons who are concerned about honor while trying to serve him. Consider it an evil gain, and, as I said,[5] honor is itself lost by desiring it, especially in matters of rank. For there is no toxin in the world that kills perfection as do these things.

8. You will say that these are natural little things to which we need pay no attention. Don't fool yourselves, they increase like foam, and there is nothing so small in which there is so obvious a danger as this concern about honor and whether we have been offended. Do you know why — besides many other reasons? Perhaps this concern begins in someone as something small and amounting to hardly anything, and then the devil stirs another to think it is something big, and this other will even think she is practicing charity by going and saying to the

offended nun, "How do you put up with such an offense? God give you patience to offer it up; a saint wouldn't suffer more." The devil puts such deceptive talk on the other Sister's tongue that, though you barely overcome the offense, you are still tempted to vainglory, when in reality you did not suffer with the perfection with which you should have suffered.

9. And this nature of ours is so weak that merely by telling ourselves the offense should not be tolerated, we think and believe we have done something; how much more is this so when we see that others feel this way for us. As a result, the soul loses the occasions it had for meriting; it becomes weaker and opens the door for the devil to come again with something worse. And it could even happen, when you want to suffer the injury, that they will come to you and say: "Are you a beast or what? It's good for you to feel things." [Huh, and if one of them is a friend!] Oh, for love of God, my Sisters! May no one be moved by an indiscreet charity to show pity for another in something that touches upon these false injuries, for such pity is like that of Job's wife and friends.[6]

DETACHMENT FROM SELF
(FROM LIFE AND HONOR)

Treating first of an interior detachment gained by losing concern for oneself, Teresa then calls for a particular kind: detachment from rank and "honor."

12.1: Interior mortification (not giving in to our own will and appetites):

- Makes everything else more meritorious and perfect.

- Enables us to do other things with greater ease and repose.

12.2: The least a true servant of the Lord can do is offer him one's life.

- True persons of prayer do not turn from the desire to die for God.

- The life of one who desires to be a true friend of God is a long martyrdom; although all life is short.

12.3: How extremely rigorous it seems to say that we shouldn't please ourselves in anything when we do not mention the delight this carries in its wake.

12.4–5: Be on guard against the pestilence having to do with privileges of rank.

- I do not call "giving up everything " entering religious life.

- The perfect soul can be detached and humble anywhere.

- If there is any vain esteem for honor or wealth, you will never grow or enjoy the true fruit of prayer.

12.6–9: A. The devil will not tempt the truly humble person about rank.

B. To counteract such temptations, volunteer for some lowly task.

C. No toxin in the world kills perfection as do these things (concerns about honor and rank).

- There is nothing so small (in this matter) in which there is so obvious a danger.

- Beware of false friends who urge you to take offence.

INTERPRETIVE NOTES. 1. Teresa's words about losing concern for both ourselves and our own satisfactions find their support in the teaching of Jesus: "Those who find their life will lose it, and those who lose their life for my sake will find it" (Mt 10:39); "For those who want to save their life will lose it, and those who lose their life for my sake will find it" (Mt 16:25; Mk 8:35; Lk 9:24); "Those who love life lose it, and those who hate their life in this world will keep it for eternal life" (Jn 12:25).

2. In the Castile of Teresa's day, honor and money went hand in hand. So much so, the two realities usually got reduced simply to honor. Though the word "honor" as used by Teresa carries different shades of meaning, she is thinking mainly of prestige, of all that raises one above the other. It mattered little whether persons lived up to the renown accorded them. What mattered was that others, by their words and deeds, pay them honor and believe they were deserving of it, whether they were in fact or not.

3. Honor was essentially an attribute of nobility. At the top of the ladder came the *grandees,* a group drawn from the oldest families of Castile and Aragón. Immediately below them came other titled aristocrats, the *títulos,* who were the dukes, marquises, and counts. The lesser aristocracy, whose members distinguished themselves with the title "Don" (or "Doña") were called either *caballeros* or *hidalgos.*

4. With so much value placed on birth and rank, the ordinary folk in society sought compensation and found it in the doctrine of *limpieza de sangre* (purity of blood). They reasoned that it was preferable to be born of humble but pure Christian parentage than to be a *caballero* of "suspicious" background (Moorish or Jewish), for it was possible to buy privileges of *hidalguía.* Pure ancestry provided for those in the lower ranks what noble ancestry did for those in the higher ranks. The achievement of honor could come from proving the purity of one's ancestry.

5. In her *Life,* Teresa wrote: "What friendship there would be among all if there were no self-interest about honor and money! I think this absence of self-interest would solve all problems" (20.27).

QUESTIONS FOR DISCUSSION. 1. In what ways might I try to lose concern about myself?

2. What are some of the defects of our culture that may be similar to those of Teresa's time?

Chapter 13

Continues to discuss mortification and how one must flee from the world's maxims and rules about honor in order to arrive at true wisdom.

I HAVE OFTEN TOLD YOU, Sisters, and now I want to leave it in writing here so that you will not forget it, that in this house — and even in the case of any person seeking perfection — you should run a thousand miles from such expressions as: "I was right." "They had no reason for doing this to me." "The one who did this to me was wrong." God deliver us from this poor way of reasoning. Does it seem to have been right that our good Jesus suffered so many insults and was made to undergo so much injustice? I don't know why the nun who doesn't want to carry the cross, except the one that seems to her reasonable, is in the monastery. Let her return to the world, although even there they will not respect such reasonings. Could you by chance suffer as much as you deserve? What kind of reasoning is this? I certainly don't understand it.

2. Let us reason in such a way when some honor is paid to us, or when we are given some comfort or receive good treatment; for certainly it isn't right that we be so treated in this life. When wrongs are done — that's what they call them without there being any wrong done to us — I don't know what there is to talk about. Either we are brides of so great a King or we are not. If we are, what honorable woman is there who does not share in the dishonors done to her spouse even though she

does not will them? In fact, both spouses share the honor and the dishonor. Now, then, to enjoy a part in his kingdom and want no part in his dishonors and trials is nonsense.

3. May God not allow us to refuse the latter; but the nun to whom it seems she is herself least of all should consider herself the most blessed of all. And she indeed is. If she bears dishonor as it must be borne, she will not be without honor either in this life or in the next. Believe me in this. But what nonsense I have spoken — that you believe me, when it has been said by true Wisdom, [who is Truth itself, and by the Queen of the angels.[1] Let us, at least, imitate his humility in some way. I say "in some way," for however much we might lower and humble ourselves, someone like myself does nothing; for because of her sins she has merited that the devils humiliate and despise her, even though she wouldn't like their doing so. For even if you may not have so many sins, seldom is there anyone who hasn't done something by which he has merited hell.]

Let us, my daughters, imitate in some way the great humility of the Blessed Virgin, whose habit we wear, for it is embarrassing to call ourselves her nuns. However much it seems to us that we humble ourselves, we fall far short of being the daughters of such a Mother and the brides of such a Spouse.

Thus, if you do not diligently put a stop to the things mentioned, what today seems to be nothing will tomorrow perhaps be a venial sin; and it is so dangerous that if you are careless about it you will suffer its ill effects, for it is something very bad for religious communities.

4. We who live in community should be very careful about it so as not to harm those who work to do good for us and give us good example. And if we could understand what great harm is done when a bad custom is begun, we would rather die than be the cause of it. For such a death would be a bodily one, but the loss of souls is a great loss, and it doesn't seem there is any

end to the loss. Once some are dead, others follow after; and all, perhaps, are more affected by a bad custom we have started than by many virtues. For the devil does not allow the bad custom to cease, but natural weakness causes the virtues to be lost.

5. Oh, what a great act of charity and what a great service to God a nun would perform if when she sees she cannot follow the customs of this house she would recognize the fact and leave! And she ought to do so if she doesn't want to go through a hell here on earth; and, please God, there won't be another in the next life,[2] for there are many reasons to fear such perdition, and perhaps neither she nor the others will understand this as I do.

6. Believe me in this matter; and if you don't, time will be my witness. For the style of life we aim to follow is not just that of nuns but of hermits, and thus you detach yourselves from every creature. I see the Lord gives this favor of detachment in a special way to the one he has chosen for this life. Even though the detachment may not be entirely perfect from the beginning, it is seen that she is advancing toward it by the great contentment and happiness she finds in not having to deal again with anything of the world and by how she relishes everything about the religious life.

I repeat that if she is inclined to the things of the world and not seen to be making progress that she should leave. If she still desires to be a nun, let her go to another monastery; and if she doesn't she will see what will happen to her. Don't let her complain about me, who started this way of life, for not having warned her.

7. This house is a heaven, if one can be had on this earth. Here we have a very happy life if one is pleased only with pleasing God and pays no attention to her own satisfaction. If a nun desires something in addition to pleasing God, all will be

lost because that something cannot be had. The discontented nun is like the sick who feel great loathing for food; however good the food may be, it nauseates them, and the food that healthy people find great pleasure in eating is repugnant to the sick. This nun will be saved better elsewhere, and it may be that little by little she will reach the perfection that here she couldn't endure because she had to undertake it all at once. For although interiorly it takes time to become totally detached and mortified, exteriorly it must be done immediately. I fear that any nun who walks in such good company and sees that all the other nuns are detached but does not herself make progress in a year will not make more progress in many years, but less. I don't say that the detachment need be as complete as it is with the other nuns, but that you recognize that health is returning; for when the sickness is mortal, the fact becomes immediately obvious.

DETACHMENT FROM SELF
(FROM THE ESTEEM OF OTHERS)

Continuing on her theme, Teresa now writes forcefully to warn against the habit of complaining over being wronged, which she surely must have witnessed in her religious life.

13.1: Run a thousand miles from complaints about whether someone was right in doing this to you or not.

- It's not a matter of right or wrong.

- Look at what Jesus suffered.

- Don't stay in the monastery if you want to carry only reasonable crosses.

- Return to the world, but even there they won't listen to your reasonings.

13.2: Our reasoning should rather lead us to the awareness that we don't deserve good treatment.

- We are brides of Christ, and as such share the dishonors done to our Spouse, as is the case with husbands and wives.

- To want a part in his kingdom but not a part in his dishonors and trials is nonsense.

13.3: The nun who considers herself the least of all is the most blessed of all.

- If she bears dishonor as she ought, she will not be without honor (from assuring words of Christ and the Blessed Virgin).

- Let us imitate the humility of the Blessed Virgin.

13.4–6: Do not allow this kind of complaining to become customary.

- Anyone who can't give up this complaining should leave.

- Our style of life is not just that of nuns but of hermits (demanding total detachment).

13.7: Our life is a heaven if one is pleased only with pleasing God. The discontented nun will be saved better elsewhere.

INTERPRETIVE NOTES. 1. In the chapter heading Teresa uses the term *mortification* in place of the word *detachment*. Throughout the history of Christian spirituality, authors, adding their own nuances, used a number of terms to refer to detachment: *abnegation, renunciation, mortification, self-denudation, self-forgefulness, self-sacrifice,* and *humility.* Terms frequently used today are *spiritual freedom* and *availability for apostolic work.* For Teresa the reality behind these expressions is freedom from enslavement, from all that would hinder anyone in doing God's will.

2. Teresa's words here may seem hard; nonetheless, it doesn't take much imagination to envision what a disturbance it would be for a small strictly enclosed community to have to bother with nuns always worried and complaining about their being slighted. "Love does not brood over injury" (1 Cor 13:5).

3. Teresa speaks of the style of life she had established, not just that of nuns but of hermits. Many in her day

thought of a hermit lifestyle as emphasizing corporal penance. The classic examples from Teresa's own writings are St. Peter of Alcantara (L 27.16–20), who slept only an hour and a half during the night and ate only every third day; and Catalina de Cardona (F 28.21–36), who took the discipline with heavy chains and wore extremely sharp ones. But for the style of hermit life Teresa founded, she chose instead various practices of detachment that did not threaten one's health, that everyone in the community could pursue without harm, and that would lead to perfect love. Her hermit life–style made no allowances for a nun unwilling to bear offense without complaining.

QUESTIONS FOR DISCUSSION. 1. What are some of the ways in which I can practice the advice Teresa gives here?

2. Have I had any experience of bearing injury, as Teresa advises, and ending up being esteemed?

Chapter 14

The importance of not allowing anyone to make profession whose spirit goes contrary to the things mentioned.

I TRULY BELIEVE that the Lord highly favors the one who has real determination. Thus, the intention of the new member should be considered, lest she merely be looking for a secure future, as will be the case with many,[1] although the Lord can bring this intention to perfection if she has good intelligence; but if she doesn't, in no way should she be accepted, for neither will she understand why she is entering, nor afterward will she understand those who desire to lead her along the best spiritual path. For the most part those who have this fault always think they know more about what suits them than do those who are wiser. And the fault is an evil I consider incurable, for it would be a wonder if those having this fault ever gave up their malice. Where there are many nuns this fault could be tolerated, but where there are so few it shouldn't be allowed.

2. When a nun with good intelligence begins to grow attached to good, she takes hold of it with fortitude because she sees that doing so is most appropriate. And if her intelligence doesn't help her to attain a high degree of spirituality, it will be useful for giving good counsel and for many other services without being a bother to anyone. If this good intelligence is lacking, I don't know how she can be of any use to the community, and she could be the cause of much harm.

This lack of intelligence is not so quickly noticed. For many speak well but understand poorly; others speak little and without polish but they have the intelligence for a great deal of good. In fact, there is a holy simplicity that knows little about the affairs and style of the world but a lot about dealing with God. Hence much information is necessary before accepting new members and a long probation before admitting them to profession. Let the world understand once and for all that you have the freedom to dismiss the new members and that in a monastery where austerities are practiced, there are many occasions for doing so. And when decisions of this sort become the custom, no one will take the dismissal as an affront.

3. I say this because we are living in such miserable times and our nature is so weak that we don't want to offend relatives, and so it is not enough that we have a command from our forebears to stop paying attention to what people nowadays take for honor. May it please God that we do not pay in the next life for the new members we admit in this life; there is never lacking a pretext for convincing ourselves that we can't do otherwise. [And in a matter so important no pretext is good, for when the bishop without attachment or passion looks after the good of the house, I don't think God will ever let him be mistaken. And I do believe that there will always be some mistake made if he is affected by such pity and foolish ideas about one's honor.]

4. And this is a matter that each one should consider, recommend to God, and encourage the prioress about, for it's something so important. Thus, I beg God to give you light. You are very fortunate that you do not receive dowries, for it can happen that in monasteries where they are accepted the nuns, so as to avoid giving back the money — which they no longer have — leave the thief in the house who steals the treasure from them; which is a great pity. In this matter you shouldn't take pity on anyone, for you would be doing harm to the person you are trying to help.

THE DISCERNMENT OF VOCATION

The subject of the previous chapter led Teresa to insist that a nun with the kind of complaints mentioned was unfit for the style of life established at St. Joseph's: "not just that of nuns but of hermits." It is easy to see how Teresa's mind turns now to the question of the discernment of vocations, even though the topic is somewhat of a digression from the theme of detachment.

14.1: The intention of the new member should be considered, lest she be merely looking for a secure future.

- Where good intelligence is present, there is hope that a defective intention can be corrected.

- Where good intelligence is lacking, an aspirant should not be accepted.

- Such a person will not understand why she is entering or those who desire to lead her along the spiritual path.

- Such persons always think they know more about what suits them than those who are wiser.

14.2: If good intelligence doesn't help one to attain a high degree of spirituality, it will be useful for giving good counsel and other services.

- Lack of intelligence is not so quickly noticed.

- Many speak well but understand poorly; others speak little but have the intelligence for a great deal of good.

- Much information is necessary and a long probation before profession.

• The world should know you are free to dismiss new members and that in your style of life many occasions arise for doing so.

14.3: Our times are so miserable and our natures so weak that we do not want to offend relatives.

14.4: A. The community should be concerned about this matter and encourage the prioress.

B. You are fortunate that you do not receive dowries.

INTERPRETIVE NOTES. 1. In Teresa's "miserable times," Castilian men followed the lure of adventure and fortune in lands across the sea. (Not one of Teresa's nine brothers stayed in Avila.) The ensuing lack of opportunities for women in the married life led to the overpopulation of nuns' monasteries. In monasteries women could feel secure and socially accepted. Not much thought was given to their intentions for entering. Sometimes they entered not because they couldn't find a husband but because they did not want to accept the one their parents had selected for them. Doña Elvira de Guzmán entered the monastery of the Incarnation to spite her mother who "took away the husband she desired and selected another one for her against her will."

2. In 1522, the community of the Incarnation numbered 40 nuns. By 1552 the number had reached 180. In 1565, a petition to the mayor of Avila for help mentioned that there were about 200 nuns in the monastery. Of course, as the numbers increased the expenses

rose. The monastery began contracting debts with the result that one of the sources of income, the dowries of new nuns, had to go immediately to pay contracted debts or to buy food. The permanent source of income thereby could never grow. Sending someone home would require repayment of the dowry; that presented a problem because the dowry had already been spent.

3. The Council of Trent in 1563 called for a limit in numbers, stating that the norm would be the number that could be sustained by the income. But the Incarnation, unable to comply with these rules, resorted to a principle from the Carmelite rule: "Necessity has no law."

4. In calling for good intelligence in a candidate for the style of life she founded, Teresa is not making demands for any particular amount of education. Educational opportunities for women did not form a part of the culture of her times. Education itself did not hold a place of esteem among the people; indeed, they often looked on it with suspicion. Blessed Anne of St. Bartholomew, who came to be Teresa's assistant and also an important figure in the establishment of the Teresian Carmel in France and the Netherlands, was illiterate when she entered Carmel as a lay sister. What Teresa singled out as essential was the intelligence to be able to grasp the meaning of the religious life and, in particular, the Teresian Carmelite style of life. Included also in her idea of good intelligence would be the capacity to make sound practical judgments in applying the theory in particular situations.

5. A few passages from the *Foundations* help us understand some of the things Teresa had in mind by good intelligence:

"At another time, when I was present, the nuns were going to confession, and one who was waiting for the other to finish came to speak to the prioress. The prioress asked her why she was doing that and if it was a good way to recollect herself and told her to go stick her head in a well that was nearby and there think of her sins. The nun thought she was to jump into the well and went so quickly to do so that if they hadn't hurried to hold her back she would have done so thinking she was doing God the greatest service in the world. Other similar things, requiring much mortification, were done. This made it necessary for learned men to restrain the nuns and explain to them the matters in which they were obliged to obey. For these nuns did some things that were imprudent, so that if their good intention had not redeemed them, they would have lost rather than gained merit. The above is true not only of this monastery, but it occurred to me to speak of the matter here" (16.3).

"Another counsel I give you, and it is a very important one. Do not give any order that could be a sin (even venial) if carried out, and not even if you do so just to test obedience. (I've heard that some things would have involved mortal sin if done). At least the nuns, because of their innocence perhaps, are without blame; but not the prioress, because there is no order she gives that they will not carry out immediately. And since they hear and read about what the saints of the desert did, everything seems to them well done if ordered by obedience, at least in their own case. And also let subjects be advised that anything that would be a mortal sin when not ordered by the superior would still be one if the superior orders it, unless the matter involves omitting Mass or the church fast, or things like that, in which the prioress may have reasons for dispensing. But something like jumping into the well and things of that sort are wrong to do. No one should think that God must work miracles, as he did with the saints; there are many other things in which perfect obedience may be practiced" (18.11).

QUESTIONS FOR DISCUSSION. 1. What should have been my intention in the life God called me to and how am I carrying it out in my daily activites?

2. How can my intelligence and the learning of other persons help me?

Chapter 15

The great good that lies in not excusing oneself even when blamed without fault.

[B UT WHAT DISORDER IN THE WAY I write! Really, it's as though the work were done by one who doesn't know know what she's doing. The fault is yours, Sisters, because you are the ones who ordered me to write this. Read it as best you can, for I am writing it as best I can. And if you find that it is all wrong, burn it. Time is necessary to do the work well, and I have so little as you see, for eight days must have gone by in which I haven't written anything. So I forget what I have said and also what I was going to say. Now it is wrong for me to ask you to avoid doing what I have just finished doing, that is, making excuses. For I see that not making excuses for oneself is a habit characteristic of high perfection, and very meritorious; it gives great edification. And although I have often taught it to you, and by God's goodness you practice it, His Majesty has never given it to me.] *·· this is gift*

I am very embarrassed about what I am going to try to persuade you of, for I should have practiced at least something of what I am about to tell you concerning this virtue. The fact is, I confess, that I have made very little progress. It always seems to me there is some reason for my thinking it is greater virtue to make an excuse for myself. Since at times it is lawful to give an excuse and it would be wrong not to do so, I don't have the discretion or, to put it better, humility to do so when

161

fitting. Indeed, it calls for great humility to be silent at seeing oneself condemned without fault. This is a wonderful way to imitate the Lord who took away all our faults. So, I ask you to take great care about this practice; it brings with it great benefits. I see no reason at all for us to try to excuse ourselves, unless, as I say, in some cases where not telling the truth would cause anger or scandal. When to excuse oneself will be recognized by those who have more discretion than I.

2. I believe it's very advantageous to get in the habit of practicing this virtue, or to strive to attain from the Lord the true humility that comes from it. The truly humble person must in fact desire to be held in little esteem, persecuted, and condemned without fault even in serious matters. If she desires to imitate the Lord, in what better way can she do so? For here there is no need of bodily strength or help from anyone but God.

3. I should like us, my Sisters, to strive very much for these great virtues; and let us do this penance, for you already know that I am rather strict when there is question of your doing too many penances. They can do harm to one's health if done without discretion. In this practice there is nothing to fear. However great the interior virtues may be, they do not take away the bodily strength necessary to keep the religious observance; on the contrary, they strengthen the soul. And from very little things, as I have said at other times,[1] one can gain the light so as to come out the victor in great things. [But how easily one writes of this and how poorly I practice it!] Indeed, in these great things I have not been able to test this myself, for I have never heard anything evil said of me that I didn't see that it fell short; for even though I had not failed in the things they accused me of, I have offended God in many other areas, and it seemed to me they were being quite kind by not mentioning these other offenses. I am always happier that they speak about what is not true of me than the truth.[2]

4. It is a great help to reflect upon the many things that are gained through all the various ways and how — if we observe carefully — we are never, never blamed without there being faults on our part, for we always go about full of them since the just man falls seven times a day, and it would be a lie to say we have no sin.[3] Thus even though we are blamed for faults we haven't committed, we are never entirely without fault, as was the good Jesus.

5. O my Lord, when I think of the many ways you suffered and how you deserved none of these sufferings, I don't know what to say about myself, nor do I know where my common sense was when I didn't want to suffer, nor where I am when I excuse myself. You already know, my Good, that if I have some good it is a gift from no one else's hands but yours. Now, Lord, what costs you more, to give much or little? If it is true that I have not merited this good, neither have I merited the favors you have granted me. Is it possible that I have wanted anyone to feel good about a thing as bad as I after so many evil things have been said about you who are the Good above all goods? Don't allow, don't allow, my God — nor would I ever want you to allow — that there be anything in your servant that is displeasing in your eyes. Observe, Lord, that mine are blind and satisfied with very little. Give me light and grant that I may truly desire to be abhorred by all since I have so often failed you who have loved me so faithfully.

6. What is this, my God? What do we expect to obtain from pleasing creatures? What does it matter if we are blamed a lot by all of them if in your presence we are without fault? O my Sisters, we never completely understand this virtue; so, we are never completely perfect if we do not reflect and think a great deal upon what is and what is not. For when you have no other gain than the embarrassment of the person who after having blamed you sees that you are in fact without fault and yet allow yourself to be condemned, that gain is extremely

great. At times something like this elevates a soul more than ten sermons. We must all try to be preachers through our deeds since the Apostle[4] and our incapacity prevent us from being preachers through our words.

7. However enclosed you are, never think that the good or evil you do will remain a secret. And do you think, daughters, that when you do not excuse yourselves there will be lacking someone to defend you? Observe how the Lord answered for the Magdalene both in the house of the Pharisee and when her sister accused her.[5] He will not be as harsh with you as he was with himself, for at the time that one of the thieves defended him, he was on the cross.[6] So His Majesty will inspire someone to defend you; and when he doesn't, the defense won't be necessary. I have seen this, and it is true. But I wouldn't want you to be thinking about being defended, but that you rejoice in being blamed; and time will be the witness to the benefit you will see in your soul. For you begin to obtain freedom and don't care whether they say good or evil of you but rather think of what is said as though it were another's affair. The situation is like that in which we have two persons talking together but not to us; we then don't care about answering. So it is here; with the habit that has been acquired of not responding, it doesn't seem they are speaking to us.

This will seem impossible to those of us who are very sensitive and little mortified. In the beginning it is difficult; but I know that such freedom, self-denial, and detachment from ourselves can, with God's help, be attained.

HUMILITY (ACCEPTING FALSE ACCUSATIONS)

Without explicitly saying so, Teresa turns to the third virtue that must accompany a life of prayer. She has already pointed out how closely connected humility and detachment are.

15.1: After an eight-day interruption she takes up her work again, deploring the disorder in what she is writing and her lack of time.

- After excusing herself she becomes aware that she is doing the very thing she is going to ask the nuns not to do.

- She confesses her embarassment as she approaches this topic because of her own lack of progress in humility.

- Not making excuses for oneself is a habit characteristic of high perfection.

- It calls for great humility to be silent at seeing oneself condemned without fault.

- It is a wonderful way to imitate the Lord.

- The acceptable exception: if not telling the truth would cause anger or scandal.

15.2–4: The truly humble person must desire to be held in little esteem, persecuted, and condemned without fault even in serious matters.

- There is no better way to imitate the Lord.

- Interior virtues like this are the penance we should perform; they do us no bodily harm.

- Her experience was that her true failings were always worse than the untrue ones she was sometimes accused of.

- We are never entirely without fault; only the good Jesus was.

15.5–6: A. She enters into a devout colloquy with the Lord, recalling the many sufferings he bore without having deserved any of them; she wonders what difference it makes if we are blamed as long as we are without fault in his presence.

B. We must all try to be preachers through our deeds.

15.7: A. When you do not excuse yourself the Lord will inspire someone else to defend you, or the defense will be unnecessary.

B. But your joy should not lie in being defended but in being blamed; this leads to freedom.

INTERPRETIVE NOTES. 1. In her *Life* Teresa says that while in the novitiate she was often accused without being at fault. She confesses that she did not bear this easily but with much pain and imperfection (5.1). Some 30 years later, her humility clearly manifests itself in the way she dealt with misunderstandings and false accusations stemming from her new foundation in Avila. She describes the inner state of mind she had when she was called before the provincial to be reprimanded for what she had done:

"They sent everything to the provincial and the case was left up to him. When he came, I went before him very happy to know I was suffering something for the Lord because in this case I didn't find I had committed any offense either against His Majesty or against the order.... I recalled the judgment pronounced on Christ and saw how it amounted to nothing at all, I accused myself of the fault as one who was very much to blame, and this seemed true to anyone who didn't know all the reasons. After having received a serious reprimand, although not one as severe as the transgression deserved or in accordance with what many told the provincial, I didn't want to excuse myself; I had been determined about what I did. Rather, I begged to be pardoned and punished and that he not be vexed with me" (36.12).

But the provincial told Teresa to go before the nuns at the Incarnation and present her side of the story. Of this she writes:

"Since I felt interiorly calm and the Lord helped me, I gave my explanation in such a way that neither the provincial nor those who were present found anything to condemn me for. Afterward I spoke to him more freely, and he was very satisfied and promised — if all went well — to give me permission to go there once the city quieted down, for the clamor throughout the whole city was vehement.... " (36.13).

2. The Word comes forth from the silent mystery of God as God's own self-expression in and to humanity. Similarly, the words and deeds of Jeus, the Word Incarnate, come forth out of his silence. At times the silence of Jesus speaks: his silence before his accusers, his silent suffering (Mt 26:63; Is 53:7).

3. The followers of Jesus must have the mind of Christ Jesus: "Learn from me, for I am meek and humble of heart" (Mt 11:29). His deepest expression of humility lay in his own silent acceptance of the cross: "He humbled himself, becoming obedient to death, even death on a cross" (Phil 2:8).

QUESTIONS FOR DISCUSSION. 1. Can I recall any instances in my life where keeping silent might have been the better thing to do?

2. What are some of the ways in which I might avoid making excuses for myself?

3. What does being silent when falsely accused have to do with humility?

Chapter 16

The difference that must lie between the perfection of the life of contemplatives and that of those who are simply content with the practice of mental prayer. How it is possible that God may at times raise a distracted soul to perfect contemplation and the reason for his doing so. This chapter and the following one are very noteworthy.[1]

[D]ON'T THINK THAT WHAT I HAVE SAID so far is all I have to say, for I am just setting up the game, as they say. You asked me to mention something about the foundation for prayer. Even though God did not lead me by means of this foundation, for I still don't have these virtues,[2] I know of no other. Now realize that anyone who doesn't know how to set up the pieces for a game of chess won't know how to play well. And without knowing how to check the king, one won't know how to checkmate it either. Well, you will reprimand me because I am speaking about a game we do not have in this house, nor should we have it. Here you see the kind of Mother God has given you, that she even knows about this vanity; although they say that sometimes the game is permissible. And oh, how permissible this kind of game will be for us; and how quickly, if we play it often, will we checkmate this divine King, who will not be able to escape, nor will he want to.

2. The queen is the piece that can carry on the best battle in this game, and all the other pieces help. There's no queen like humility for making the King surrender. Humility drew the King from heaven to the womb of the Virgin, and with it, by one hair,[3] we will draw him to our souls. And realize that the one who has more humility will be the one who possesses

him more; and the one who has less will possess him less. For I cannot understand how there could be humility without love or love without humility; nor are these two virtues possible without detachment from all creatures.

3. You will ask me, daughters, why I am speaking to you about virtues when you have enough books to teach you about them, and you will say that you want to hear only about contemplation. I say that had you asked about meditation I could have spoken about it and counseled all to practice it even though they do not possess the virtues, for meditation is the basis for acquiring all the virtues, and to undertake it is a matter of life and death for all Christians. And no one, however lost, should set it aside if awakened by God to so great a good, as I have already written elsewhere[4] and as have many others who know what they are writing about; for I certainly don't know what I'm writing about — God knows.

4. But contemplation is something else, daughters. This is the mistake we all make, that those who spend a little time each day thinking about their sins — for they are obliged to do that if they are Christians more than in name — are immediately said to be very contemplative and are expected to possess at once virtues as great as those a very contemplative soul is obliged to have; and even these persons themselves expect this, but are mistaken. In the beginning they didn't know how to set up the game. They thought it was enough to know the pieces in order to checkmate the King. But that was impossible, for this King doesn't give himself but to those who give themselves entirely to him.]

5. Therefore, daughters, if you desire that I tell you about the way that leads to contemplation, you will have to bear with me if I enlarge a little on some other matters even though they may not seem to you so important; for in my opinion they are. And if you don't want to hear about them or put them into

practice, stay with your mental prayer for your whole life, for I assure you and all persons who aim after true contemplation (though I could be mistaken since I am judging by myself for whom it took twenty years) that you will not thereby reach it.

6. I now want to explain — because some of you don't know — what mental prayer is, and please God we shall practice this as it ought to be practiced. But I fear that mental prayer also involves much labor if the virtues are not obtained — although it's not necessary that they be possessed in as high a degree as is required for contemplation. I say that the King of glory will not come to our soul — I mean to be united with it — if we do not make the effort to gain the great virtues. I want to explain this because if you should catch me saying something that isn't true you wouldn't believe anything, and you would be right if I did so knowingly; but God forbid! If I should say something that isn't true, it would be a matter of my not knowing more or not understanding. I want to say, then, that there are times when God will want to grant some great favor to persons who are in a bad state so as to draw them by this means out of the hands of the devil.[5]

7. O my Lord, how often do we make you fight the devil in arm to arm combat! Isn't it enough that you allowed him to take you in his arms when he carried you to the pinnacle of the temple[6] so that you might teach us how to conquer him? But what would it be like, daughters, to see him, with his darknesses, next to the Sun. And what fear that unfortunate one must have borne without knowing why, for God didn't allow him to understand it.[7] Blessed be such compassion and mercy. What shame we Christians ought to have for making him wrestle arm to arm, as I have said, with so foul a beast. It was truly necessary, Lord, that you have such strong arms. But how is it that they didn't weaken by the many torments you suffered on the cross? Oh, how everything that is suffered with love is healed again! And so I believe that had you survived,

the very love you have for us would have healed your wounds, for no other medicine was necessary. [It seems I am speaking nonsense, but I'm not; for divine love can do greater things than these. But to avoid seeming strange — which I really am — and so as not to give you bad example, I'll say no more.] O my God, grant that I might put medicine like this in everything that causes me pain and trial! How eagerly I would desire these if I could be sure that I'd be healed with so soothing a balm!

8. To return to what I was saying,[8] there are souls that God thinks he can win to himself by these means. Since he sees they are completely lost, His Majesty desires that nothing be wanting on his part. And even though they are in a bad state and lacking in virtue, he gives them spiritual delight, consolation, and tenderness that begin to stir the desires. And he even places them in contemplation sometimes, though he does so rarely and it lasts only a short while. He does this, as I say, so as to try them to see if with that favor they will want to prepare themselves to enjoy him often. But if they don't prepare themselves — pardon me; or better, may you pardon us, Lord, for it is a great evil when after you bring a soul like this to yourself it approaches and becomes attached to some earthly thing.

9. For myself I hold that there are many to whom our Lord God gives this test, but few who prepare themselves for the enjoyment of the favor of contemplation. When the Lord grants it and we do not fail on our part, I hold as certain that he never ceases to give until we reach a very high degree. When we do not give ourselves to His Majesty with the determination with which he gives himself to us, he does a good deal by leaving us in mental prayer and visiting us from time to time like servants in his vineyard.[9] But these others are favored children. He would not want them to leave his side, nor does he leave them, for they no longer want to leave him. He seats them at

his table, he shares with them his food even to the point of taking a portion from his own mouth to give them.

10. Oh, blessed care, my daughters! Oh, blessed renunciation of things so small and so base that reaches so high a state. What would it matter, when you are in the arms of God, if the whole world blamed you! He has the power to free you from everything, for once he commanded that the world be made, it was made; his will is the deed. Now do not fear that he will allow others to speak against you except for the benefit of the one who loves him. His love for those who love him is not so small. Well why, my Sisters, shouldn't we show our love for him as much as we can? Behold it is a beautiful exchange to give our love for his. Consider that he can do all things, and we can't do anything here below but what he enables us to do. Well, what is this that we do for you, Lord, our Maker? It amounts to almost nothing, just a little determination. Well, if from that which is nothing His Majesty desires us to merit everything, let's not be foolish.

11. O Lord, how true that all harm comes to us from not keeping our eyes fixed on you; if we were to look at nothing else but the way, we would soon arrive. But we meet with a thousand falls and obstacles and lose the way because we don't keep our eyes — as I say — on the true way. It seems so new to us that you would think we had never walked on it. It's certainly something to excite pity, that which sometimes happens. [I say that it doesn't seem we are Christians or that we ever in our lives read the Passion. God help me, if I neglect a little rule concerning someone's honor! Then, anyone who tells you not to worry about your honor seems to be unchristian. I laughed to myself — or rather was distressed — at what I sometimes saw in the world and even, because of my sins, in religious communities.] For any slight loss in one's honor is not tolerated, nor does it seem that such a loss should be tolerated. They immediately say: "We're not saints."

12. God deliver us, Sisters, when we do something imperfect, from saying: "We're not angels, we're not saints." Consider that even though we're not, it is a great good to think that if we try we can become saints with God's help. And have no fear that he will fail if we don't fail. Since we have not come here for any other thing let us put our hands to the task, as they say. May we presume to use everything we learn about greater service of the Lord in his favor. The presumption I would like to see present in this house, for it always makes humility grow, is to have a holy daring; for God helps the strong and he shows no partiality.[10]

13. I have digressed a good deal. I want to return to what I was saying,[11] that is, explaining the nature of mental prayer and of contemplation. It may seem impertinent for me to be doing that, but for you everything is acceptable. It may be that you will understand the matter better through my rough style than through other more elegant styles. May the Lord help me, amen.

HUMILITY (IN REGARD TO CONTEMPLATION)

Teresa's explanation of prayer here has two perspectives: that of the one who prays, and that of God.

16.1–2: What she has said so far is like setting up the game of chess.

- The life of prayer is like the game of chess.

- The queen (which stands for humility) is the best piece for making the King surrender.

- Humility drew the King from heaven to the womb of the Blessed Virgin.

- The one who has more humility will be the one who possesses him more.

- There can be no humility without love; nor the two of them without detachment.

16.3–6: Meditation (mental prayer) is the basis for acquiring all the virtues.

- Contemplation is not given if the virtues are not present.

- But mental prayer also involves much labor if the virtues are not obtained; though contemplation requires them in a higher degree.

- However, God may grant a great favor to persons in a bad state so as to draw them out of it.

16.7: Colloquy with the Lord: everything suffered with love is healed again.

16.8–9: God gives lost souls spiritual delight, consolation, and tenderness so as to stir their desires for himself.

- God does this to see if with that favor they will want to prepare themselves to enjoy him often.

- God gives this test to many, but few prepare themselves for more.

- If we do not fail, God will never cease to give until we reach a very high degree.

- When we do not give ourselves, God does a great deal by leaving us in our mental prayer and visiting us from time to time, as servants in his vineyard; those who do give themselves, God will seat at his table.

16.10–12: Exhortation to her sisters to exchange their love for his; and to keep their eyes fixed on God.

- God deliver us from saying "we're not saints."

- Think that if you try, you can become saints with God's help.

16.13: She has digressed and now returns to her subject.

INTERPRETIVE NOTES. 1. The two major difficulties in the revision of the *Way of Perfection* concern the game of chess and the contemplation given to a sinner. Teresa made apologies about her use of the game of chess as an analogy. The censor, García de Toledo, made no marginal comment. He apparently found little reason for objecting. In her revision of the text, apparently pleased with the possibilities of the comparison, Teresa took it further. What amounted to one page she expanded to five pages. Later, however, she tore this section out, and the manuscript now jumps a chapter number and from page 59 to 64. We can only speculate about what happened here. For one thing, the game of chess was frowned upon as a game for religious to play. Padre Domingo de Valtanas in his *Apología de los Juegos (Defense of Games)* asserted that clerics or religious obliged to the recitation of the Divine Office would be doing something seriously immoral by playing chess or even watching the game. His thoughts went like this: the game greatly tires the intellect, hinders one from being attentive to the Divine Office, and impedes the experience of devotion. Perhaps opinions of such sort were the reason for Teresa's decision to jettison the whole analogy. Or possibly, Teresa became more interested in the subsequent topic, on how God may give contemplation to a lost soul, than she was in the virtues that can checkmate the king.

2. Following the gap produced in the text, two pages follow that were revised for a third time. They deal with a matter that seriously engaged Teresa's reflections: "How it is possible that God may at times raise a distracted soul to perfect contemplation." She herself had begun to experience an outpouring of God's favors while still full of weaknesses and failings. Pondering the problem, she came to the conclusion that God can give perfect contemplation to an imperfect soul to free it from its imperfections, but not to anyone in the state of sin. This was her position in the first draft. Whether

Teresa's opinion was the same when she wrote her revision is unknown. Whatever she wrote, she tore out. What we do have now represents a radical change of opinion. She admits that God may give contemplation to a person in the state of sin to draw that person out of a bad state.

3. St. John of Avila wrote in his letter (September 1568) approving Teresa's *Life:* "No one should be surprised or condemn these things outright on seeing that the persons to whom they are given are not perfect, for, according to what I have seen, it is nothing new to the goodness of God to draw one from the state of the bad to that of the just, and even from grave sins to great blessings by granting them his sweet delights. Who will place limits on the goodness of God?"

4. After Teresa's death, Fray Luis de León prepared her works for publication. When he noticed that her ingenius use of the game of chess was missing from her second redaction, he inserted the section from the first redaction into the second.

5. In the game of chess in Teresa's time the queen was called the *dama* (lady). The noted Teresian scholar Tomás Alvarez remarks that what Lady Poverty was for St. Francis of Assisi Lady Humility was for St. Teresa.

6. In this chapter, as in chapter 4, Teresa links prayer and the practice of the virtues. The latter is necessary for contemplation because the King doesn't give himself save to those who give themselves to him. A higher degree of virtue is required for contemplation, but mental prayer is itself difficult where there is no effort to

practice virtue. Although in her writings Teresa speaks of many different virtues (faith, hope, charity, religion, fortitude, chastity, obedience, poverty), the three virtues given prominence in this work (love of neighbor, detachment, and humility) lie at the heart of the other virtues. They are gospel virtues and relational, requiring us to keep our eyes fixed on the King and centered lovingly on the person of Christ. However, in the Teresian vision, it is always the Lord who gives first, and if we do our part he never ceases to give until we reach "a very high degree" of contemplation. To our ascetical efforts to practice these virtues and prepare ourselves for God's communication, Teresa holds up a promise, a conviction frequently alluded to from her privileged place at the mystical summit: "It seems to me I would want to cry out and make everyone understand what is gained by not being satisfied with a few things and how much good there is that God will give us if we dispose ourselves for it" (ST 1.4).

QUESTIONS FOR DISCUSSION. 1. Why are humility, love, and detachment so interconnected that where the one is present the others are also?

2. Why would God give his precious gift of contemplation to a sinner?

3. Can I use the game of chess as an analogy for my own prayer life, or would some other game help me to express it better?

Chapter 17

Not all souls are suited for contemplation, and some reach it late. The truly humble must be content with the path along which God leads them.

IT SEEMS I AM ALREADY DEALING with prayer. But something still remains to be said that is very important because it pertains to humility and is necessary in this house[1] where the main occupation is prayer. And, as I have said,[2] it is only right that you should try to understand how to train yourselves a great deal in humility. In fact, this is an important aspect of prayer and indispensable for all persons who practice it. How could the truly humble think they are as good as those who are contemplatives? Yes, it is true, God can make you a contemplative — through his goodness and mercy; but, in my opinion, one should always take the lowest place, for this is what the Lord told us to do[3] and taught us in deed. Prepare yourself so that God may lead you along this path if he so desires. When he doesn't, you can practice humility, which is to consider yourself lucky to serve the servants of the Lord and praise His Majesty because he brought you among them and drew you away from the devils in hell where you deserved to be a slave of these devils.

2. I don't say this without serious cause, because, as I have said,[4] it is important to understand that God doesn't lead all by one path, and perhaps the one who thinks she is walking along a very lowly path is in fact higher in the eyes of the Lord.

So, not because all in this house practice prayer must all be contemplatives; that's impossible. And it would be very distressing for the one who isn't a contemplative if she didn't understand the truth that to be a contemplative is a gift from God; and since being one isn't necessary for salvation, nor does God demand this, she shouldn't think anyone will demand it of her. So, you will not fail to be very perfect if you do what has been mentioned. Indeed, it could be that a Sister will gain much more merit because she must work harder and the Lord leads her as one who is strong, saving for her what she doesn't enjoy here below so as to give it to her all at once. Not for this reason should she grow fainthearted or give up prayer or what all the other Sisters are doing, for sometimes the Lord comes very late and pays just as well, and all at once, what he was giving to others in the course of many years.

3. I spent fourteen years never being able to practice meditation without reading. There will be many persons of this sort, and others who will be unable to meditate even with the reading but able only to pray vocally, and in this vocal prayer they will spend most of their time. There are minds so active they cannot dwell on one thing but are always restless, and to such an extreme that if they want to pause to think of God, a thousand absurdities, scruples, and doubts come to mind.

I know an elderly person who lives a good life, is penitential and an excellent servant of God, who has spent many hours for many years in vocal prayer, but in mental prayer she's helpless; the most she can do is go slowly in reciting the vocal prayers.[5] There are a number of other persons of this kind. If humility is present, I don't believe they will be any the worse off in the end but will be very much the equals of those who receive many delights; and in a way they will be more secure, for we do not know if the delights are from God or from the devil. Now if the delights are not from God, there is greater danger because the work of the devil here is to instigate pride. But if they are from God, there is nothing to fear; they bring with them humility, as I have written very much at length in another book.[6]

4. Those who do not receive these delights walk with humility, suspecting that this lack is their own fault, always concerned about making progress. They don't see anyone shed a tear without thinking that if they themselves don't shed any they are very far behind in the service of God. And perhaps they are much more advanced, for tears, even though they be good, are not all perfect. In humility, mortification, detachment, and the other virtues there is always greater security. There is nothing to fear; don't be afraid that you will fail to reach the perfection of those who are very contemplative.

5. St. Martha was a saint, even though they do not say she was contemplative. Well now, what more do you want than to be able to resemble this blessed woman who merited so often to have Christ our Lord in her home, give him food, serve him, and eat at table with him [and even from his plate]?[7] If she had been enraptured like the Magdalene, there wouldn't have been anyone to give food to the divine Guest. Well, think of this congregation as the home of St. Martha and that there must be people for every task. And those who are led by the active life shouldn't complain about those who are very much absorbed in contemplation, for these active ones know that the Lord will defend the contemplatives, even though these latter are silent[8] since for the most part contemplation makes one forgetful of self and of all things.

6. Let them recall that it is necessary for someone to prepare his meal and let them consider themselves lucky to serve with Martha. Let them consider how true humility consists very much in great readiness to be content with whatever the Lord may want to do with them and in always finding oneself unworthy to be called his servant. If contemplating, practicing

mental and vocal prayer, taking care of the sick, helping with household chores, and working even at the lowliest tasks are all ways of serving the Guest who comes to be with us and eat and recreate, what difference does it make whether we serve in the one way or the other?

7. I don't say that we shouldn't try; on the contrary, we should try everything. What I am saying is that this is not a matter of your choosing but of the Lord's. If after many years he should give to each a certain task, it would be a nice kind of humility for you to want to choose for yourselves. Leave it up to the Lord of the house; he is wise, he is mighty, he understands what is suitable for you and what is suitable for him as well. Be sure that if you do what lies in your power, preparing yourselves for contemplation with the perfection mentioned, and that if he doesn't give it to you (and I believe he will give it if detachment and humility are truly present), he will save this gift for you so as to grant it to you all at once in heaven. And, as I have said before,[9] he wants to lead you as though you were strong, giving you the cross here below, something that His Majesty always had. What better friendship than that he desire for you what he desired for himself? And it could be that you would not have received so great an award in contemplation. The judgments are his, there's no reason for us to become involved in them. It is good that the choice is not up to us, for then — since contemplation seems a more restful path — we would all be great contemplatives.

O wonderful gain, not to want to gain from following our own judgment lest we suffer any loss! God, in fact, never permits any loss to come to a person truly mortified save for a greater gain.

HUMILITY
(IN ACCEPTING THE PATH GIVEN BY THE LORD)

Still on the theme of humility, Teresa poses a question: How could a truly humble nun think she is as good as those who are contemplatives?

17.1–2: God can make you a contemplative, but you should always take the lowest place.

- Prepare yourself for this path.

- If God doesn't lead you by this path, consider yourself lucky to serve the servants of the Lord.

- God does not lead all by one path.

- The one who thinks she is on a very lowly path may be higher in the Lord's eyes.

- Not all in this house must be contemplatives.

- God does not demand that you be a contemplative.

- Do not give up prayer; the Lord may come very late.

17.3–4: Like myself for 14 years, some will be unable to meditate without reading; others will be able to pray only vocally.

- If humility is present, they may be the equals of those who receive many delights.

- If the virtues are present, you will not fail to reach the perfection of those who are very contemplative.

17.5–6: Think of this house as the house of Martha and Mary.

- Those who are led by the active life shouldn't complain about those who are very much absorbed in contemplation.

- They should consider themselves lucky to serve with Martha.

17.7: Leave the choosing to the Lord; he will give contemplation if detachment and humility are present.

INTERPRETIVE NOTES. 1. The impression left from reading this chapter may be that Teresa's communities consisted of those who were absorbed in contemplation and those who were unsuited to receive this gift from the Lord. The nuns who did not receive it were to be humble and serve those who did. Each community would have its Marthas and Marys. But Teresa wanted no class distinctions in her monastery ("All the Sisters must be equal" [27.6]; "The mother prioress should be the first on the list for sweeping so that she might give good example to all" [C 22]). She hardly could have wanted any distinctions based on favors from God. Some other questions arise as well in reading this chapter. What did Teresa mean by contemplatives? How much time was required to become one? What should one do to become a contemplative? What would be the proportion in a Teresian community between Marthas and Marys? May the Marthas, or some of them at least, slacken their efforts in prayer since "not all souls are suited for contemplation," so as to devote more time to works of service?

2. For Teresa, mental prayer (vocal prayer, meditation) refers to the effort an individual makes, with God's grace, to enter into intimate friendship with the Lord. "For mental prayer in my opinion is nothing else than an intimate sharing between friends; it means taking time frequently to be alone with him who we know loves us"(L 8.5). The effort may be made in vocal prayer or in discursive meditation or by some other means. What is essential is to be present to the one who loves us. Contemplation includes both the presence of Christ who loves us and our presence to him. It differs from mental prayer in that the awareness of God's presence is bestowed passively and experienced as a gift; it cannot be acquired. Teresa's use of the term "contemplation" carries the influence of her own mystical experience of God, of Christ in his mysteries, of an intimately delightful and graced relationship between herself and God. The experience brought with it spiritual joy, delight, and sometimes pain. For her, a "contemplative" was one who had reached perfect contemplation and entered into the depths of mystical experience. This chapter can be easily misinterpreted by not understanding this special meaning Teresa gives to the term "contemplative(s)." Some 10 years after completing this book, she had come to a deeper understanding of this "perfect contemplation" as well as a deeper level in her prayer. In a new book, *The Interior Castle,* she dealt in detail with "contemplatives" and this unitive contemplation in the fifth, sixth, and seventh dwelling places.

3. As for the amount of time that passed before she became a "contemplative," she writes in her *Life:* "It

will be seen that within only twenty-seven years in which I have practiced prayer His Majesty has given me the experience...that for others took forty-seven or thirty-seven years; they journeyed in penance and always in virtue" (10.9). However, she began experiencing the prayer of union, though for only very short periods of time, in her early twenties (4.7).

Because contemplation remains always God's gift, nothing really definite can be said about the amount of time one spends in mental prayer before contemplative prayer begins. Further on in her *Life* Teresa cautions: "These are gifts God gives when he desires and how he desires, and they depend neither on time nor on services. I do not mean that time and service are not important, but often the contemplation the Lord doesn't give to one in twenty years he gives to another in one. His Majesty knows the reason" (34.11).

After telling about the quick progress made by the nuns at St. Joseph's, she advises spiritual directors: "By noting this, I would like us to recall the many years that have passed since we made profession and began to practice prayer, and not to disturb those who in a short time make more progress, causing them to turn back in order to walk at our pace; nor would I want to make those who fly like eagles with the favors God grants them to advance like fettered chickens" (39.11).

4. In her *Foundations,* after she had founded seven monasteries in addition to St. Joseph's in Avila and had broader experience of the prayer life in her communities than when writing *The Way of Perfection,* Teresa makes the following remarks to our surprise:

"Well to return to what I was saying, for I have digressed a great deal, the favors the Lord grants in these houses are so many that if there are one or two in each that God leads now by meditation all the rest reach perfect contemplation. Some are so advanced that they attain to rapture. To others the Lord grants a favor of another kind, giving them, along with rapture, revelations and visions that one clearly understands to be from God. There is no house now that does not have one, two, or three who receive this latter favor. Well do I understand that sanctity does not lie in these favors, nor is it my intention to praise only them but to make it understood that the counsels I want to give have a purpose" (4.8).

5. Teresa's advice to her readers is that they not concern themselves with receiving favors in prayer, but leave the matter to the Lord's choosing. Some will receive more favors than others, but there is more security in humility and detachment. Finally, in the *Interior Castle*, she teaches that the purpose of all God's favors is good works, to strengthen us for service (VII.4.5,12). In a word, the true contemplative is also a Martha. This was very evident in Teresa herself. In her *Foundations* she writes: "I never would, or did, leave any monastery until it was in fit condition, had a spirit of recollection, and was adapted according to my wishes. In this matter God greatly favors me, for when there was question of work to be done I enjoyed being the first" (19.6).

6. The parenthetical declaration in number 7 that the Lord will give contemplation if detachment and humility are present is consistent with what Teresa affirms

later in chapters 19 (no. 15) and 25: "For it is God who must bestow supernatural prayer, and he will grant it to you if you do not stop short on the road but try hard until you reach the end" (no. 4).

7. The favors from God that were less common in Teresa's communities were raptures, visions, and revelations. These bring wonderful blessings to the soul, Teresa insisted. But in such matters, prioresses should let themselves be seen as prizing humble works more than the experiences of those whom God leads by this "very supernatural path of prayer" (F 8.9).

8. In her *Foundations*, Teresa speaks of some nuns who appear to be absorbed for many hours in contemplation, but their experience is attributable in fact to bodily weakness brought on, for example, by fasting. She explains the difference between this kind of absorption and rapture, and advises the prioress to take away their fasts and give them duties that will distract them (cf. 6.1–8). Rapture and the union of all the faculties are of short duration, she explains; although certain effects may last for days.

9. If God will not fail to give the waters of contemplation to those who persevere in their efforts at prayer, humility, and detachment, there is nonetheless a great variety in the way he favors individuals. Teresa was once wondering why she was receiving gifts and favors from the Lord that others who were his very good servants were not, when suddenly the Lord spoke to her for the first time: "Serve me and don't bother about such things" (L. 19.9).

10. The virtues of charity, detachment, and humility that Teresa recommends as attitudes necessary for the gift of contemplation can be practiced, *mutatis mutandis*, in all walks of life and in all cultures.

QUESTIONS FOR DISCUSSION. 1. What did Teresa mean by a "contemplative" or "those who are very contemplative"?

2. In what ways could I fail in humility through my attitude toward the gift of contemplation?

Chapter 18

Continues on the same subject and tells how the trials of contemplatives are much greater than those of persons living an active life. This chapter is very consoling for these latter.

NOW, DAUGHTERS, I TELL THOSE OF YOU whom God does not lead by this path that from what I have seen and understood concerning the lives of those who do walk along it, contemplatives do not bear a lighter cross; and you would be surprised at the ways and modes in which God gives them crosses. I know both paths, and I know clearly that the trials God gives to contemplatives are intolerable. These trials are of such a kind that if he didn't give that food with its delights, these persons wouldn't be able to endure the trials. And it is clear that since God wants to lead those whom he greatly loves by the path of tribulation — and the more he loves them the greater the tribulation — there is no reason to think that he despises contemplatives, for with his own mouth he praises them and considers them his friends.[1]

2. Well, to think that he admits into his intimate friendship people who live in comfort and without trials is foolish. I am very certain that God gives contemplatives much greater trials. Thus, since he leads them along a rough and uneven path and at times they think they are lost and must return to begin again, His Majesty needs to give them sustenance, and not water but wine so that in their inebriation they will not understand what they are suffering and will be able to endure it. So,

I see few true contemplatives who are not courageous and determined to suffer, for the first thing the Lord does, if they are weak, is to give them courage and make them unafraid of trials.

3. I believe that when those of the active life see the contemplative favored a little, they think there is nothing else to the contemplative's life than receiving favors. Well, I say that perhaps these active persons couldn't endure one day of the kind the contemplative endures. Thus, since the Lord knows what each one is suited for, he gives to each person a proper task, one that he sees as appropriate for that person's soul, for the service of the Lord himself and for the good of neighbor. And if you have done what you can to be prepared, do not fear that your effort will be lost. Keep in mind that I say we should all try to be contemplatives, since we are not here for any other reason. And we should try not for just a year, nor for only two, nor even for just ten; otherwise we leave the impression that we are giving up as cowards; and it is good for the Lord to know we are doing our best. We must be like soldiers who even though they may not have served a great deal must always be ready for any duty the captain commands them to undertake, since it is he who gives them their salary. And how much better the pay our King gives than the pay of earthly kings.[2]

4. Since the captain sees his soldiers present and eager to serve and has understood the capability of each one, he distributes the duties according to the strengths he sees. And if these soldiers were not present, he wouldn't give them anything, nor would he command them to serve.

So it is with us, Sisters; let us give ourselves to mental prayer. And let whoever cannot practice it turn to vocal prayer, reading, and colloquy with God, as I shall say afterward.[3] Do not abandon the hours of prayer we have in common;[4] you don't know when the Spouse[5] will call — let not what happened to the foolish virgins happen to you.[6] He may want to give more work, disguised in delight. If he doesn't, you should understand that this delight is not meant for you, that it is fitting for you to go without it. And here is where meriting through humility enters; you truly believe that you aren't even capable of doing the little you do.

5. You should be happy to serve in what they command you to do, as I have said.[7] And if this humility is true, blessed be such a servant in the active life, for she will not complain but of herself. [I would much rather be like her than like some contemplatives.] Let the others fight their own war, which is not small. Even though the standard-bearer doesn't fight in the battle, he doesn't for that reason fail to walk in great danger; and interiorly he must do more work than anyone. Since he carries the flag, he cannot defend himself; and even though they cut him to pieces he must not let it out of his hands. So it is with contemplatives: they must keep the flag of humility raised and suffer all the blows they receive without returning any. Their duty is to suffer as Christ did, to hold high the cross, not to let it out of their hand whatever the dangers they see themselves in, nor let any weakness in suffering be seen in them; for this reason they are given so honorable an office. Contemplatives must be careful about what they are doing, for if one lets go of the flag the battle will be lost. Thus, I believe that great harm is done to those who are not so advanced when they see that the deeds of those they consider to be captains already and friends of God are not in conformity with this office.

6. The other soldiers advance as best they can, and sometimes they retreat from where they see greater danger; and no one notices this, nor do these soldiers lose honor. As for the former ones, the eyes of all are upon them; they cannot

stir. So their office is a good one, and the king does a great honor and favor to the one he gives it to, but the obligation in accepting it is not a small one.

So, Sisters, we don't know what we are asking for. Let us leave it to the Lord. [For he knows us better than we do ourselves. And true humility is content with what is received.] There are some persons who demand favors from God as though these were due them in justice. That's a nice kind of humility! Thus, he who knows all very seldom grants such persons favors, and rightly so. He sees clearly that they are not ready to drink from the chalice.[8]

7. What each of you will understand, daughters, if you are advanced, will be that you are the most wretched of all. And this understanding will be manifested in deeds done for your own spiritual growth and for the good of others, and not in having more delights and raptures in prayer, or visions, or favors of this kind that the Lord grants; for we shall have to wait for the next world to see the value of such experiences. This understanding is like current coin, like unfailing revenue, like having a perpetual annuity and not a sum that's paid only once; for these other experiences come and go. This attitude includes the great virtues of humility and mortification, careful obedience by not in any way going against what the superior commands, for you truly know that God, in whose place the superior stands, commands it.

It is into this obedience that you must put the most effort; and, in my opinion, where there is no obedience there are no nuns. I am not saying anything about this virtue because I am speaking with nuns and, I think, good ones — at least they desire to be good. In a matter of such wisdom and importance, no more than a word so that it won't be forgotten.

8. I say that I don't know why a nun under obedience by vow is in the monastery if she doesn't make every effort to

practice this obedience with greater perfection. At least I can assure her that as long as she fails in obedience she will never attain to being a contemplative, nor will she even be a good active Sister; and I hold this as very, very certain. Even though others may not have this obligation of the vow, if they desire or aim after contemplation, it is necessary for them in order to proceed correctly to give up their will, with complete determination, to a confessor, who must be the kind [that will understand them.] Since this practice is something already well known — for there is more progress made in this way in one year than without it in many — and it is not necessary for you, there's no need to talk of it.

9. I conclude by saying that these are the virtues I desire you to have, my daughters, the ones you must strive for and about which you should have holy envy. As for those other devotions, there's no need to be sorry about not having them; having them is an uncertain matter. It could be that in other persons they may be from God, whereas in your case His Majesty may permit them to be an illusion of the devil and that you be deceived by him, as were other persons [for in women this is something dangerous]. Why desire to serve the Lord in a doubtful way when you have so much that is safe? Who places you in these dangers?

10. I have enlarged so much on this subject because I know it is important; for this nature of ours is weak, and His Majesty will strengthen anyone to whom he wishes to give contemplation. I have paused to give these counsels to those to whom he doesn't give contemplation. By practicing them, the contemplatives, also, may humble themselves. [If, daughters, you say that you don't need them, perhaps someone else will come along who will be pleased to have them.] May the Lord, because of who he is, give us light to follow his will in everything, and there will be nothing to fear.

HUMILITY (WITH REGARD TO GOD'S FAVORS)

Teresa continues the topic of humility. She turns her attention first to some of the hard realities contemplatives must face and seeks to console them.

18.1–2: Despite God's favors to them, contemplatives do not bear a lighter cross.

- The delights given by God enable contemplatives to endure trials.

- The more God loves them, the greater the tribulation.

- God loves contemplatives, praises them and considers them his friends.

- The Lord gives them wine to enable them to endure their sufferings.

18.3: Those of active life might think there is nothing more to the contemplative's life than receiving favors.

- But perhaps they wouldn't be able to endure one day of the kind endured by the contemplative.

- Nonetheless, all the nuns should try to be contemplatives, and try for their entire lives.

18.4–5: A. Be happy to serve. Some persons demand favors from God as though these were due them in justice; but they are not ready to drink from the chalice.

B. She turns to a military analogy.

- The captain (Christ, the commander-in-chief of love) distributes duties according to the strengths he observes in the soldiers.

- The sisters, like soldiers, must not abandon prayer, for they know not when the Spouse (captain) will call; they should be available for service.

- The contemplatives are like the standard bearer in a military battle: they must keep the flag of humility raised and suffer all the blows they receive without returning any.

- They must hold high the cross and not let any weakness in suffering be seen in them.

- If they let go of the flag, the battle will be lost.

18.6–9: We don't know the value of spiritual delights, raptures, visions, and revelations.

- These experiences come and go.

- Obedience added to a humble and happy spirit are what her readers should strive for and not these other devotions (spiritual delights, visions, revelations).

18.10: These counsels were for the non-contemplatives; but contemplatives may also practice them.

INTERPRETIVE NOTES: 1. In the last dwelling-place of the *Interior Castle*, Teresa explains the purpose of God's favors in this world. Their purpose is to allow him to bestow the greatest favor of all, a life "that would be an imitation of the life his Beloved Son lived." She concludes: "Thus I hold for certain that these favors are meant to fortify our weakness, as I have said a number of times, that we may be able to imitate him in his great sufferings" (IC VII. 4.4).

2. The standard-bearer was the soldier to whom the captain entrusted the banner. It was the office of the captain to carry the banner, but since he had many other tasks to attend to he called on a substitute, who was not to move except on orders from the captain. The banner held high by the standard-bearer served to rally the troops who followed him into battle. In Teresa's application, contemplatives are the standard-bearer who must hold high the banner of humility and the cross.

3. "You should be happy to serve" (no. 5), recalls Teresa's advice to beginners in her *Life:* "to walk in joy and freedom" (13.1). There are other gifts besides those of contemplative prayer that could become either objects of our desires or occasions for envy and sadness; for example, intellectual and artistic gifts. Humility urges you to leave the choices of gifts to the Lord. Besides, Teresa points out, gifts bring with them, in addition to their benefits, responsibilities and sufferings. "Can you drink the cup that I am going to drink?" (Lk 20:22).

4. Humility and obedience, it seems, are gospel virtues unattractive on the whole to the modern mind. Nonetheless, Vatican Council II calls not only priests (*Presbyterorum Ordinis,* 15) and religious (*Perfectae caritatis,* 5) to obedience but the laity as well: "Let lay men and women follow Christ's example, who by his obedience unto death, opened the blessed way of the liberty of the children of men to all" (*Lumen Gentium,* 37). Humility and obedience: these virtues became so much admired by Teresa because of their resplendent occurrence in Christ on the cross. The will and ability to be humble and obey is a gift from God, a

grace made possible because God's sacrificial obedience has preceded and anticipated our own.

5. In the sixth dwelling places of the *Interior Castle,* Teresa speaks more specifically of the sufferings of contemplatives. She draws heavily from her own experiences. The trials come from both exterior and interior sources: opposition carried on by others; praise (itself becoming a trial); severe illnesses; misunderstanding from the confessor; the consequent anxiety about being deceived; and a feeling of unbearable inner oppression and even of being rejected by God. We have seen the pain over the split in the church that pulsed through the opening chapters of this work. But what added to her pain was the feeling that this calamity was a result of her own sins: "It seemed to me I was so evil that all the wickedness and heresies that had arisen were due to my sins" (L 30.8)

QUESTIONS FOR DISCUSSION. 1. Why are humility and obedience unattractive to our world?

2. Does the analogy of the standard-bearer in a military battle speak to me?

3. What is the greatest of all God's favors?

Chapter 19

Begins to discuss prayer. Speaks to souls unable to reason with the intellect.

SO MANY DAYS HAVE GONE BY since I wrote the above, days in which I haven't had time to return to it, that if I don't reread it I won't know what I was saying. So as not to take up time, I'll have to let this work turn out in whatever way it does, without any order. There are so many good books written by able persons for those who have methodical minds and for souls that are experienced and can concentrate within themselves that it would be a mistake if you paid attention to what I say about prayer. As I say, there are books in which the mysteries of the Lord's life and Passion are divided according to the days of the week, and there are meditations about judgment, hell, our nothingness, and the many things we owe God together with excellent doctrine and method concerning the beginning and end of prayer.[1] There is nothing for me to say to any of you who can form the habit of following this method of prayer, or who has already formed it, for by means of so good a path the Lord will draw you to the haven of light. And through such a good beginning the end will be reached. All who are able to walk along this path will have rest and security, for when the intellect is bound one proceeds peacefully.

But what I would like to speak about and offer a remedy for, if the Lord should will that I succeed — and if I don't, at least you will understand that there are many souls who undergo this trial, and those of you who suffer it will not grow weary — is the following.

2. There are some souls and minds so scattered they are like wild horses no one can stop. Now they're running here, now there, always restless. [And if the rider is skillful, there is not always a danger — just sometimes. But even though his life is in no danger, he is not free from some dishonor in mounting the wild horse; and there is always some hardship.] This restlessness is either caused by the soul's nature or permitted by God. I pity these souls greatly, for they seem to be like very thirsty persons who see water in the distance, but when they want to go there, they meet someone who prevents their passing from the beginning through the middle to the end. It happens that after they have conquered the first enemy through their labor — and through a great deal of labor — they let themselves be conquered by the second; they would rather die of thirst than drink water so costly. Their efforts cease, their courage fails. And when some have the courage to conquer the second class of enemy as well, their strength gives way when they meet the third, and perhaps they were no more than two steps from the fount of living water, of which the Savior said to the Samaritan woman, "whoever drinks of it will never thirst."[2] How right and true, as words coming from the mouth of Truth Itself, that such a person will not thirst for anything in this life — although thirst for the things of the next life increases much more than can ever be imagined through natural thirst! How thirsty one becomes for this thirst! The soul understands the great value of this thirst, and even though the thirst is a most painful, wearying one, it brings with it the very satisfaction by which it is assuaged, in such a way that it is a thirst unquenchable except in earthly things. Indeed, this thirst slakes in such a way that when God satisfies the thirst, the greatest favor he can grant the soul is to leave in it this same need — and a greater one — to drink the water again.

3. Water has three properties that I now recall as applicable to our subject, for it must have many more. The first is that it refreshes; for, no matter how much heat we may experience, as soon as we approach the water the heat goes away. If there is a great fire, it is extinguished by water — unless the fire burns from pitch; then it is enkindled more. Oh, God help me, what marvels there are in this greater enkindling of the fire by water when the fire is strong, powerful, and not subject to the elements. For this water doesn't impede the fire, though it is fire's contrary, but rather makes the fire increase! It would be a great help here to be able to speak with someone who knows philosophy, for in knowing the properties of things he would be able to explain to me what I enjoy thinking about but don't know how to speak of or even perhaps understand.

4. Those of you, Sisters, who drink this water and you others, once the Lord brings you to drink, will enjoy it and understand how the true love of God — if it is strong, completely free of earthly things, and if it flies above them — is lord of all the elements and of the world. And since water flows from the earth, don't fear that it will extinguish this fire of the love of God; such a thing does not lie within its power. Even though the two are contraries, this fire is absolute lord; it isn't subject to water. Hence do not be surprised, Sisters, about the many things I have written in this book so that you might obtain this liberty. Isn't it wonderful that a poor nun of St. Joseph's can attain dominion over all the earth and the elements? No wonder the saints, with the help of God, were able to do with the elements whatever they wanted. Fire and water obeyed St. Martin; even the birds and the fish, St. Francis; and so it was with many other saints. There was clear evidence that they had dominion over all worldly things because they labored to take little account of them and were truly subject with all their strength to the Lord of the world. So, as I say, the water that rises from the earth has no power over the love of God; the flames of this love are very high, and the source of it is not found in anything so lowly.

There are other little fires of love of God that any event will extinguish. But extinguish this fire? No, not at all! Even though a whole sea of temptations comes, the fire will not be put out and thereby made to lose control over these temptations.[3] [For with the help of God and doing what lies in their power, people can almost seek this love by right. Do you think that because the Psalmist says that all things are subject to us mortals and put under our feet that it is so with everyone? Not at all! On the contrary, I see many individuals subject to and trampled upon by things. In fact, I knew a gentleman who was killed in a quarrel over a few dimes. What a miserable price he was subject to. There are many things you will see every day from which you will know that I am speaking the truth. If the psalmist couldn't lie — for what he says is from the Holy Spirit — it seems to me that the saying, "they will rule over all earthly things," pertains to the perfect. It could be that I don't understand and am foolish, but I have read this.[4]]

5. Well, if it is water that rains from heaven, so much less will it extinguish this fire; the two are not contraries but from the same land. Have no fear that the one element will do harm to the other; rather, they help each other produce their effect. For the water of true tears, those that flow in true prayer, readily given by the King of heaven, helps the fire burn more and last longer; and the fire helps the water bring refreshment. Oh, God help me, what a beautiful and marvelous thing, that fire makes one feel cooler! Yes, and it even freezes all worldly attachments when it is joined to the living water from heaven. Heaven is the source of the tears that were mentioned, for they are given and not acquired through our own efforts. Therefore, this living water will certainly not let the heat from worldly things detain the soul — unless to allow the soul to communicate this fire to others. For by its nature this fire is not content with little; it would burn up the whole world if it could.

6. Another property of water is that it cleans dirty things. What would the world be like if there were no water for washing? Do you know how clean this water is, this heavenly water, this clear water, when it isn't cloudy, when it isn't muddy, but falls from heaven? Once this water has been drunk, I am certain that it leaves the soul bright and cleansed of all faults. Since this divine union is something very supernatural, it is not a matter of our own choosing. As I have written,[5] God doesn't permit a soul to drink this water unless to cleanse it and leave it clean and free from all the mud and misery in which, through its own faults, it was stuck. Other delights that come through the medium of the intellect, however much they may accomplish, come from water running on the ground; they do not come from drinking at the fount. There is never a lack of muddy things to detain one on this path, and the water is not so pure and clean. Living water is not what I call this prayer in which, as I say, there is reasoning with the intellect; I mean from the way I understand things. For something from the road that we don't want will stick to our soul and be helped to cling there by our body and natural lowliness, however much we may want to avoid this.

7. Let me explain myself further: suppose that in order to despise the world we are thinking about its nature and how all things come to an end. Almost without our realizing it we find ourselves thinking about the things we like in the world; and in desiring to flee them, we are at least hindered a little by thinking about how they were and how they will be and what we will do; in order to think of what we must do to free ourselves, we place ourselves in danger again. Not that this reasoning must be abandoned, but one must be fearful; it's necessary to proceed with care.

By means of this living water the Lord himself takes up these cares, for he doesn't want to entrust them to us.[6] He so esteems our soul that he doesn't allow it to be occupied with things that can harm it during the time he wishes to favor it. Rather, he immediately places it near himself and shows it in an instant more truths, and gives it clearer understanding of what everything is, than we could have here below in many years. For our eyes don't see clearly; the dust blinds us as we walk. By this living water the Lord brings us to the end of the journey without our understanding how.

8. The other property of water is that it satisfies to the full and takes away thirst. To me it seems that thirst signifies the desire for something of which we are in great want, so that if the thing is completely lacking its absence will kill us. How strange that if water is lacking, this lack kills us; and if there is too much, we die, as is seen through the many who drown. O my Lord, and who will be so immersed in this living water as to die! But is this possible? Yes, because the love of God and desire for him can increase so much that the natural subject is unable to endure it, and so there have been persons who have died from love. I know of one who would have died if God hadn't succored her immediately with such an abundance of this living water, for she was almost carried out of herself with raptures.[7] I say that she was almost carried out of herself because in this water the soul finds rest. It seems that while she is drowning from not being able to endure the world, she is revived in God; and His Majesty enables her to enjoy what in herself she couldn't without dying.

9. It should be understood here that since there can be nothing imperfect in our supreme Good, everything he gives is for our good; and however great the abundance of this water he gives, there cannot be too much in anything of his. If he gives a great deal, he gives the soul, as I said,[8] the capacity to drink much; like a glassmaker who makes the vessel a size he sees is necessary in order to hold what he intends to pour into it.

In desiring this water there is always some fault, since the desire comes from ourselves; if some good comes, it comes from the Lord who helps. But we are so indiscreet that since the pain is sweet and delightful, we never think we can have enough of this pain. We eat without measure, we foster this desire as much as we can, and so sometimes it kills. How fortunate such a death! But perhaps by continuing to live we can help others die of desire for this death. And I believe the devil causes this desire for death, for he understands the harm that can be done by such a person while alive; and so at this stage he tempts one to perform indiscreet penances so that one's health will be lost, which would be no small gain for the devil.

10. I say that anyone who reaches the experience of this thirst that is so impelling should be very careful because I believe this temptation will be experienced. And even though such persons may not die of thirst, their health will be lost and they will give exterior manifestations of this thirst, even though they may not want to; these manifestations should be avoided at all costs. Sometimes our diligence is of little avail, for we will be unable to hide everything we would like to hide. But when these impulses that so greatly increase this desire to die come, we should be careful not to add to the desire, but gently cut the thread with another consideration. For our nature at times can be as much at work as the love; there are persons who will vehemently desire anything, even if it is bad. I don't believe these persons will be very mortified, for mortification helps in everything. It seems foolish to cut short something good; but it isn't. For I do not say that the desire is taken away, but that it is cut short, and perhaps by another desire as meritorious as the former.

11. I wish to say something in order to explain myself better: a great desire is given to see oneself with God and to be loosed from this prison, like the desire St. Paul had.[9] Pain

for a reason like this must in itself be very delightful; no small amount of mortification is needed to break it off, and one will be unable to do so completely. Sometimes the pain is seen to afflict so much that it almost takes away one's reason. Not long ago I saw a person of an impetuous nature who, even though she was experienced in going against her will — I think she had already lost it, as was seen in other things — was deranged for a while by the great pain and the effort that was made to conceal this pain. I hold that in so extreme a case, even though the experience may come from the Spirit of God, the humble thing is to be fearful, for we shouldn't think we have so much charity that it will put us in such straits.

12. If they are able — for perhaps such persons will not always be able — I say that I wouldn't consider it wrong if they were to remove the desire by the thought that if they live they will serve God more and enlighten some soul that would have been lost, and that by serving more they will merit the capacity to enjoy God more. And let them fear the little that they have served. These consoling thoughts are good for so great a work. The affliction will be mitigated, and one will gain very much. For in order to serve the Lord himself, one should desire to suffer here below and live with the Lord's affliction. It's as when you comfort one having a great trial or a heavy sorrow by advising patience and that one should leave the matter in the hands of God and that the Lord's will is being done by it, for in every event the best we can do is leave ourselves in the hands of God.

13. It would be possible for the devil in some way to foster such a great desire. The account is given, I believe in Cassian, of a hermit who lived a most austere life. The devil made him think that by throwing himself into a well he would see God more quickly. I truly believe that this hermit could not have served with humility or goodness; for the Lord is faithful, and

His Majesty would not consent that one be blinded in a matter so obvious. But clearly, if the desire were from God, it wouldn't cause any harm: such a desire bears light, discretion, and measure. But this adversary and enemy of ours tries to cause harm wherever he can; and since he doesn't go about carelessly, neither should we. This is an important point for many reasons. Thus the time of prayer should be shortened, however delightful the prayer may be, when it is seen that the bodily energies are failing or that the head might suffer harm. Discretion is very necessary in all.

14. Why do you think, daughters, that I have tried to explain the goal and show you the reward before the battle, by telling you about the good that comes from drinking of this heavenly fount, of this living water? So that you will not be dismayed by the trial and contradiction there is along the way, and advance with courage and not grow weary. For, as I have said, it can happen that after having arrived you will have nothing left to do but stoop and drink from the fount; and yet you will abandon everything and lose this good, thinking that you have not the strength to reach it and that you are not meant for it.

15. Behold, the Lord invites all. Since he is truth itself, there is no reason to doubt. If this invitation were not a general one, the Lord wouldn't have called us all, and even if he called all, he wouldn't have promised, "I will give you to drink." He could have said, "Come all of you, for in the end you won't lose anything, and to those whom I choose I will give to drink." But since he spoke without this condition to all, I hold as certain that all those who do not falter on the way will drink this living water. May the Lord, because of who he is, give us the grace to seek this living water as it should be sought, for he promises it.

PRAYER AND PERFECT CONTEMPLATION

After a considerable period in which her work was interrupted, Teresa now returns to it without the time to reread and reorient herself. She actually turns now to the subject of prayer, at first commending all the good books on prayer with their methodical arrangement of the material. Good meditation books on the Lord's life and Passion, and so on, were available. She does not intend to try to improve on them. Instead she will speak to those whose minds are as scattered as wild horses. But then, instead of beginning with the first stages of contemplation, she gets carried along by the image of water and speaks of some of the characteristics of perfect contemplation (union and rapture).

19.1: When the intellect is bound through meditation one proceeds peacefully.

19.2: Many have minds as restless as wild horses.

- They are like thirsty persons who see water in the distance and are prevented from going there.

- Their strength and courage fail them.

- The water is from the fount of living water of which Christ speaks to the Samaritan woman.

- It takes away thirst for the things of this life, but increases thirst for the things of the next life.

- When God satisfies the thirst with this water, he increases one's desire to drink of it again.

19:3–5: A. Three of water's properties: it refreshes (4–5); it cleans (6–7); it satisfies (8).

B. The first property of water: it cools, but also enkindles.

- This water enkindles the fire (of love) more.

- This true love of God is lord of all the elements
  of the world.

- Fire and water obeyed St. Martin; the birds and
  the fish, St. Francis.

- Water from the earth has no power over the
  love of God.

- Little fires of love of God may be extinguished
  by any event, but not this fire.

- A brief interpretation of Psalm 8.7 as speaking
  of the perfect: "they will rule over all things."

- Water and fire from heaven are not contraries
  but help each other produce their effect.

19.6–7: The second property of this water (of divine
union): it leaves the soul bright and cleansed of all
faults.

- Reasoning with the intellect always carries some
  mud with it.

- The Lord in this prayer shows it truths in an instant and gives it clearer understanding than we
  could have here below in many years.

19.8–13: The third property of this water: it satisfies.

- The lack of this water will kill us; too much of
  it will also cause us to die.

- There cannot be too much in anything of God's; if he gives much, he gives the capacity to receive much.

- This great thirst could cause one to desire death; and some might be tempted by the devil to perform indiscreet penances.

- When the loving impulses increase one's desire to die, they should be cut short gently with another consideration, such as the thought that by living one can serve God more.

- When it seems that the bodily energies are failing, the prayer should be shortened.

19.14: She has explained the goal first so as to encourage the nuns not to grow weary.

19.15: The Lord has called all unconditionally and promised that he will give them to drink of this water.

- She holds as certain that all those who do not falter on the way will drink this living water.

- May the Lord give us the grace to seek this living water.

INTERPRETIVE NOTES. 1. Teresa's use of water as an image for God's gift of contemplation brings to mind her use of the image in her *Life.* Expounding the degrees of prayer, she chose as her allegory the four ways in which a garden may be watered (11.7–8). Speaking of the fourth degree of prayer, in which the soul is immersed in rain from heaven, she depicts the same kind of experience described in this chapter. In such prayer, God draws the soul up from the earth and gives it dominion over every earthly thing (21.8). The divine love increased in her to such a degree that she was dying with desire to see God (29.8). She experienced mystically St. Paul's words: "Miserable one that I am, who will deliver me from this mortal body?" (Rom 7:24). Like St. John of the Cross, she wrote verses around the refrain "Muero porque no muero" (I die because I do not die):

> Ah, how bitter a life
> When the Lord is not enjoyed!
> While love is sweet,
> Long awaiting is not.
> O God, take away this burden
> Heavier than steel,
> I die because I do not die.
>
> Only with that surety
> I will die do I live,
> Because in dying
> My hope in living is assured.
> Death, bringing life,
> Do not tarry; I await you,
> I die because I do not die.
>
> (*Poetry* 1, st. 4–5)

2. In her *Life*, she turned as well to the image of fire to describe this prayer of union and rapture that she calls perfect contemplation: "It receives great delight in seeing that the driving force of that fire is quenched by a water that makes the fire increase" (19.1).

3. The intense longings and thirst to see God are a purification; a soul "is purged of what otherwise it would have to be purged of in purgatory" (L 20.16). This purgative prayer can take away the fear of death, and Teresa says that she had always greatly feared death: "Now death seems to me to be the easiest thing" (L 38.5).

The dread of death and of the process of dying has had a direct influence on the spiritual and pastoral life of the church. The Second Vatican Council regards human beings as "tormented not only by pain and by the gradual breaking up of the body but also and even more so by the dread of forever ceasing to be" (*Gaudium et Spes*, 18). Further along, the document tells how faith relieves our anxieties by making us aware of God's revelation that human beings were created for a blessed destiny beyond the limits of their sad state on earth. Christ won the victory when he rose to life; by his death he freed us from death. Faith also enables us to live united with our loved ones who have already died and gives hope that they have found true life with God.

4. This impassioned love even to the point of one's wanting to die so as to be fully united with the Lord needs to be tempered at times, Teresa warns, because there is something of our human weakness present in it. She cautions against trying to mitigate the longings through excessive bodily penances. In her *Foundations* she tells of how two nuns, actually examples of virtue, felt such thirst and longing for the Lord that, it seemed to them, only the Eucharist could alleviate it. In those times, daily Communion was not a practice among nuns. One of the nuns thought that she had to receive

Communion not only daily but early in the morning in order to live. Teresa had to try to convince the two that they would still live if they didn't receive Communion. She did so by explaining that she too had such desires to receive and that they could all three die together by not receiving on the next day. When the two saw that they did not die on days when they did not receive Communion, the compulsion to receive gradually diminished (see F 6.9–13).

5. This prayer described by Teresa consists not only of love; it has a cognitive element too. A cloud of God's great Majesty raises the soul up and begins to show it the things of the kingdom prepared for it (L 20.2). The ideas and reasonings of philosophers and theologians always carry some mud along with them; that is, they are drawn through the sieve of earthly experience and easily stir the human emotions and limit one's knowledge. On the other hand, the understanding given by this pure water is clear. God shows the soul more truths and gives it clearer understanding than you could otherwise have in many years.

6. In her *Life*, written for her confessors and meant to be a secret book, Teresa discusses her experiences openly. In this *Way of Perfection*, as in the *Interior Castle*, she hides her identity — not too successfully — and speaks of experiences that happened to someone she knew. In this chapter, she is explaining the prayer of union and rapture as it was experienced by herself. Although this prayer belongs with the fourth water or last stage in her *Life*, her spiritual journey in prayer continued. As time went on, the ardent longings for death turned

into longings for the salvation of souls and the service and praise of God. Now her "glory lies in being able in some way to help the Crucified" (IC VII.3.6; F 1.7).

QUESTIONS FOR DISCUSSION: 1. What happens to the thirst of one who reaches this fount of living water?

2. What are the properties of this water and how can it help me to know about them?

3. Why did Teresa speak about the goal before explaining the steps to it?

4. How might the image of fire help me in considering my own prayer life?

Chapter 20

How in different ways consolation is never lacking on the path of prayer. Counsels the Sisters to let their conversations deal always with prayer.

IT SEEMS I CONTRADICTED in the previous chapter what I had said before. When I was consoling those who were not contemplatives,[1] I said that the Lord had different paths by which to go to him just as there are many dwelling places.[2] So I repeat it now. Since His Majesty has understood our weakness, he has provided after the manner of who he is. But he did not say: "some come by this path, and others by another." Rather, his mercy was so great he excluded no one from striving to come to this fount of life to drink. May he be blessed forever! And how rightly might he have excluded me!

2. Now, since he didn't stop me when I started to walk along this path, nor order me to be thrown into the abyss, surely he excludes no one; rather, he calls us publicly, crying aloud.[3] But since he is so good, he does not force us; on the contrary, in many ways he gives drink to those who wish to follow him so that no one will go without consolation or die of thirst. Rivers stream from this overflowing fount, some large, others small; and sometimes little pools for children — for that is enough for them, and moreover it would frighten them to see a lot of water. These children are the ones who are at the beginning. So, Sisters, do not fear that you will die of thirst on this road. Never is the lack of consoling water such that it cannot

be endured. Since this is so, take my advice and do not stop on the road but, like the strong, fight even to death in the search, for you are not here for any other reason than to fight. You must always proceed with this determination to die rather than fail to reach the end of the journey. If even though you so proceed, the Lord should lead you in such a way that you are left with some thirst in this life, in the life that lasts forever he will give you to drink in great plenty and you will have no fear of being without water. May it please the Lord that we ourselves do not fail, amen.

3. Now, that you might so walk along this path of prayer that you do not go astray at the beginning, let us deal a little with how this journey must begin; for the beginning is the more important part — indeed it is the most important part for everything. I don't say that if you don't have the determination of which I shall speak here, you should stop trying; for the Lord will continue perfecting you. And if you should do no more than take one step, the step will contain in itself so much power that you will not have to fear losing it, nor will you fail to be very well paid.

This situation can be compared to that of using beads to count indulgenced prayers. If you use them once, you gain the indulgences; if you use them more often, you gain more; but if you never use them, keeping them rather in a chest, it would be better for you not to have them. So it is here: even though afterward some may not continue on the same road, the little progress they may have made on it will have provided them with light so that they may walk well on other paths; and the greater the progress, the more light. In sum, even if later they give up, they may be certain that it will not have done them any harm to have begun; for good never produces evil.

Thus, daughters, in reference to all the persons who speak with you, if they are disposed and there is some friendship, try to remove any fear they may have of beginning to use so great a good. And for the love of God I beg you that your conversation always be directed toward bringing some good to the one with whom you are speaking, for your prayer must be for the benefit of souls. And since the good of souls is what you must always beg the Lord for, it would seem wrong, Sisters, if you did not strive for this in every way.

4. If you want to be a good relative, this desire to be of benefit to the relative is where true friendship lies; if you want to be a good friend, know that you cannot be one save by this path. Let truth dwell in your hearts, as it should through meditation, and you will see clearly the kind of love we are obliged to have for our neighbor.

There's no longer time, Sisters, for children's games, for these worldly friendships, even though they may be good, seem to be nothing else. Unless there is a very good reason and it is for the benefit of that soul, don't let your conversation be of the sort in which you ask, "Do you like me?" or "Don't you like me?" It can happen that in order that your relative or brother or a similar person listen to and admit a truth you want to point out, you will have to dispose that person by means of these words and demonstrations of love that are always pleasing to sensuality. It will happen that a good word, as these are called, will do more and dispose one more than will many about God so that afterward these latter may be accepted. And thus if you use them knowingly for the benefit of others, I do not forbid them. But if they are not used for this reason, they will be of no avail and may do harm without your realizing it. Others already know that you are religious and that your business is prayer. Don't think to yourself that you don't want them to consider you good, for what they see in you is to the benefit or harm of all. And it is a serious wrong for those who have so great an obligation to speak of God, as do nuns, to think that it is good for them to hide their feelings about God; although they may be allowed to do this sometimes for a greater good. God is your business and language. Those who want to speak to you must learn this language; and if they don't, be on your guard that you don't learn theirs; it will be a hell.

5. If they should think you're unsophisticated, what does it matter? If they take you for hypocrites, it matters even less. You will gain in that no one will want to see you except the one who understands this language. There wouldn't be much reason for anyone who doesn't know Arabic to enjoy speaking a great deal with one who knows only that language. And so, neither will they make you weary or do you harm, for to begin to speak a new language would cause no small amount of harm, and all your time would be spent in learning it. And you cannot know as I do, for I have experience of it, the great evil this new language is for the soul; in order to know the one, the other is forgotten. The new language involves a constant disturbance from which you ought to flee at all costs, for what is very suited to this path that we are beginning to discuss is peace and tranquillity of soul.

6. If those who speak with you wish to learn your language, though it is not your business to teach anyone, you can tell about the riches that are gained in learning it since telling of this is beneficial to the other, and when others learn about the great gain that is to be had, they may go and seek out a master who will teach them. It would be no small favor from the Lord if you were to succeed in awakening some soul to this good.

But how many things come to mind in beginning to discuss this path, even to the mind of one who has walked it as poorly as I. [Would that I had many hands with which to write so that while putting down some of these things I wouldn't forget the others.] May the Lord be pleased, Sisters, that I know how to speak of it better than I have practiced it, amen.

THE CALL TO CONTEMPLATION

After concluding the previous chapter by assuring her readers that God has invited all to drink from the fount of living water and promised to give it to them, Teresa now explains further.

20.1–2: She repeats that God excludes no one from striving to come to this fount of life.

- Since he didn't stop me, he excludes no one.

- God calls us publicly, crying aloud (Jn 7:37).

- Rivers (large and small and sometimes little pools) stream from this fount.

- Never is there a lack of water sufficient for this road.

- Proceed with the determination to fight and even die rather than fail to reach the end of the journey.

- Even if you are left with some thirst in this life, in eternal life the water will be plentiful.

20.3: The importance of beginning the journey.

- It does no one any harm to begin, even if they later give up.

- With persons who speak to you, try to remove their fears of beginning.

20.4: The previous thought leads her into a discussion of the kinds of friendships the nuns should have.

- Words of friendship that show others the nuns' love for them should be used only to dispose them to receive some words about God and prayer.

- Others know that the business of the nuns is prayer.

- It is a serious wrong for the nuns to think they must hide their feelings about God.

- God is not only your business but also your language.

20.5–6: A. Let them think you are unsophisticated or hypocrites.

- You will gain by this: No one will want to speak to you except the one who understands this language.

- In this matter, to learn another's language means forgetting your own.

- The new language would also disturb the peace of soul you need for the path of prayer.

- If those who speak with you wish to learn your language, you can tell them of its riches.

B. But how many things come to mind in beginning to discuss this path.

INTERPRETIVE NOTES. 1. For Teresa the fount of living water is Christ; to reach the end of the journey is to reach union with Christ. The water is contemplation. Drinking from the fount is equivalent to the prayer of union or pure contemplation. In speaking of the differences of paths, Teresa surely has in mind her own contemplative journey in which she came to receive an overflow of water, bountiful in its variety of mystical graces. She is the prime example of one whose prayer life is "very supernatural." Who would have the capacity for a contemplative life like hers? Such a life could not be the call of everyone. But all are invited — no one is forced — to drink from the fount, to drink the living waters of contemplation. Therefore they must begin to walk along the path of prayer, be determined to persevere, to struggle and fight and even die rather than give up. She assures us that the Lord will give water to all those who continue on this path, whether from rivers, or streams, or little pools. This living water of contemplation, wherever it is obtained, flows from that inexhaustible fount, who is Christ.

2. Jesus made his dramatic invitation to come to him and drink (Jn 7:37) in the context of the feast of Tabernacles. This feast was the third and last major pilgrimage feast of the Jewish year. Coming at the end of the dry season (September and October), the feast naturally became the occasion to pray for the return of the rains which would guarantee the crops for the following year. On each of the seven days of the festival there were water-ceremonies and prayers for rain.

To describe the future God had in store for his people, Zechariah used the images and ceremonies of the Feast of Tabernacles (Zec 9-14). He tells us that on the great and final Feast of Tabernacles the messianic king would enter Jerusalem triumphantly (Zec 9:9), the Lord would open up a fountain of water for the House of David (Zec 13:1) and would make living waters flow out abundantly from Jerusalem (Zec 14:8).

Each day of the festival, water was ceremonially drawn from a spring at the bottom of the hill on which Jerusalem is built and taken in solemn procession to the Temple. There it was poured into the ground. As the water was drawn a choir sang, "You will draw water joyfully from the springs of salvation" (Is 12:3).

The ceremonies corresponded to much more than petitions for rain and abundant harvests; along with hymns they expressed the hopes and expectations of the people, their longing, their "thirst" for the Messiah. On the last day of the festival, when the emotions of all his listeners were at their peak, Jesus proclaimed that he is the One for whom they and their forebears had waited so long.

3. After his invitation, Jesus goes on: "As the Scripture has said, 'Out of the believer's heart, shall flow rivers of living water'" (Jn 7:38). Jesus is the true rock, the one from whom the living waters flow. In the context of the Feast of Tabernacles, the wandering in the desert and the incident of the Lord providing water from the rock were recalled. The rock which gushed forth water was a sign of Christ from whom flow the true waters of life.

4. The commercialization of talk through television and radio shows dedicated to this pastime can remind us of Teresa's frustration with her life in the monastery parlor of the Incarnation. She urges her nuns strongly to speak a language different from the standard one, to talk freely about God, who must be their business and language. In chapter 7 of her *Life,* she laments at length the amount of time she spent in the parlor in empty talk. She later exhorted beginners at prayer to cultivate friendships and associate with others having the same interests. In her days, there were those who thought that talking about God and prayer could lead to vainglory and advised against it. But Teresa's defense of spiritual friendship and conversation about God and prayer is forceful:

"This is something most important even though the association with other persons may be only to help one another with prayers" (20).

"I don't know why it is not permitted that persons beginning truly to love and serve God talk with some others about their joys and trials, which all who practice prayer undergo" (20).

"Those who experience vainglory in speaking of these things will also experience it in attending Mass with devotion if they are seen and in doing other things they must do if they want to be Christian; and these deeds they are not allowed to abandon for fear of vainglory" (21).

"Since this spiritual friendship is so extremely important for souls not yet fortified in virtue — since they have so many opponents and friends to incite them to evil — I don't know how to urge it enough" (21).

"If any begin to give themselves to God, there are so many to criticize them that they need to seek companionship to defend themselves until they are so strong that it is no longer a burden for them to suffer this criticism" (22).

"And it is a kind of humility not to trust in oneself but to believe that through those with whom one converses God will help and increase charity while it is being shared" (22).

"And there are a thousand graces I would not dare speak of if I did not have powerful experience of the benefit that comes from this sharing" (22).

5. Teresa gives the example in her writings, passing easily to and fro between conversation with her readers about God and conversation with God.

QUESTIONS FOR DISCUSSION. 1. What things could prevent us from drinking of the fount of living water?

2. In what ways might a prayer group help us?

3. What would be some essential elements in a spiritual friendship?

4. What are some ways in which the image of water speaks to me about prayer?

Chapter 21

Tells how important it is to begin the practice of prayer with great determination and not pay any attention to obstacles set up by the devil.

D O NOT BE FRIGHTENED, daughters, by the many things you need to consider in order to begin this divine journey which is the royal road to heaven. A great treasure is gained by traveling this road; no wonder we have to pay what seems to us a high price. The time will come when you will understand how trifling everything is next to so precious a reward.

2. Now returning to those who want to journey on this road[1] and continue until they reach the end, which is to drink from this water of life,[2] I say that how they are to begin is very important — in fact, all important.[3] They must have a great and very determined determination to persevere until reaching the end, come what may, happen what may, whatever work is involved, whatever criticism arises, whether they arrive or whether they die on the road, or even if they don't have courage for the trials that are met, or if the whole world collapses. You will hear some persons frequently making objections: "there are dangers"; "so-and-so went astray by such means"; "this other one was deceived"; "another who prayed a great deal fell away"; "it's harmful to virtue"; "it's not for women, for they will be susceptible to illusions"; "it's better they stick to their sewing"; "they don't need these delicacies"; "the Our Father and the Hail Mary are sufficient."

3. This last statement, Sisters, I agree with. And indeed they are sufficient! It is always good to base your prayer on prayers coming from the mouth of the Lord. In this matter those who warn us are right, for if our nature were not so weak and our devotion so lukewarm there wouldn't be any need to compose other prayers, nor would there be need for other books. As I say,[4] I am speaking to souls that cannot recollect their minds in the thought of other mysteries because they think some kind of skill is needed, and there are some minds so ingenious that they're never satisfied with any of their thoughts. So it seems to me now that I should proceed by setting down some points here about the beginning, the means, and the end of prayer. I will not take time to dwell on more sublime things. No one will be able to take from you these books (the Our Father and the Hail Mary), and if you are eager to learn you won't need anything else provided you are humble.[5] I have always been fond of the words of the Gospels [that have come from that most sacred mouth in the way they were said] and found more recollection in them than in very cleverly written books. I especially had no desire to read these books if the author was not well approved. If, then, I draw near to this Master of wisdom, he will perhaps teach me some worthwhile thoughts that will please you.

4. I don't say that I'm going to write a commentary on these divine prayers,[6] for I wouldn't dare. Many commentaries have been written; and even if they hadn't been, it would be absurd for me to write one. But I will mention some thoughts on the words of the Our Father. For sometimes, with regard to many books, it seems we lose devotion in the very exercise in which it is so important for us to have devotion. Clearly, when a master teaches something he gets to love his disciple and is pleased if that which he teaches satisfies his pupil, and he helps him a great deal to learn the material. The heavenly Master will do the same with us.

5. Hence, don't pay any attention to the fears they raise or to the picture of the dangers they paint for you. Wouldn't it be nice if while desiring to procure a great treasure I should want to walk without danger along a path where there are so many robbers. It would be a pleasant world if they would let you get the treasure in peace. But for a penny's worth of self-interest they will go many nights without sleep and disturb you in body and soul. For when you are about to gain the treasure — or steal it, since the Lord says that the violent take it away[7] — by a royal road and by a safe road, the road chosen by our King and all his elect and saints, they will tell you that there are so many dangers and so many things to fear. How many more dangers are there for those who think they obtain this good without following a road?

6. Oh, my daughters! There are incomparably more dangers for such persons, but people don't know about them until they bump blindly into the true danger when there is no one to give them a hand; and they lose the water entirely without drinking either little or much — neither from a small pool nor from a stream.

So you see, how will one journey without a drop of this water on a road where there are so many struggles? It is clear that when it is needed most they will not have it and will die of thirst. Because whether we like it or not, my daughters, we must all journey toward this fount, even though in different ways. Well, believe me; and don't let anyone deceive you by showing you a road other than that of prayer.

7. I am not speaking now about whether the prayer should be mental or vocal for everyone. In your case, I say that you need both. Such is the duty of religious. Should anyone tell you that prayer is dangerous, consider him the real danger and run from him. Don't forget this counsel, for perhaps you will need it. There will be danger in not having humility and

the other virtues. But that the way of prayer be a way of danger — God would never will that. It seems the devil has invented these fears, and so he has been skillful, apparently, in making some who have practiced prayer fall away.

8. And see how blind the world is, for they fail to consider the many thousands who have fallen into heresies and great evils because they didn't practice prayer but engaged in distractions. And if in order to carry on his work better the devil has caused, among this multitude of persons, some of those who practiced prayer to fall, he has caused as much fear in others about virtuous things. Those who take this reasoning as a refuge in order to free themselves should be on their guard, for they are running away from good in order to free themselves from evil. Never have I seen such a wicked contrivance; it really seems to come from the devil. O my Lord, defend yourself! See how they understand your words in reverse. Don't permit such weaknesses in your servants. [Hold fast, daughters, for they cannot take from you the Our Father and the Hail Mary.]⁸

9. There's one great blessing: you will always find some who will help you, because this is a characteristic of the real servant of God to whom His Majesty has given light concerning the true way; in the midst of these fears the desire not to give up increases within him. He understands clearly where the devil is going to strike, flees from him and crushes his head. The devil feels more regret over this than he does satisfaction over the many pleasures that others give him. In a time of disturbance, of discord caused by the devil — for it seems all are following him half blind because they do so under the guise of zeal — God will raise up someone to open the eyes of these half-blind people and tell them that the devil has placed a cloud in front of them to prevent their seeing the way. Oh, the greatness of God, for sometimes one or two men alone can do more when they speak the truth than many together! Little

by little, souls discover again the way; God gives them courage. If they are told there is danger in prayer, one of these servants of God will strive, if not in words then in deeds, to make known how good prayer is. If they are told that frequent Communion is not good, that servant will receive more frequently. Thus, since there are one or two who fearlessly do what is best, the Lord at once begins to win back gradually the ground that was lost.

10. Therefore, Sisters, give up these fears; never pay attention in like matters to the opinion of the crowd. Behold, these are not the times to believe everyone; believe only those who you see are walking in conformity with Christ's life. Try to preserve a pure conscience, humility, and contempt for all worldly things; believe firmly what Holy Mother Church holds, and you can be sure you will be walking along a good path.

Leave aside, as I said,[9] your fears where there is no reason for fear. If someone should raise these fears to you, humbly explain the path to him. Tell him you have a rule that commands you to pray unceasingly — for that's what it commands us[10] — and that you have to keep it. If they tell you that the prayer should be vocal, ask, for the sake of more precision, if in vocal prayer the mind and heart must be attentive to what you say. If they answer "yes" — for they cannot answer otherwise — you will see how they admit that you are forced to practice mental prayer and even experience contemplation if God should give it to you by such a means.

DETERMINATION WITHOUT FEAR

She returns to the beginning to tell us how one must journey along this way (or path or road) of prayer.

21.1: A great treasure is gained by traveling this road: everything is trifling next to the precious reward.

21.2: A. To reach the end they need a *muy determinada determinación* (literally, a very determined determination) to persevere until reaching the end (the fount of living water).

B. Continue on no matter what the obstacles are and despite the objections raised by others.

21.3–4: If they object by saying that the Our Father and the Hail Mary are sufficient, I agree.

- It is good to base our prayer on words from the mouth of the Lord.

- I'm speaking to souls who cannot recollect their minds in the thought of other mysteries.

- No one will be able to take from you these books (the Our Father and the Hail Mary).

- If you are eager to learn, you won't need anything else except humility.

- I have always found more recollection in words from the Gospels than in cleverly written books.

- Drawing near to the Master of wisdom, I may receive some thoughts to help you understand the words of the Our Father.

- But I will not be writing a commentary on them.

- The heavenly Master will be our loving teacher.

21.5–8: Pay no attention to the fears others try to stir up about prayer.

- The road of prayer is a royal and safe road.

- It is the road Christ (our King) and his saints chose.

- All must journey toward this fount, like it or not.

- There are incomparably more dangers for those who refuse to take the road of prayer.

- Consider anyone who tells you the way of prayer is dangerous to be the true danger.

- They run away from good to free themselves from evil.

- No one can take from you the Our Father and the Hail Mary.

21.9: God will always raise up someone to open the eyes of the half-blind.

21.10: Give up these fears and pay no attention to the opinion of the crowd.

- These are not the times to believe everyone, but those you see walking in conformity with Christ's life.

- Believe firmly what Holy Mother Church holds.

- Tell others you have a rule that comands you to pray unceasingly.

- If they say the prayer should be vocal, ask if in vocal prayer the mind and heart must be attentive.

- They will have to answer "yes" and thereby admit your obligation to practice mental prayer and be open to contemplation if the Lord gives it.

INTERPRETIVE NOTES: 1. Teresa's impassioned defense of mental prayer in this chapter springs from her own experience. The section on the historical context in the introduction for this volume contains information about the hostile environment one who practiced mental prayer could encounter in certain circles in Teresa's times, especially if a woman. When Teresa began to receive an inundation of God's mystical graces, as explained by her in the *Life*, a group of spiritual consultants concluded that the devil was the culprit behind her experiences. They advised her to renounce frequent Communion, avoid being alone, and abandon mental prayer (25.14–15). After the Lord liberated her from these fears that her directors had caused her, she was able to write:

"I don't understand these fears, 'The devil! The devil!', when we can say 'God! God', and make the devil tremble.... Without doubt, I fear those who have such great fear of the devil more than I do the devil himself" (L 25.22).

This opposition to her prayer on the part of good men was, in her words, one of the most severe trials she had to undergo: "There were enough things to drive me insane" (L 28.18).

2. In her writings, then, Teresa speaks forcefully against those who seek to turn mental prayer into something to be feared. Attempting to live without prayer, for her, amounts to undergoing the trials of life with greater trial and closing the door on God and thereby preventing him from making us happy (L 8.8): "Whoever has not begun the practice of prayer, I beg for the love of the Lord not to go without so great a good" (L 8.5).

3. After encouraging us to break free from all fear about mental prayer, Teresa presses us to persevere. For her, prayer is a *camino* (a road, path, or way) leading to perfection, or the fount of living water. Once you overcome your fears of starting out on this road, you must continue to travel on it no matter what the obstacles. It is along this line of thought that Teresa makes her classic assertion that travelers on this road must do so with a *muy determinada determinación* (a very determined determination) to persevere until reaching the end whatever the effort and despite any criticism.

4. Traveling in sixteenth-century Spain was both dangerous and uncomfortable. It was not an unusual thing for a traveler, as part of his preparation for a journey, to make out a will. Added to the dangers inherent in the physical terrain and the climate were those from bandits and murderers. In her *Foundations*, Teresa remarks regarding the discomforts: "I am not recording in these foundations the great hardships endured in the traveling: the cold, the heat, the snow...sometimes

getting lost, and at other times being very sick and having a fever" (18.4). There was no planned network of roads. The existing roads were in miserable condition and it was easy to get lost. A royal road, then, was a road kept in excellent condition because it was traveled by the king; it was the easiest of all roads to travel on. In saying that prayer is a royal and safe road, the road chosen by our King, Teresa reminds all Christians how much prayer belonged to the essence of Jesus' life and mission. In his prayer he was completely obedient to his Father, spontaneously grateful, full of praise, altogether trusting, and intent on carrying out the mission given him. Through prayer he united himself to the Father in thought, purpose, and affection. References from the gospels to Jesus praying could fill a number of pages. Thus, not only because Teresa herself received a lavish outpouring of grace by following this road does she recommend it with such assurance, but she does so also because it was the road taken by the Lord himself and by his saints.

5. Much has come to light about the distrust of and even hostility toward mental prayer prevalent in Teresa's times. Nowadays people in general are not likely to fear deception by the devil. Their more common objection to mental prayer is the lack of time. The prevailing trend is to dismiss mental prayer as something, on the whole, unnecesary; it consumes the time we need for our many responsibilities. But whatever the excuse one might make against the practice of prayer, Teresa objects: Without prayer, you will die of thirst.

6. More specifically than the Carmelite rule, the Lord himself told his followers that they must pray always and not lose heart (Lk 18:1). Teresa confesses that she found more recollection in the words and prayers of the Lord than in her other books, even when cleverly written. This did not mean that she had found no enjoyment in reading spiritual books. In 1559, Fernando Valdés, the Inquisitor General, published an index of forbidden books among which were included almost all books dealing with prayer. Among them were books by some of Teresa's favorite authors: Luis de Granada, Juan de Avila, the Carthusian (Ludolph of Saxony), and Francisco de Osuna. Shortly after, while she was keenly feeling this loss, the Lord told her not to be sad, that he would become for her a living book (L 26.5).

QUESTIONS FOR DISCUSSION: 1. Have I experienced any fears or noticed them in others regarding the practice of mental prayer?

2. What are some of the reasons for which we might give up the practice of mental prayer?

3. What does Teresa mean by mental prayer?

Chapter 22

Explains what mental prayer is.

R EALIZE, DAUGHTERS, that the nature of mental prayer isn't determined by whether or not the mouth is closed. If while speaking I thoroughly understand and know that I am speaking with God and I have greater awareness of this than I do of the words I'm saying, mental and vocal prayer are joined. If, however, others tell you that you are speaking with God while you are reciting the Our Father and at the same time in fact thinking of the world, then I have nothing to say. But if you are to be speaking, as is right, with so great a Lord, it is good that you consider whom you are speaking with as well as who you are, at least if you want to be polite. How can you call the king "your highness" or know the ceremonies to be observed in addressing a highest ranking nobleman if you do not clearly understand what his position is and what yours is? For it is in conformity with these facts that you must show respect, and in conformity with custom — because you also need to know even the customs. If you don't know them, you will be sent away as a simpleton and will fail to negotiate anything. [And what's more, if you don't know these things well, you will need to find out and even rehearse what you must say. Once it happened to me[1] that, not having been accustomed to speaking with lords and ladies I had to speak with someone who was to be addressed as your ladyship; and so they had to show me

241

how to say it. Since I am dull and was not used to these titles, I didn't get it right when the time came. I decided to tell her what happened and, laughing at myself, asked her to allow me to address her with the ordinary form "you"; and so I did.]

Well, what is this, my Lord? What is this, my Emperor? How can it be tolerated? You are King forever, my God; your kingdom is not a borrowed one. When in the Creed the words, "and his kingdom will have no end," are said, it is almost always a special delight for me. I praise you, Lord, and bless you forever; in sum, your kingdom will last forever. Well then, may you never permit, Lord, that anyone who is about to speak to you consider it good to do so only vocally.

2. What is this, Christians, that you say mental prayer isn't necessary? Do you understand yourselves?[2] Indeed, I don't think you do, and so you desire that we all be misled. You don't know what mental prayer is, or how vocal prayer should be recited, or what contemplation is, for if you did you wouldn't on the one hand condemn what on the other hand you praise.

3. I shall always have to join mental prayer to vocal prayer —when I remember— so that others don't frighten you, daughters. I know how this criticism of mental prayer will end up, for I have suffered some trials in this matter, and thus I wouldn't want anyone to disturb you. It is harmful to walk on this road with fear. It is very important for you to know that you are on the right road. When a traveler is told that he has made a mistake and lost his way, he is made to go from one end to another, and all his searching for the way tires him, and he wastes time and arrives late.

Who can say that it is wrong, when we begin to recite the Hours or the rosary, to consider whom we are going to speak with, and who we are, so as to know how to speak with him? Now I tell you, Sisters, if before you begin your vocal prayer you do the great deal that must be done in order to understand these two points well, you will be spending a good amount of time in mental prayer. Yes, indeed, for we must not approach a conversation with a prince as negligently as we do one with a farm worker, or with some poor thing like ourselves for whom any manner of address is all right.

4. It is only right that we consider these two points since, because of his humility, this King listens to me and lets me approach him; and his guards do not throw me out, even though as an uneducated person I don't know how to speak to him. The angels who assist him know well the attitude of their King, for he delights more in the unpolished manners of a humble shepherd who he realizes would say more if he knew more than he does in the talk of very wise and learned men, however elegant their discourse, if they don't walk in humility. But just because he is good doesn't mean that we should be rude. At least, in order to thank him for the bad odor he must endure in consenting to allow one like myself to come near him, we should strive to be aware of his purity and of who he is. It's true that upon approaching him one understands immediately, just as with lords here below; for when they tell us who their father was and about the millions they get in rent and of their title of dignity, there's no more to know. In fact, here below people in paying honor don't take into account the persons themselves, however much these persons may deserve the honor, but their wealth.

5. O miserable world! Praise God very much, daughters, because you have left something so wretched, where people pay attention not to what they have within themselves but to what their tenant farmers and vassals have; and if these persons lack subordinates then no honor is paid them. It's something amusing to relax over when you all have to take some recreation. For this is a good pastime: to notice how blindly those who are in the world spend their time.

6. Oh, our Emperor, supreme Power, supreme Goodness, Wisdom itself, without beginning, without end, without any limit to your works; they are infinite and incomprehensible, a fathomless sea of marvels, with a beauty containing all beauty, strength itself ! Oh, God help me, who might possess here all human eloquence and wisdom together in order to know how to explain clearly — insofar as is possible here below, because in this case all knowledge is equivalent to knowing nothing — a number of the many things we can consider in order to have some knowledge of who this Lord and Good of ours is!

7. Yes, bring yourselves to consider and understand whom you are speaking with, or, as you approach, with whom you are about to speak. In a thousand lives we would never completely understand the way in which this Lord deserves that we speak with him, for the angels tremble before him. He commands all; he can do all; for him, to will is to do. Well then, it is only right, daughters, that we try to delight in these grandeurs our Spouse possesses and that we understand whom we are wedded to and what kind of life we must live. Oh, God help me, here below before getting married a person will know who the other party is and what he possesses. We are already betrothed and before the wedding must be brought to his house. Here below they don't try to make those who are betrothed renounce such thoughts. Why should they try to prevent us from thinking about who this man is, who his Father is, what country he is going to bring me to, what good things he promises to give me, what his status is, how I can make him happy, and in what ways I can please him, and from studying how I can conform my way of life to his? Now if a woman is to be happily married, she must, according to the advice she receives, strive for this conformity even though her husband is a man of lowly estate.

8. Well, my Spouse, must they in everything pay less attention to you than to men? If paying more attention to you doesn't seem right to them, let them at least leave your brides alone, for these latter must live their lives with you. Indeed, their life is a good one. If a spouse is so jealous that he doesn't want his bride to talk to anyone, it would be a fine thing if she didn't think about how she might please him in this matter and the reason she has for putting up with this jealousy and for wanting to avoid speaking with another since in him she has all that she could want!

This is mental prayer, my daughters: to understand these truths. If you should want to grow in understanding these things and pray vocally, well and good. You should not be thinking of other things while speaking with God, for doing so amounts to not knowing what mental prayer is. I believe the matter has been explained. May it please the Lord that we know how to put it into practice. Amen.[3]

THE NATURE OF MENTAL PRAYER

In the previous chapter Teresa indicated the theme she will now go into more at length. She tells what this theme is in the briefest of all her chapter headings: "Explains what mental prayer is."

22.1–2: A. The nature of mental prayer is not determined by whether or not the mouth is closed.

B. I must have greater awareness that I am speaking with God than of the words.

- You must consider who the one you are speaking with is and who you are.

- You must know another's rank in society and your own to show respect in conformity with custom.

- An example of her own difficulties in this regard.

C. She then begins to speak to God, recognizing him as the King whose Kingdom will last forever, and begs him not to allow anyone speaking to him to think it good to do so only vocally.

D. She then addresses Christians who say that mental prayer is unnecessary.

22.3–5: She addresses her readers urging them not to be intimidated into thinking that mental prayer is the wrong road.

- When we begin the Hours (of the Office) or the rosary, we must consider whom we are addressing.

- If we are going to speak to a prince, our approach will be different from speaking to some poor thing like ourselves.

- Our King is more pleased with the unpolished manner of a humble shepherd than with the elegant talk of the learned who have no humility.

- But just because he is good doesn't mean we should be rude.

- Here below, in paying honor, people don't take into account the persons themselves, but their wealth.

- For your relaxation, laugh at how blindly people in the world pay more attention to what others possess than to what others are within themselves.

22.6–7: She turns to God, addressing him by many of his titles, lamenting her lack of the eloquence and wisdom necessary to convey some understanding of who he is.

- Consider with whom you are about to speak.

- In a thousand lives we could never completely understand what the Lord deserves in our way of speaking with him.

- The angels tremble before him.

- She introduces his title of Spouse.

- They don't prevent a woman from knowing about her husband-to-be.

22.8: She again turns to the Lord begging him to let them leave his brides alone; his brides must be paying attention to him.

INTERPRETIVE NOTES: 1. What Teresa calls mental prayer is an awareness that we are speaking with God, of who he is, and who we are. Even vocal prayer, then, can be (and must be, for Teresa) accompanied by mental prayer. Mental prayer may be present when you pray in common as well as when you pray alone. Vocal prayer at first referred to prayer expressed with the voice, but then came to mean prayer to which outward expression was given, such as moving the lips. Nowadays, vocal prayer is often understood to be prayer with preset formulas. In contrast to these conceptions, mental prayer would be silent prayer, or interior prayer, or prayer unbound by any formulas.

2. Teresa's understanding of mental prayer as our being aware of who God is and who we are entails, of course, no small matter. In her *Life*, she gives another definition of mental prayer which has become classic: "For mental prayer in my opinion is nothing else than an intimate sharing between friends: it means taking time frequently to be alone with him who we know loves us" (8.5). The Spanish words *tratar de amistad* suggest a communion or exchange suffused with intimacy and love. The communion is between two. And the Other is one who we know loves us.

As Christians, we believe that God initiated a dialogue at a deeper level than the one between Creator and creature. "In this way the love of God was revealed to us: God sent his only Son into the world so that we might have life through him. In this is love: not that we have loved God, but that he loved us and sent his Son as expiation for our sins" (1 Jn 4:9–10). Building on this thought Teresa writes in her *Life:* "As often as we think of Christ we should recall the love with which he bestowed on us so many favors and what great love God showed us in giving us a pledge like this of his love, for love begets love" (22.14). Divine Love invites us to a communion of life, a sharing in divine life itself. That this communion might be more perfect, God took on our human nature to participate fully in our human life. Teresa's first consideration is not that we *must* pray. What is so awesome for her is that we *can* pray because God in addressing his Word, his Son, to us has made it possible for us to enter into intimacy with him and his divine life. Prayer for Teresa is a relationship, a communion between friends. "Listen, I am standing at the door knocking; if you hear my voice and open the door, I will come in to you and eat with you, and you with me" (Rv 3:20). At the core of all prayer, Teresa insists, is this awareness that we stand in the presence of this God of Majesty who so loves us.

3. The journey in prayer calls as well for a journey in understanding so that the awareness of who God is and who we are is necessary not only at the beginning of prayer. This awareness develops into the fruit of prayer because the one who prays becomes more deeply aware of the divine mysteries. Prayer is "the place where the Lord gives the light to understand truths" (F 10.13).

QUESTIONS FOR DISCUSSION. 1. Who are we in relation to God our Creator and who are we in relation to Christ our Redeemer?

2. What should we be most aware of when we pray?

Chapter 23

Treats of how important it is for one who has begun the path of prayer not to turn back and speaks once more of the great value that lies in beginning with determination.

❦

WELL NOW, I SAY there are so many reasons why it is extremely important to begin with great determination that I would have to go on at much length if I mentioned them all. Sisters, I want to mention only two or three.

One is that if we resolve to give something, that is, this little care, to someone who has given so much to us and continually gives — giving this little care is certainly to our advantage and we thereby gain so many wonderful things — there is no reason for failing to give with complete determination. There's no reason for being like the lender who gives something with the intention of getting it back again. Lending doesn't seem to me to amount to giving; rather, there is always some displeasure felt by the borrower when the object is taken back, especially if it is needed and has already been used as one's own, or if the lender is a friend, or if the borrower has given the lender many gifts without any self-seeking. The borrower would rightly think there was very little love in the lender who won't even let a little thing be kept, not even as a sign of love.

2. What bride is there who in receiving many valuable jewels from her bridegroom will refuse to give him even a ring, not because of what it is worth, for everything belongs to him, but to give it as a pledge that she will be his until

death? Does this Lord deserve less, that we should mock him by giving and then taking back the trifle that we gave him? But this little bit of time that we resolve to give him, which we spend on ourselves and on someone who will not thank us for it, let us give to him, since we desire to do so, with our thoughts free of other things and unoccupied by them. And let us be wholly determined never to take it back from him, neither because of trials on this account, nor because of contradictions, nor because of dryness. I should consider the time of prayer as not belonging to me and think that he can ask it of me in justice when I do not want to give it wholly to him.

3. In saying "wholly," I do not mean that abandoning it for a day or for a few days on account of some just occupations or because of some indisposition is the equivalent of taking it back. Let the intention be firm; my God is not at all touchy; he doesn't bother about trifling things. Thus you will have something to be grateful for; this intention amounts to giving something. As for others, for those who are not generous but so stingy that they don't have the spirit of giving, it is enough for them to lend. In the end, one who lends does do something, and this Lord of ours takes everything into account. He adjusts himself to our way of giving. In taking account of us, he is not at all petty, but generous. However great our debt may be, he finds it easy to pardon; but when there is a question of his repaying us, he's so careful that you need have no fear. Just the raising of our eyes in remembrance of him will have its reward.

4. Another reason for beginning with determination is that the devil will not then have so free a hand to tempt. He's extremely afraid of determined souls, for he has experienced the great harm they do him. And all the harm he plans to do them turns out to their benefit and to that of others as well; and he comes out with a loss. But we should not be careless or trust in this fact, for we are dealing with traitors, and they don't

dare attack so often those who are well prepared; they are very cowardly. But if the devil should see carelessness, he would do great harm. And if he knows that someone is changeable and unstable in being good and not strongly determined to persevere, he will keep after him day and night; he will cause fears and never-ending obstacles. I know this very well through experience, and that's why I'm able to say, and do say, that no one knows how important determination is.

5. The other reason for beginning with determination is — and it is very much to the point — that persons who do so struggle more courageously. They know that come what may they will not turn back. As in the case of one who is in a battle, he knows that if he is conquered they won't spare him his life and that if he doesn't die in battle he will die afterward. He struggles with greater determination and wants to fight like a desperado — as they say — and he doesn't fear the blows so much, because he is convinced of how important victory is and that for him to conquer is to live. It's also necessary to begin with the assurance that if we don't let ourselves be conquered, we will obtain our goal; this without a doubt, for no matter how small the gain, one will end up being very rich. Don't be afraid that the Lord will leave you to die of thirst, for he calls us to drink from this fount.[1] I have already said this[2] and would like to say it many times, for the devil intimidates persons who don't yet fully know the goodness of the Lord through experience, even though they know it through faith. But it is a great thing to have experienced the friendship and favor he shows toward those who journey on this road and how he takes care of almost all the expenses.

6. I'm not surprised that those who have not experienced this want the assurance of some gain for themselves. Well, you already know there is the hundredfold even in this life[3] and that the Lord says, "ask, and you will receive."[4] If you don't believe His Majesty in the sections of his Gospel that insure this

gain, it will be of little benefit, Sisters, for me to break my head in trying to tell you about it. Nevertheless, I say that should anyone have some doubt little would be lost in trying the journey of prayer; for this journey brings with it the following good: more is given than is asked for, beyond what we could desire. This is absolutely true; I know. And those of you who know it by experience, through the goodness of God, can be my witnesses.[5]

THE VALUE OF DETERMINATION

After her digression on the union of mental prayer with vocal prayer, Teresa returns to the subject she began to deal with in chapter 21: the "very determined determination" not to give up.

23.1–4: Reasons for the importance of determination.

A. First, we are only giving a little care to one who has given so much to us.

- We must not be like lenders, who intend to get back what they give; especially if the borrower has given the lender many gifts without self-seeking.

- Let us give the Lord this little bit of time wholly determined not to take it back.

- I should consider the time of prayer as not belonging to me.

- The intention to give something must be firm.

B. Second, the devil fears determined souls.

- Day and night he will keep after those who are unstable.

- He will cause fears and never-ending obstacles to those not strongly determined to persevere.

23.5–6: Determined persons will struggle more courageously.

- A soldier in battle, knowing that if he is conquered he will be killed, fights for his life.

- The Lord will not allow us to die of thirst and will show us his favor if we journey on this road.

- There is a hundredfold even in this life.

- The Lord gives much more than he asks of us; this is absolutely true.

INTERPRETIVE NOTES: 1. In chapter 11 of her *Life*, in which she begins her little treatise on prayer, Teresa asks the question why we don't reach quickly the perfect love of God, which brings with it every blessing. She answers that the whole fault lies with us because we are largely miserly about giving ourselves entirely to God (11.1). The journey in prayer leads to the complete gift of ourselves, but it more often proceeds slowly because it is through giving that we open ourselves to receive. In a conversation with God, Teresa asks: "Who is more fond of giving than you, or of serving even at a cost to yourself, when there is someone open to receive?" (F 2.7).

2. What we give in the beginning is "this little bit of time...with our thoughts free of other things and unoccupied by them" (3). Prayer like love is gratuitous. Some who look for its usefulness find that it is not "cost-effective" and abandon it. The determination called for by Teresa means that even if none of our plans and projects work out and our prayer is poor, without so much as a thought worthy of God, we continue. It is God alone whom we should be seeking. We have to know how to "lose our time" so as to dedicate it to God. Prayer calls people to renounce the useful things its

practice might do for them, and to renounce as well the useful things they might otherwise do. Love needs time in which nothing more is done than loving and being with the other.

3. In addition to giving our time to God in prayer, we allow God to be with us, Teresa adds. In one of her spontaneous prayers to God in her *Life*, she reveals her thought:

"I do not know, my Creator, why it is that every one does not strive to reach you through this special friendship, and why those who are wicked, who are not conformed to your will, do not, in order that you make them good, allow you to be with them at least two hours each day, even though they may not be with you, but with a thousand disturbances from worldly cares and thoughts, as was the case with me" (8.6).

4. Teresa took up this daily practice of mental prayer after having read about it in the *Third Spiritual Alphabet* by Francisco de Osuna (L 4.7). In the constitutions she composed for the new contemplative communities she founded, she prescribed, in addition to Mass and the Hours of the Divine Office, two hours of mental prayer a day, one in the morning and the other in the evening (whether the mental prayer be in the form of vocal prayer, meditation, or contemplation). For many years the hours of prayer seemed to lag for Teresa, and she had to help herself get through them with a book. But after she began "to taste how sweet the Lord is," she found it "more pleasing for the body to be resting without work and for the soul to be receiving" (F 5.4).

At first, she was distressed when obedience and many responsibilities took her away from this contemplative prayer that was no longer arduous. In chapter 5 of her *Foundations*, she explains how she came to learn that when solitude becomes a delight — and the desire for solitude, she teaches, is continually present in souls that truly love God — one must be ready to renounce it for the works of obedience and charity. "The true lover loves everywhere and is always thinking of the Beloved" (5.16). Time spent well in good works prepares a soul for prayer:

"And let souls believe that it is not the length of time spent in prayer that benefits one; when the time is spent as well in good works, it is a great help in preparing the soul for the enkindling of love. The soul may thereby be better prepared in a very short time than through many hours of reflection" (5.17).

In this context, Teresa makes that well known comment: "Come now, my daughters, don't be sad when obedience draws you to involvement in exterior matters. Know that if it is in the kitchen, the Lord walks among the pots and pans helping you both interiorly and exteriorly" (5.8).

QUESTIONS FOR DISCUSSION: 1. How much time should I spend in prayer?

2. Why is the determination to persevere so important?

Chapter 24

How vocal prayer must be recited with perfection, and mental prayer joined with it.

NOW, THEN, LET US SPEAK AGAIN[1] to those souls I mentioned that cannot recollect or tie their minds down in mental prayer or engage in reflection. Let's not mention here by name these two things, since you are not meant to follow such a path. As a matter of fact there are many persons seemingly terrified by the mere term "mental prayer" or "contemplation," and perhaps one of these might come to this house, for as I have also said[2] not everyone walks by the same path.

2. Well, what I now want to counsel you about (I can even say teach you, because as a Mother, having the office of prioress, I'm allowed to teach) is how you must pray vocally, for it's only right that you should understand what you're saying. And because it can happen that those who are unable to think about God may also find long prayers tiring, I don't want to concern myself with these. But I will speak of those prayers we are obliged as Christians to recite (such as the Our Father and the Hail Mary) so that people won't be able to say of us that we speak and don't understand what we're speaking about — unless we think it is enough for us to follow the practice in which merely pronouncing the words is sufficient. I'm not concerned with whether this is sufficient or not; learned men will explain [the matter to those persons to

whom God gives light to ask the question. And I'm not meddling with what doesn't belong to our state.] What I would like us to do, daughters, is refuse to be satisfied with merely pronouncing the words. For when I say, "I believe," it seems to me right that I should know and understand what I believe. And when I say, "Our Father," it will be an act of love to understand who this Father of ours is and who the Master is who taught us this prayer.

3. If you reply that you already know this and that there is no reason to recall it, you are wrong. There is a large difference in teachers; but it is even a great misfortune if we forget those who teach us here below. Especially, if they are saints and spiritual masters and we are good disciples, it is impossible to forget them [but we love them very much and even take pride in them and often speak of them.] Well, God never allows us to forget the Master who taught us this prayer, and with so much love and desire that it benefit us. He wants us to remember him often when we say the prayer, even though because of our weakness we do not remember him always.

4. Now with regard to vocal prayer you already know that His Majesty teaches that it be recited in solitude.[3] This is what he always did when he prayed,[4] and not out of any need of his own but for our instruction. It has already been mentioned[5] that one cannot speak simultaneously to God and to the world; this would amount to nothing more than reciting the prayer while listening to what is being said elsewhere or to letting the mind wander and making no effort to control it. There can be exceptions at times either because of bad humors — especially if the person is melancholic — or because of faint feelings in the head so that all efforts become useless. Or it can happen that God will permit days of severe temptation in his servants for their greater good. And though in their affliction they are striving to be quiet, they cannot even be attentive to what

they are saying, no matter how hard they try; nor will the intellect settle down in anything, but by the disordered way it goes about, it will seem to be in a frenzy.

5. Those who experience the affliction these distractions cause will see that the fault does not lie with them; they should not grow anxious, which makes things worse, or tire themselves trying to put order into something that at the time doesn't have any, that is, their minds. They should just pray as best they can; or even not pray, but like sick persons strive to bring some relief to their souls; let them occupy themselves in other works of virtue. This advice now is for persons who are careful and who have understood that they must not speak simultaneously to both God and the world.

What we ourselves can do is to strive to be alone; and please God it will suffice, as I say, that we understand to whom we are speaking and the answer the Lord makes to our petitions. Do you think he is silent? Even though we do not hear him, he speaks well to the heart when we beseech him from the heart.

And it is good for us to consider that he taught this prayer to each of us and that he is showing it to us; the teacher is never so far from his pupil that he has to shout, but he is very close. I want you to understand that it is good for you, if you are to recite the Our Father well, to remain at the side of the Master who taught this prayer to you.

6. You will say that doing so involves reflection and that you neither can nor want to pray any other way but vocally; for there are also impatient persons who like to avoid any suffering. Since such individuals do not have the habit, it is difficult for them to recollect their minds in the beginning; and so as to avoid a little fatigue, they say they neither can nor know how to do anything else than pray vocally.

You are right in saying that this vocal prayer is now in fact mental prayer. But I tell you that surely I don't know how mental prayer can be separated from vocal prayer if the vocal prayer is to be recited well with an understanding of whom we are speaking to. It is even an obligation that we strive to pray with attention. Please God that with these remedies we shall recite the Our Father well and not end up in some other irrelevant thing. I have experienced this sometimes, and the best remedy I find is to strive to center the mind upon the One to whom the words are addressed. So, be patient and strive to make a habit out of something that is so necessary [if you are to be good nuns, and even pray as good Christians, in my opinion.]

HOW TO PRAY VOCALLY

In chapter 21, Teresa had promised to comment on the Our Father. She now returns to that promise and writes for those who cannot engage in discursive reflection.

24.1: Let us speak to those who cannot tie their minds down to reflection.

- Many are terrified by the mere term "mental prayer" or "contemplation."

- Not everyone walks by the same path.

24.2–3: I want to give counsel and teaching about how you should pray vocally.

- I will speak of those prayers we are obliged as Christians to recite (the Our Father and the Hail Mary).

- I'm not concerned with whether it is sufficient merely to pronounce the words.

- We should refuse to be satisfied with merely pronouncing the words.

- When I say "Our Father," it will be an act of love to understand who this Father of ours is and who the Master is who taught us this prayer.

- God wants us to remember often the Master who taught us this prayer.

24.4–5: His Majesty taught us to recite vocal prayer in solitude.

- This is what he always did when he prayed.

- One cannot speak simultaneously to God and to the world.

- There may be times when our efforts are useless: when one is suffering from bad humours, faint feelings in the head, or severe temptations. In these times:

  - One should pray as best one can.

  - Or even not pray, but find some relief in works of virtue.

- What we ourselves can do is strive to be alone and understand to whom we are speaking and the answer the Lord makes to our petitions.

- He speaks well to the heart when we beseech him from the heart.

- Remain at the side of the Master who taught the Our Father to you.

24.6: You cannot separate vocal prayer from mental prayer.

- Strive to center the mind on the one to whom the words are addressed.

- Be patient and seek to make a habit out of your obligation as a Christian to pray with attention.

INTERPRETIVE NOTES: 1. Writing for those who cannot bind their minds to reflection in prayer, Teresa speaks out of her own experience. In her *Life*, she states clearly that she could not reflect discursively with the intellect. Added to this handicap was her inability to picture things to herself with the imagination (cf. L 9.4,6). Discursive meditation where you both reason with the intellect and picture things and persons in the imagination is the kind of prayer generally thought suited to beginners. Teresa recommended this meditation to those who were capable of it and recognized that good books were available on the subject. But she does not teach it here; she cannot speak of its merits from her own experience. She must have been learning that a number of others were having difficulties like hers, enough of her nuns at least to prompt her to turn to vocal prayer as an excellent means of practicing mental prayer.

2. The introduction in this volume provides some information about several of the controversies surrounding prayer in Teresa's times. There were those who thought that women because of their lack of training in theology and Scripture should be content with reciting their vocal prayers. Women were not to get involved with mental prayer. At the other end of the spectrum were those who disparaged vocal prayer, including liturgical prayer. Teresa dismisses both extremes. Not all Christians can practice discursive meditation, but all are required to pray vocally at times, prayers such as the Our Father, the Hail Mary, and the Creed. If they pray these prayers the way they ought, they will be practicing true mental prayer.

3. Those who belittled vocal prayer also devalued external ceremonies and devotional images. Precisely because of her poor ability to picture things to herself with the imagination, Teresa highly valued religious images. Still preserved today are many of the

religious images she had acquired for her monasteries as well as devotional paintings that she had commissioned artists to paint. Acknowledging this inability to picture things to herself with her imagination, she writes in her *Life:* "This was the reason I liked images so much. Unfortunate are those who through their own fault lose this great good. It indeed appears that they do not love the Lord, for if they loved him they would rejoice to see a portrait of him, just as here on earth it really gives joy to see one whom you deeply love" (9.6). A number of the important mystical graces given to her were bestowed during the celebration of the liturgy (L 30.14; 31.4; 32.11;33.13–14; 38.23; 39.25–27; 40.5).

4. Teresa and her nuns passed hours each day reciting the Divine Office in Latin, a language they did not understand. The difficulty of their having to do this is illustrated by her description of the holy women in Villanueva de la Jara who were trying to live as Carmelites and begging Teresa to accept them among her daughters: "They recited the Divine Office most of the time despite their little ability to read, for only one of them read well. And they did not have identical breviaries. Some used old Roman breviaries that were given by priests who no longer used them; others used whatever they could find. And since they did not know how to read, they spent many hours at this. They did not recite the Office in a place where they could be heard by outsiders. God must have accepted their good intention and effort, for they must have said little that was correct" (F 28.42). But Teresa did not favor the theories holding that, since liturgical prayer was the church's prayer, it was sufficient to follow the rubrics and

pronounce the words. If the nuns could not understand the words, they could try to be aware of whom
they were speaking to and remain at the side of the
Master. Then they would be combining mental prayer
with their vocal liturgical prayers.

5. From Teresa's definition of mental prayer, solitude
is required. It is "an intimate sharing between friends;
it means taking time frequently to be alone with him
who we know loves us" (L 8.5). But this "being alone
with" of which Teresa speaks does not consist essentially in physical solitude. The solitude can be present
also in liturgical prayer celebrated in community. How
is this possible? She explains her thinking when she
brings to notice how one must be alone with God in
one's awareness or thoughts: "Now with regard to vocal prayer you already know that His Majesty teaches
that it be recited in solitude.... one cannot speak simultaneously to God and to the world; this would amount
to nothing more than reciting the prayer while listening to what is being said elsewhere or to letting the
mind wander and making no effort to control it" (4).
In point of fact, prayer in physical solitude with the
mind on the world would not be the solitude Teresa
requires for prayer. The key to solitude in reciting the
Our Father is "to remain at the side of the Master who
taught this prayer" and "is showing it to us" (5).

QUESTIONS FOR DISCUSSION: 1. Why is it insufficient merely to pronounce the words?

2. What are some of the things we can do to make our
vocal prayer true mental prayer?

Chapter 25

Tells how much the soul gains through a perfect recitation of vocal prayer and how God happens to raise it from this prayer to supernatural things.

TO KEEP YOU FROM THINKING that little is gained through a perfect recitation of vocal prayer, I tell you that it is very possible that while you are reciting the Our Father or some other vocal prayer, the Lord may raise you to perfect contemplation. By these means His Majesty shows that he listens to the one who speaks to him. And it is his grandeur that speaks to the soul, suspending one's intellect, binding one's imagination, and, as they say, taking the words from one's mouth; for even though the soul may want to do so, it cannot speak unless with great difficulty.

2. The soul understands that without the noise of words this divine Master is teaching it by suspending its faculties, for if they were to be at work they would do harm rather than bring benefit. They are enjoying without understanding how they are enjoying. The soul is being enkindled in love, and it doesn't understand how it loves. It knows that it enjoys what it loves, but it doesn't know how. It clearly understands that this joy is not a joy the intellect obtains merely through desire. The will is enkindled without understanding how. But as soon as it can understand something, it sees that this good cannot be merited or gained through all the trials one can suffer on earth. This good is a gift from the Lord of earth and

heaven, who, in sum, gives according to who he is. What I have described, daughters, is perfect contemplation.

3. Now you will understand the difference that lies between perfect contemplation and mental prayer. Mental prayer consists of what was explained: being aware and knowing that we are speaking, with whom we are speaking, and who we ourselves are who dare to speak so much with so great a Lord. To think about this and other similar things, of how little we have served him and how much we are obliged to serve him, is mental prayer. Don't think it amounts to some other kind of gibberish, and don't let the name frighten you.

To recite the Our Father or the Hail Mary or whatever prayer you wish is vocal prayer. But behold what poor music you produce when you do this without mental prayer. Even the words will be poorly pronounced at times. In these two kinds of prayer we can do something ourselves, with the help of God. In the contemplation I now mentioned, we can do nothing; His Majesty is the one who does everything, for it is his work and above our nature.

4. Since I explained contemplation very much at length and as best I could in the account of my life that I said I wrote for my confessors[1]— for they had ordered me to write that account — I will not speak of contemplation here or do any more than touch upon it. Those of you who have been so fortunate as to be brought by the Lord to the state of contemplation may, if you can get that account, find there some advice and counsel which God granted that I be able to give; it will be very consoling and beneficial to you. This is what I think, and so do some of those who have seen it — for they have the account in order to make a judgment about it. What shame I feel in telling you that you should pay attention to something I have done, and the Lord knows the embarrassment with which I write much of what I write. May he be blessed for so putting

up with me! Those of you who, as I say, experience supernatural prayer may obtain that account after my death; those of you who do not, need not worry about obtaining it but only about striving after what is contained in this present book and leave the rest to God; for it is he who must bestow supernatural prayer, and he will grant it to you if you do not stop short on the road but try hard until you reach the end.[2]

VOCAL PRAYER AND CONTEMPLATION

After insisting on the link between mental and vocal prayer, Teresa turns to their connection with contemplation.

25.1–2: It is possible that while you are reciting the Our Father or some other vocal prayer the Lord may raise you to perfect contemplation.

- By this means His Majesty shows that he listens to the one who speaks to him.

- It is his grandeur that speaks.

  - By suspending the intellect.

  - By binding one's imagination.

  - By taking the words from one's mouth.

- The Master is teaching the soul by suspending its faculties.

- The soul is enjoying and being enkindled with love without knowing how.

- This good is a gift from God that cannot be merited; it is perfect contemplation.

25.3: A. In vocal prayer and mental prayer we do something ourselves, with the help of God.

B. In perfect contemplation, His Majesty is the one who does everything.

25.4: Teresa points out that she explained contemplation at length in the book she wrote for her confessors (the *Life*).

- Those of you who have been brought to the state of contemplation may find there some beneficial advice.

- You may be able to get the account after my death.

- Those of you who do not experience supernatural prayer need not worry about it; leave yourself to God who will grant it to you if you do not stop short on the road.

INTERPRETIVE NOTES: 1. Quite clearly, Teresa sees vocal prayer as leading into contemplation. She experienced this herself and put aside the common notion that vocal prayer is a practice for those at the bottom rung of the ladder of perfection. "One day, having spent a long time in prayer and begging the Lord to help me please him in all things, I began the hymn [*Veni Creator Spiritus*]; while I was saying it, a rapture came upon me so suddenly that it almost carried me out of myself" (L 24.5). Vocal prayer, mental prayer, and contemplation all must have the essential ingredient of prayer: communion with God. The difference lies in the fact that contemplation (or in Teresa's other term, "supernatural" prayer) cannot be acquired through human efforts; it is experienced as God's gift. It is a way in which God shows he is listening and speaks in turn to us. Vocal prayer should include mental prayer. Mental prayer can be meditative (thinking about who God and his mysteries, who he is and who I am) or a simple loving awareness of the Master's presence while reciting our vocal prayer. Vocal prayers may consist of many words or few words or even one word, with a preference for words from Scripture or used in the church's liturgy.

2. Teresa envisaged her book as an effort to educate for contemplation. She is laying the groundwork for contemplative prayer without intending to deal at length with the topic of contemplation itself, because she had already done so in another book of hers (the *Life*), which was written for her spiritual directors. That book, she thinks, will help and console the nuns who experience contemplation. But the nuns were not able to read the *Life* during Teresa's remaining days on earth. At this moment in her spiritual journey, she thought that her days on earth were about to come to an end because of the desires for death that goaded her: "O Jesus! Who could give a good explanation of this prayer to your Reverence so that you could explain it to me? It is what my soul is now always experiencing. Usually when unoccupied it is placed in the midst of these anxious longings for death.... I sometimes really think that if this prayer continues as it does now, the Lord would be served if my life came to an end. In my opinion, a pain as great as this is sufficient to put an end to life, but I don't merit death. All my longing then is to die" (L 20.12–13). In thinking that her nuns could at least read the book after her death, she probably wasn't thinking of a time far off but a time soon to come. However, Teresa's experience in prayer underwent a change, and she actually lived about fifteen more years.

3. During the remainder of her years, Teresa's manuscript of the *Life* was withheld from readers. In 1574,

out of spite, the erratic princess of Eboli, one of the most difficult persons Teresa had to cope with, denounced the *Life* to the Inquisition. Actually, the Inquisition commissioned Domingo Báñez, one of Teresa's confessors, to examine the book. In an assessment of it, Báñez gave his cool approval: "I have consistently observed caution in examining this nun's account of her prayer and her life, and no one has been more incredulous than I concerning her visions and revelations, though not in respect of her virtues and good desires.... I have decided that this book should not be shown to all and sundry, but only to men of learning and experience and Christian discretion."

4. Since the manuscript of her *Life*, after examination by the Inquisition, remained in secret archives, Teresa was told in 1577 by Padre Gracián, then her superior, to write another book explaining contemplative prayer as she did in her *Life*. But he advised her to put down her thoughts in a general way and not as an account of her own experience. In the final analysis, Teresa thought of *The Way of Perfection*, as a book leading up to the fount of living waters (contemplation); it prepared the way for her later masterpiece, *The Interior Castle*, to be written ten years later.

QUESTIONS FOR DISCUSSION: 1. What is my experience with vocal prayer?

2. Have I placed it at the bottom rung of the ladder?

3. What is the difference between vocal prayer, mental prayer, and contemplation?

Chapter 26

Explains a method for recollecting one's mind. Sets down some ways of doing this. The chapter is very useful for beginners in prayer.

NOW THEN LET US RETURN to our vocal prayer that it may be so recited that, without our being aware of the fact, God may grant us everything together and also enable us to say vocal prayers as we should, as I have mentioned.[1]

As is already known, the examination of conscience, the act of contrition, and the sign of the cross must come first. Then, daughters, since you are alone, strive to find a companion. Well what better companion than the Master himself who taught you this prayer? Represent the Lord himself as close to you and behold how lovingly and humbly he is teaching you. Believe me, you should remain with so good a friend as long as you can. If you grow accustomed to having him present at your side, and he sees that you do so with love and that you go about striving to please him, you will not be able — as they say — to get away from him; he will never fail you; he will help you in all your trials; you will find him everywhere. Do you think it's some small matter to have a friend like this at your side?

2. O Sisters, those of you who cannot engage in much discursive reflection with the intellect or keep your mind from distraction, get used to this practice! Get used to it! See, I know that you can do this; for I suffered many years from the trial —

and it is a very great one — of not being able to quiet the mind in anything. But I know that the Lord does not leave us so abandoned; for if we humbly ask him for this friendship, he will not deny it to us. And if we cannot succeed in one year, we will succeed later. Let's not regret the time that is so well spent. Who's making us hurry? I am speaking of acquiring this habit and of striving to walk alongside this true Master.

3. I'm not asking you now that you think about him or that you draw out a lot of concepts or make long and subtle reflections with your intellect. I'm not asking you to do anything more than look at him. For who can keep you from turning the eyes of your soul toward this Lord, even if you do so just for a moment if you can't do more? You can look at very ugly things; won't you be able to look at the most beautiful thing imaginable? Well now, daughters, your Spouse never takes his eyes off you. He has suffered your committing a thousand ugly offenses and abominations against him, and this suffering wasn't enough for him to cease looking at you. Is it too much to ask you to turn your eyes from these exterior things in order to look at him sometimes? Behold, he is not waiting for anything else, as he says to the bride,[2] than that we look at him. In the measure you desire him, you will find him. He so esteems our turning to look at him that no diligence will be lacking on his part.

4. They say that for a woman to be a good wife toward her husband she must be sad when he is sad, and joyful when he is joyful, even though she may not be so. (See what subjection you have been freed from, Sisters!) The Lord, without deception, truly acts in such a way with us. He is the one who submits, and he wants you to be the lady with authority to rule; he submits to your will. If you are joyful, look at him as risen. Just imagining how he rose from the tomb will bring you joy. The brilliance! The beauty! The majesty! How victorious! How joyful! Indeed, like one coming forth from a battle where he has

gained a great kingdom! And all of that, plus himself, he desires for you. Well, is it such a big thing that from time to time you turn your eyes to look upon one who gives you so much?

5. If you are experiencing trials or are sad, behold him on the way to the garden: what great affliction he bore in his soul; for having become suffering itself, he tells us about it and complains of it. Or behold him bound to the column, filled with pain, with all his flesh torn in pieces for the great love he bears you; so much suffering, persecuted by some, spit on by others, denied by his friends, abandoned by them, with no one to defend him, frozen from the cold, left so alone that you can console each other. Or behold him burdened with the cross, for they didn't even let him take a breath. He will look at you with those eyes so beautiful and compassionate, filled with tears; he will forget his sorrows so as to console you in yours, merely because you yourselves go to him to be consoled, and you turn your head to look at him.

6. O Lord of the world, my true Spouse! (You can say this to him if he has moved your heart to pity at seeing him thus, for not only will you desire to look at him but you will also delight in speaking with him, not with ready-made prayers but with those that come from the sorrow of your own heart, for he esteems them highly.) Are you so in need, my Lord and my Love, that you would want to receive such poor company as mine, for I see by your expression that you have been consoled by me? Well then, how is it, Lord, that the angels leave you and that even your Father doesn't console you? If it's true, Lord, that you want to endure everything for me, what is this that I suffer for you? Of what am I complaining? I am already ashamed, since I have seen you in such a condition. I desire to suffer, Lord, all the trials that come to me and esteem them as a great good enabling me to imitate you in something. Let us walk together, Lord. Wherever you go, I will go;[3] whatever you suffer, I will suffer.

7. Take up that cross, daughters. Don't mind at all if the Jews trample upon you, if his trial can thereby be lessened. Pay no attention to what they say to you, be deaf to their gossip. In stumbling, in falling with your Spouse, do not withdraw from the cross or abandon it. Consider carefully the fatigue with which he walks and how much greater his trials are than those trials you suffer, however great you may want to paint them and no matter how much you grieve over them. You will come out consoled because you will see that they are something to be laughed at when compared to those of the Lord.

8. You will ask, Sisters, how you can do this, saying that if you had seen His Majesty with your bodily eyes at the time he walked in this world that you would have looked at him very willingly and done so always. Don't believe it. Whoever doesn't want to use a little effort now to recollect at least the sense of sight and look at this Lord within herself (for one can do so without danger but with just a little care) would have been much less able to stay at the foot of the cross with the Magdalene, who saw his death with her own eyes. But how much the glorious Virgin and this blessed saint must have suffered! How many threats, how many wicked words, how much shoving about and rudeness! For the people around them were not exactly what we would call courteous! No, they were people from hell, ministers of the devil. Indeed, what these two suffered must have been terrible; but in the presence of another greater affliction they didn't feel their own.

So, Sisters, don't think you are capable of such great trials if you are not capable of such little ones. By exercising yourselves in these little trials, you will come to be able to suffer other greater ones. [And believe that I am speaking the truth in saying that you can speak with him, for I have passed through this difficulty.]

9. What you can do as a help in this matter is try to carry about an image or painting of this Lord that is to your liking,

not so as to carry it about on your heart and never look at it but as to speak often with him; for he will inspire you with what to say. Since you speak with other persons, why must words fail you more when you speak with God? Don't believe they will; at least I will not believe they will if you acquire the habit. Otherwise, the failure to communicate with someone causes both estrangement and a failure to know how to speak with that person. For it seems then that we don't know the person who may even be a relative; family ties and friendship are lost through a lack of communication.

10. It is also a great help to take a good book written in the vernacular in order to recollect one's thoughts and pray well vocally, and little by little accustom the soul with coaxing and skill not to grow discouraged. Imagine that many years have passed since the soul left the house of its Spouse and that until it returns to this house there's a great need that it know how to deal with him. For so we sinners are: our soul and our thoughts are so accustomed to wandering about at their own pleasure — or grief, to put it better — that the poor soul doesn't understand itself. In order that it get to love remaining at home once again, a great deal of skill is necessary. If little by little this is not accomplished, we will never do anything.

And I again assure you that if with care you grow accustomed to what I have said[4] your gain will be so great that even if I wanted to explain this to you I wouldn't know how. Draw near, then, to this good Master with strong determination to learn what he teaches you, and His Majesty will so provide that you will turn out to be good disciples. He will not abandon you if you do not abandon him. Consider the words that divine mouth speaks, for in the first word you will understand immediately the love he has for you; it is no small blessing and gift for disciples to see that their Master loves them.

ON RECOLLECTING THE MIND

Teresa moves now to explain her own method of interiorizing mental prayer, which she calls recollection.

26.1–3: Vocal prayer should be so recited that God may grant us everything at once.

- The examination of conscience, act of contrition, and sign of the cross must come first.

- You must find the Master himself who taught you the Our Father.

- Represent him as close to you.

- Behold how lovingly and humbly he is teaching you.

- Grow accustomed to having him present.

- I am not asking that you think about him.

- I am asking that you look at him.

- He never takes his eyes off you; your abominations didn't make him cease looking at you.

- He waits for nothing else but that we look at him.

- In the measure you desire him, you will find him.

26.4–5: A good wife must be sad when her husband is, and joyful when he is.

- The Lord acts this way with us.

- If you are joyful, look at him as risen; all of that plus himself he desires for you.

- If you are experiencing trials or are sad, behold him on the way to the garden; or bound to the column; or burdened with the cross.

- He will forget his sorrows so as to console you in yours.

26.6: In the presence of her readers Teresa descriptively beholds Christ in his sufferings; and this leads her into spontaneous and loving colloquy with her Lord.

- She expresses compassion.

- She expresses the desire to imitate him and follow him.

26.7: She exhorts her daughters to take up their cross.

- They can thereby lessen Christ's trial.

- Consider how much greater his trials are than yours.

26.8: She answers an objection: Had we been on earth at the same time he was, we would have gladly looked at him.

- Don't believe it.

- If you can't make the little effort required for recollection now, how would you have been able to stand at the foot of the cross with the Magdalene and the glorious Virgin?

26.9–10: A. A painting of the Lord that is to your liking can be a help.

- The failure to communicate with a person causes estrangement.

- Friendship is lost through a lack of communication.

B. A good book can be another help toward communication.

C. The soul must get used to staying in the house of its Spouse.

- Our soul and thoughts are accustomed to wandering about.

- They must get used to remaining at home.

- Draw near to this Master with strong determination to learn what he teaches you.

- In the first word he speaks, you will understand immediately the love he has for you.

INTERPRETIVE NOTES: 1. In urging us to draw near to the Master who is looking at us, Teresa places this effort at recollection in the setting of a dialogue or communion between two. It is the Master who has taken the initiative and first looks at us and continues to do so. On his part the presence, the communication, is never broken off. He has given his teaching in the words of the Our Father and helps us to understand them if we open ourselves to his love. Teresa's readers must acquire the habit of keeping Christ present. This is done not by thinking about him but by looking at him. Representing Christ does not, in the Teresian sense, refer to picturing him carefully in the imagination but to becoming personally present to him who is always present to us. He never takes his eyes off us. She asks: "Is it too much to ask you to turn your eyes from these exterior things in order to look at him sometimes?" To look at another helps one to be present in a personal way. Mutual presence happens when two persons begin to communicate with each other. The personal presence, intimacy between friends, is what Teresa emphasizes as she begins to teach us about recollection. Her method has to do with relationship more than technique. This presence to Christ is, indeed, what Christians must always bring to prayer, no matter what stage they may be in. It is as good for the novice as it is for the seasoned contemplative. In her *Life*, she points this out explicitly: "This method of keeping Christ present with us is beneficial in all stages and is a very safe means of advancing in the first degree of prayer, of reaching in a short time the second degree, and of walking secure against the dangers the devil can set up in the last degrees. Keeping Christ present is what we of ourselves can do" (12.3–4).

2. We acquire a habit through repetition. In her awareness of this truth, Teresa exhorts her sisters to get accustomed to having Christ present at their side. They must converse with him as with a friend and do everything with him, and get into the habit of doing so. Gaining a habit requires effort. But Teresa notes here much more than a unilateral effort on our part. Once again the personal element is paramount. When he sees you making this effort, she assures us, he will help you so that you find him everywhere.

3. That the Lord is first looking at us and waiting for us to turn our eyes toward him belongs to the mystery of God's love and omniscience. In addition, Teresa directs our minds to the manifestation of the divine humility when God draws near to us and invites us to be his friends. "Draw near to him"; "Behold how lovingly and humbly he is teaching you." The humility of Christ in drawing near to us — remember the class distinctions in Teresa's times, each class clinging tightly to their rung on the ladder — is, of course, unfathomable. But something of it can be apprehended if with Teresa the Christian understands how impossible it is ever to transcend Christ.

4. Teresa knew her nuns well and the kind of objection they were ready to make. How can we look at him, since we do not see him? Had we lived when he was on earth we would have wanted to look at him always. Those who lived during the lifetime of the Lord also had to look at Jesus with faith, and to look at him always was not easy for them, Teresa observes. You must at least make the little effort necessary to recollect the sense of sight to look in faith at the Lord within. In the measure that you desire to be with him, in that measure you will find him. But looking at, beholding him, is not enough, for he speaks to us. In recollection you also listen to him, for he is teaching you. You listen as attentively as you gaze upon him.

5. Christ was not always as manifest to Teresa as he apparently is while she writes this chapter: "Are you so in need, my Lord and my Love, that you would want to receive such poor company as mine, for I see by your

expression that you have been consoled by me?" Of her early experience with prayer, she plainly confessed "I don't know what heavy penance could have come to mind that frequently I would have gladly undertaken rather than recollect myself in the practice of prayer" (L 8.7). Remembering these difficulties she recognizes the help the sisters may find from a book or a picture in seeking out this presence.

6. Teresa's prayer in number 6 reaches its height in the words "Lord wherever you go, I will go; whatever you suffer, I will suffer." She then encourages her daughters to take up their cross and not mind their difficulties if his trial can thereby be lessened. What she is so alert to is that in the solitude of her being before God, the Master in his revelation speaks not to just anyone at all but to her. For her Christ is born; for her Christ dies on the cross. It is to prepare a place for her that he ascends into glory. Her nuns must keep vividly before their minds this element of here and now, and each nun must rule out any idea that she is simply one of a number of people. The nun must understand that the Word of God in the turmoil of human history turns to her his countenance and speaks to her personally. All that in her contemplation she adores, insofar as she receives some understanding of the unsearchable mystery before her, enters as a living element into the church's own adoration. It may escape her detection, but she must be the person of the church in her own person, the church as Bride and Handmaid (or servant). She helps Christ carry his cross particularly when in her contemplation she is given experiences, difficulties, and trials not

intended for her personally, but for persons unknown to her. Or she may be assuming the burden of definite individuals who are helped by her assuming what was intended for them. Teresa's difficulties in prayer and her many graces have been a source of blessing for other members of the Body of Christ; innumerable individuals have been touched. All of this becomes possible by our deep union in the church.

QUESTIONS FOR DISCUSSION: 1. What are some of the things we should do when we recite the Our Father?

2. How is friendship with Christ or with others fostered and how does it slip away from us?

3. Is it possible to be as much present to Christ as were those who walked with him while he was on this earth?

Chapter 27

Deals with the great love our Lord showed us in the first words of the Our Father and how important it is for those who truly want to be children of God to pay no attention whatsoever to lineage.

OUR FATHER WHO ART IN HEAVEN.[1] O my Lord, how you do show yourself to be the Father of such a Son; and how your Son does show himself to be the Son of such a Father! May you be blessed forever and ever! This favor would not be so great, Lord, if it came at the end of the prayer. But at the beginning, You fill our hands and give a reward so large that it would easily fill the intellect and occupy the will in such a way that one would be unable to speak a word.

Oh, daughters, how readily should perfect contemplation come at this point! Oh, how right it would be for the soul to enter within itself in order to rise the better above itself[2] that this holy Son might make it understand the nature of the place where he says his Father dwells, which is in the heavens. Let us go forth from the earth, my daughters, for there is no reason that a favor like this should be so little esteemed that after we have understood how great it is, we should still want to remain on earth.

2. O Son of God and my Lord! How is it that you give so much all together in the first words? Since you humble yourself to such an extreme in joining with us in prayer and making yourself the Brother of creatures so lowly and wretched, how is it that You give us in the name of your Father everything that

can be given? For you desire that he consider us his children, because your word cannot fail.[3] You oblige him to be true to your word, which is no small burden since in being Father he must bear with us no matter how serious the offenses. If we return to him like the prodigal son, he has to pardon us.[4] He has to console us in our trials. He has to sustain us in the way a father like this must. For, in effect, he must be better than all the fathers in the world because in him everything must be faultless. And after all this he must make us sharers and heirs with you.[5]

3. Behold, my Lord, that since with the love you bear us and with your humility, nothing will stop you ... in sum, Lord, you are on earth and clothed with it. Since you possess our nature, it seems you have some reason to look to our gain. But behold, your Father is in heaven. You yourself said so. It is right that you look to his honor. Since you have vowed to undergo disgrace for us, leave your Father free. Don't oblige him to do so much for a people so wretched, like myself, who will not thank you properly [and there are no others who will do better.]

4. O good Jesus! How clearly you have shown that you are one with him, and that your will is his and his, yours![6] How clear your declaration, my Lord! How magnificent it is, the love you bear us! You made use of roundabout ways, hiding from the devil the fact that you are the Son of God; and with the great desire you have for our good, nothing was able to stop you from granting us so very great a favor. Who could have done it but you, Lord? I don't know how the devil failed to understand in these words who you were, and had doubts about it. At least I see it clearly, my Jesus. You have spoken, as a favored son, for yourself and for us; and you are powerful enough so that what you say on earth will be done in heaven. May you be blessed forever, my Lord, for you are so willing to give that nothing will stop you from doing so.

5. Well, daughters, doesn't it seem to you that this Master is a good one, since in order to make us grow fond of learning what he teaches us he begins by granting us so wonderful a favor? Does it seem right to you now that even though we recite these first words vocally we should fail to let our intellects understand and our hearts break in pieces at seeing such love? What son is there in the world who doesn't strive to learn who his father is when he knows he has such a good one with so much majesty and power? If our Father had not so much majesty, it wouldn't surprise me if we refused to be known as his children. The world has come to such a state that if the father is of a lower status than his son, the son doesn't feel honored in recognizing him as his father.

6. Such an attitude doesn't belong here. In this house, please God, may there never be any thought about such a thing; it would be a hell. But the one who is from nobler lineage should be the one to speak least about her father. All the Sisters must be equal.

O college of Christ, where St. Peter, being a fisherman, had more authority — and the Lord wanted it so — than St. Bartholomew, who was a king's son![7] His Majesty knew what would take place in the world where people dispute over lineage. These disputes in reality amount to nothing much more than a debate about whether the mud is better for making bricks or adobes. God help me, what a great trial we bear! God deliver us, Sisters, from similar disputes, even though they be in jest; I hope in His Majesty that he will do so. When this concern about lineage is noticed in a Sister, apply a remedy at once and let her fear lest she be Judas among the apostles. Give her penances until she understands that she doesn't deserve to be thought of as made from even a very wretched kind of mud.[8]

You have a good Father, for he gives you the good Jesus. Let no one in this house speak of any other father but him.

And strive, my daughters, so to behave that you will deserve to find your delight in him; and cast yourselves into his arms. You already know that he will not reject you if you are good daughters. Who, then, would fail to strive so as not to lose such a Father?

7. Oh, God help me! How much there is in these words to give you consolation. So as not to enlarge any more on this matter, I want to leave it to your own reflection. For no matter how unruly one's mind may be, the truth is — leaving aside our gain in having so good a Father — that the Holy Spirit must be present between such a Son and such a Father, and he will enkindle your will and bind it with a very great love.

THE FIRST WORDS OF THE OUR FATHER

Teresa is ready now to present her thoughts on the Lord's Prayer. The first words of the prayer take her out of herself in a loving outpouring of admiration and praise.

27.1: She marvels at the revelation of the relationship between Father and Son.

- At the outset you give a reward so absorbing to the intellect and will that one is rendered speechless.

- Perfect contemplation readily comes right at the beginning.

- How right it would be to enter within oneself so as to rise above oneself and understand the nature of the Father's dwelling place.

- After understanding a favor like this, there's no reason for us to want to remain on earth.

27.2–4: She speaks to the Lord and wonders how he gives us so much altogether in the first words.

- You join with us in prayer.

- You make yourself the Brother of creatures so lowly.

- You give in the name of the Father everything that can be given.

- You desire that he consider us his children.
  - He has to sustain us, pardon us as the father of the prodigal son.

– In him everything is faultless.

- You make us sharers and heirs with you.

- In your love and humility you are clothed with earth since you possess our nature.

- Don't oblige your Father to do so much for a people so wretched, like myself.

- How clearly you have shown that you are one with him.

- Nothing was able to stop you from granting us so great a favor.

27.5–6: A. Teresa turns to address her nuns.

- This Master begins teaching us by granting us so wonderful a favor.

- Shouldn't we in these first words let our intellects understand and our hearts break in pieces at seeing such love?

B. She enters into a digression on lineage and class distinctions.

- Disputes over lineage amount to nothing more than a debate about whether the mud is better for making bricks or adobes.

- If concern about lineage appears in the community, apply a remedy at once.

- Let no one in this house speak of any other father than the Father who gives us the good Jesus.

- Cast yourselves into his arms; he will not reject you.

27.7: How much there is in these words; between such a Father and such a Son, the Holy Spirit must be present, and he will enkindle your will and bind it with a very great love.

INTERPRETIVE NOTES: 1. Teresa does not try to teach us here as a theologian or exegete about the meaning of the text or our nature as adopted children of God. Setting aside the effort to explain the truth seen by her as too great to be explained, she teaches through her own spontaneous prayer. Her ardent words bear the heat of the Spirit's love as she stands in awe before the Father's love in giving us his Son and the Son's love in making us children of this Father. Being made coheirs with the Son, we can call God our Father. The opening words could readily lead her into perfect contemplation. But her prayer carries the traits of that state in which she says the soul would want to be all tongues so as to praise the Lord. Her outpourings of love flow from the mystical understanding she received of the truths contained in the opening words, an understanding that at first hardly allows her to speak.

2. In hearing the words of Christ, his word and his truth, Teresa encounters God with the eye of faith and is inwardly illumined by the Spirit. Grace, which is objectively a participation in the divine nature, is especially, for Teresa, a participation in the life of mutual love within the Trinity. Her fervent words show her as one made a participant in the subjective relationship of the Son, as human, to his heavenly Father in the Holy Spirit. And since the Holy Spirit must be present between "such a Son and such a Father," the grace of

prayer for Teresa is trinitarian; in it she receives the gift of all three Persons.

3. Thus illumined, she seeks to impress on her nuns the dignity they have as children of the divine Father, a status given them through the favor of the good Jesus. Then Teresa begins to lament once more her society's anxieties about lineage and class differences. None of these claims of superiority can add anything to the mud. What makes the nuns authentically worthy of respect is the gift they have received from Jesus by which they all have the same Father. Every society finds within itself, though perhaps in different expressions, these same tendencies to value persons by reason of their background, gender, nationality, or race, factors that in themselves make no one superior to another.

4. "In his fatherly care for all of us, God desired that all human beings should form one family and deal with each other in a spirit of brotherhood. All, in fact, are destined to the very same end, namely God himself, since they have been created in the likeness of God who 'made from one every nation of men and women who live on the face of the earth' (Acts 17:26).... Furthermore, the Lord Jesus, when praying to the Father 'that they may all be one ...even as we are one' (Jn 17:21–22), has opened up new horizons closed to human reason by implying that there is a certain parallel between the union existing among the divine persons and the union of the children of God in truth and love. It follows, then, that if human beings are the only creatures on earth that God has wanted for their own sake, they can fully discover their true self only in a sincere giving of themselves" (*Gaudium et Spes*, 24).

QUESTIONS FOR DISCUSSION. 1. From what we know through Jesus, what is our Father like in his relationship with us?

2. What does our Father give us? What does Jesus give us? What does the Holy Spirit do for us?

3. What are some of the things similar to honor and lineage on which we today might tend to pride ourselves?

Chapter 28

Explains the nature of the prayer of recollection and sets down some ways of getting accustomed to this form of prayer.

NOW CONSIDER WHAT YOUR MASTER SAYS: *Who art in heaven.*[1] Do you think it is of little importance to know what heaven is and where you must seek your most sacred Father? Well, I tell you that for wandering minds it is very important not only to believe these truths but to strive to understand them by experience. Doing this is one of the ways of greatly slowing down the mind and recollecting the soul.

2. You already know that God is everywhere. It's obvious, then, that where the king is, there is his court; in sum, wherever God is, there is heaven. Without a doubt you can believe that where His Majesty is present, all glory is present. Consider what St. Augustine says, that he sought him in many places but found him ultimately within himself.[2] Do you think it matters little for a soul with a wandering mind to understand this truth and see that there is no need to go to heaven in order to speak with one's Eternal Father or find delight in him? Nor is there any need to shout. However softly we speak, he is near enough to hear us. Neither is there any need for wings to go to find him.[3] All one need do is go into solitude and look at him within oneself, and not turn away from so good a Guest but with great humility speak to him as to a father. Beseech him as you would a father; tell him about your trials;

ask him for a remedy against them, realizing that you are not worthy to be his daughter.

3. Leave aside any of that faintheartedness that some persons have and think is humility. You see, humility doesn't consist in refusing a favor the King offers you but in accepting such a favor and understanding how bountifully it comes to you and being delighted with it. What a nice kind of humility! I have the Emperor of heaven and earth in my house (for he comes to it in order to favor me and be happy with me), and out of humility I do not want to answer him or stay with him or take what he gives me, but I leave him alone. Or, while he is telling me and begging me to ask him for something, I do not do so but remain poor; and I even let him go, for he sees that I never finish trying to make up my mind.

Have nothing to do with this kind of humility, daughters, but speak with him as with a father, or a brother, or a lord, or as with a spouse; sometimes in one way, at other times in another; he will teach you what you must do in order to please him. Don't be foolish; take him at his word. Since he is your Spouse, he will treat you accordingly. [Consider that it is well worthwhile for you to have understood this truth: that the Lord is within us, and that there we must be with him.]

4. The intellect is recollected much more quickly with this kind of prayer even though it may be vocal; it is a prayer that brings with it many blessings. This prayer is called "recollection," because the soul collects its faculties together and enters within itself to be with its God. And its divine Master comes more quickly to teach it and give it the prayer of quiet than he would through any other method it might use. For centered there within itself, it can think about the Passion and represent the Son and offer him to the Father and not tire the intellect by going to look for him on Mount Calvary or in the garden or at the pillar.

5. Those who by such a method can enclose themselves within this little heaven of our soul, where the Maker of heaven and earth is present, and grow accustomed to refusing to be where the exterior senses in their distraction have gone or look in that direction should believe they are following an excellent path and that they will not fail to drink water from the fount; for they will journey far in a short time. Their situation is like that of one who travels by ship; with a little wind, the end of his journey is reached in a few days. But those who go, by land take longer. [It's the path of heaven. I say "of heaven," because they are there in the palace of the King; they are not on earth and are more secure against many occasions.]

6. Those who know how to recollect themselves are already out to sea, as they say. For even though they may not have got completely away from land, they do what they can during that time to get free from it by recollecting their senses within. If the recollection is true, it is felt very clearly; for it produces some effect in the soul. I don't know how to explain it. Whoever has experienced it will understand; the soul is like one who gets up from the table after winning a game, for it already sees what the things of the world are. It rises up at the best time, as one who enters a fortified castle to be safe from enemies. There is a withdrawing of the senses from exterior things and a renunciation of them in such a way that, without one's realizing it, the eyes close so as to avoid seeing them and so that the sight might be more awake to things of the soul.

So, those who walk by this path keeps their eyes closed almost as often as they pray. This is a praiseworthy custom for many reasons. It is a striving so as not to look at things here below. This striving comes at the beginning; afterward, there's no need to strive; a greater effort is needed to open the eyes while praying. It seems the soul is aware of being strengthened and fortified at the expense of the body, that it leaves the body alone and weakened, and that it receives in this recollection a supply of provisions to strengthen it against the body.

7. And even though it isn't aware of this at the beginning, since the recollection is not so deep — for there are greater and lesser degrees of recollection — the soul should get used to this recollection; although in the beginning the body causes difficulty because it claims its rights without realizing that it is cutting off its own head by not surrendering. If we make the effort, practice this recollection for some days, and get used to it, the gain will be clearly seen; we will understand, when beginning to pray, that the bees are approaching and entering the beehive to make honey. And this recollection will be effected without our effort because the Lord has desired that, during the time the faculties are drawn inward, the soul and its will may merit to have this dominion. When the soul does no more than give a sign that it wishes to be recollected, the senses obey it and become recollected. Even though they go out again afterward, their having already surrendered is a great thing; for they go out as captives and subjects and do not cause the harm they did previously. And when the will calls them back again, they come more quickly, until after many of these entries the Lord wills that they rest entirely in perfect contemplation.

8. May what has been said be well understood; even though it seems obscure, it will be understood by anyone who desires to practice it. Therefore, those who know how to recollect themselves are like those who travel by sea; and since it is important for us not to proceed so slowly, let us speak a little about how we should get accustomed to a method that's so good. These souls are safer from many occasions. The fire of divine love is more quickly enkindled when they blow a little with their intellects. Since they are close to the fire, a little spark will ignite and set everything ablaze. Because there is

no impediment from outside, the soul is alone with its God; it is well prepared for this enkindling. [I would like you to understand clearly this manner of prayer, which, as I have said, is called recollection.]

9. Well, let us imagine that within us is an extremely rich palace, built entirely of gold and precious stones; in sum, built for a lord such as this. Imagine, too, as is indeed so, that you have a part to play in order for the palace to be so beautiful; for there is no edifice as beautiful as is a soul pure and full of virtues. The greater the virtues the more resplendent the jewels. Imagine, also, that in this palace dwells this mighty King who has been gracious enough to become your Father; and that he is seated upon an extremely valuable throne, which is your heart.

10. This may seem trifling at the beginning; I mean, this image I've used in order to explain recollection. But the image may be very helpful — to you especially — for since we women have no learning, all of this imagining is necessary that we may truly understand that within us lies something incomparably more precious than what we see outside ourselves. Let's not imagine that we are hollow inside. And please God it may be only women that go about forgetful of this inner richness and beauty. I consider it impossible for us to pay so much attention to worldly things if we take the care to remember we have a Guest such as this within us, for we then see how lowly these things are next to what we possess within ourselves. Well, what else does an animal do upon seeing what is pleasing to its sight than satisfy its hunger by taking the prey? Indeed, there should be some difference between them and us.

11. You will laugh at me, perhaps, and say that what I'm explaining is very clear, and you'll be right; for me, though, it was obscure for some time. I understood well that I had a soul. But what this soul deserved and who dwelt within it, I

did not understand because I had covered my eyes with the vanities of the world. For, in my opinion, if I had understood as I do now that in this little palace of my soul dwelt so great a King, I would not have left him alone so often. I would have remained with him at times and striven more so as not to be so unclean. But what a marvelous thing, that he who would fill a thousand worlds and many more with his grandeur would enclose himself in something so small! [And so he wanted to enclose himself in the womb of his most Blessed Mother.] In fact, since he is Lord he is free to do what he wants, and since he loves us he adapts himself to our size.

12. So that the soul won't be disturbed in the beginning by seeing that it is too small to have something so great within itself, the Lord doesn't give it this knowledge until he enlarges it little by little and it has the capacity to receive what he will place within it. For this reason I say he is free to do what he wants since he has the power to make this palace a large one. The whole point is that we should give ourselves to him with complete determination, and we should empty the soul in such a way that he can store things there or take them away as though it were his own property. And since His Majesty has the rights of ownership, let us not oppose him. [Even here below guests in the house are a bother when we cannot tell them to leave.] And since he doesn't force our will, he takes what we give him; but he doesn't give himself completely until we give ourselves completely.

This fact is certain; and because it is so important, I bring it to your minds so often. He never works in the soul as he does when it is totally his without any obstacle, nor do I see how he could. He is the friend of all good order. Now, then, if we fill the palace with lowly people and trifles, how will there be room for the Lord with his court? He does enough by remaining just a little while in the midst of so much confusion.

13. Do you think, daughters, that he comes alone? Don't you see that his Son says, "who art in heaven"? Well, since he is such a King, certainly his court attendants would never leave him alone, but they will always be with him; and they beseech him on our behalf since they are full of charity. Don't think that things in heaven are like they are here below; for if here below a lord or prelate, because of certain of his own aims or because he wants to, favors someone, the envy of others is immediately stirred, and that poor person is hated without having done anything against them.

THE PRAYER OF RECOLLECTION
(CONTINUED)

The words "who art in heaven" bring Teresa back to the prayer of recollection that she began to explain in Chapter 26.

28.1–3: It is important to know where your Father is and where you must seek him.

- For wandering minds it is very important.

    - They must not only believe these truths.

    - They must strive to understand them by experience.

- Wherever God is, there is heaven and all glory.

- St. Augustine says that he sought him in many places but ultimately found him within himself.

- All one need do is go into solitude and look at him within oneself and with great humility speak to him as with a father.

- Accept the favor offered by the King.

- Speak to him as with a father, brother, lord, or spouse.

- Understand this truth: the Lord is within us, and there we must be with him.

28.4–5: The prayer of recollection: the soul collects the faculties and enters within itself to be with its God.

- In it the divine Master comes more quickly to give the prayer of quiet than he would through any other method.

- Those who grow accustomed to enclosing themselves within the little heaven of their souls are following an excellent path.

  - They refuse to go where their exterior, distracted senses have gone or even look in that direction.

  - They will not fail to drink water from the fount.

28.6: A. Those who practice recollection:

- Travel quickly like a ship;

- Are like one who gets up quickly after winning a game; the things of the world are like a game;

- Are like one who enters a fortified castle to be safe from enemies.

B. Anyone who walks by this path usually keeps the eyes closed when praying.

28.7–8: There are greater and lesser degrees of recollection.

- The soul should get used to this recollection even though in the beginning the body causes difficulty.

- Gradually the senses will come to obey the soul when given a sign by the soul that it wants to be recollected, even though they may go out again.

- When the will calls them back they come more quickly.

- These comings and goings take place until the Lord wills that it rest entirely in perfect contemplation.

- Since these souls are close to the fire, a little spark will ignite and set everything ablaze.

- Since the soul is alone with its God, it is well prepared for this enkindling.

28.9: Let us imagine that within us is an extremely rich palace built of gold and precious stone.

- You have a part to play in its beauty: the greater the virtues the more resplendent the jewels.

- In the palace dwells the King gracious enough to become your Father.

- He is seated upon an extremely valuable throne, which is your heart.

28.10: For those without learning this imagining is necessary:

- That we truly understand that within us lies something incomparably more precious than what we see outside;

- That we not imagine that we are hollow inside;

- That we take care to remember we have a Guest such as this within.

28.11–13: A. For me this truth was obscure for some time.

- I understood I had a soul.

- What this soul deserved and who dwelt within it, I did not understand.

- I had covered my eyes with the vanities of the world.

- If I had understood as I do now, I would not have left this great King alone so often.

- What a marvelous thing, that he who would fill a thousand worlds with his grandeur would enclose himself in something so small!

- The Lord doesn't give this knowledge until he enlarges the soul little by little.

- He has the power to make this palace a large one.

B. The whole point is that we should give ourselves to him with complete determination.

- We should empty the soul in such a way that he can store things there.

- We should let him take things away as though they were his own property.

C. He doesn't give himself completely until we give ourselves completely to him.

- He never works in the soul as he does when it is without obstacle.

- If we fill the palace with lowly people and trifles, how will there be room for the Lord and his court?

- He remains just a little while in so much confusion (He is a friend of good order).

- His court attendants never leave him alone.

- They will beseech him on our behalf since they are full of charity.

INTERPRETIVE NOTES. 1. In Chapter 26, taking up recollection for her subject, Teresa spoke mainly of being present to the Lord. Toward the end of the chapter she went a step further and envisioned it as staying at home with one's Spouse. In this chapter her thought advances, and she urges her readers to enter within themselves as though their souls were a beautiful palace for the King. This image helps her explain her thoughts on recollection. In her *Interior Castle*, which she was to write some ten years later, she uses the image of a castle rather than a palace to develop her theological vision of human existence, of life in general, and of life with God. In this latter work she pictures for us a beautiful crystal globe like a castle in which are seven dwelling places. In the seventh, which is the center, the King of Glory dwells in the greatest splendor. From there he beautifies and illumines all the dwelling places to the outer wall. The inhabitants receive more light the nearer they come to the center. Outside the castle, everything is darkness, with toads, vipers, and other poisonous vermin. In each of the seven dwelling places there are "many others, below and above and to the sides, with lovely gardens and fountains and labyrinths, such delightful things that you would want to be dissolved in praises of the great God who created the soul in his own image and likeness" (IC Epilogue.3).

2. In some of Teresa's visions of Christ, he mightily revealed to her his majesty. When she refers to the Lord as King and so frequently speaks of him as His Majesty, she is showing the influence of some powerful visions (imaginative and intellectual) she had of Christ as majestic Lord. She writes in her *Life:* "Sometimes he comes with such great majesty that no one could doubt but that it is the Lord himself. Especially after receiving Communion — for we know that he is present, since our faith tells us this — he reveals himself as so much the lord of this dwelling that it seems the soul is completely dissolved; and it sees itself consumed in Christ. O my Jesus! Who could make known the majesty with which you reveal yourself! And, Lord of all the world and of the heavens, of a thousand other worlds and of numberless worlds, and of the heavens that you might create, how the soul understands by the majesty with which you reveal yourself that it is nothing for you to be Lord of the world!" (L 28.8).

3. In this chapter Teresa does not speak of the King as dwelling in the center of the soul but as seated on an extremely valuable throne. That throne is one's own heart. He is the one who ought to rule over the heart, have dominion over all our activities. Everything must be given to him as belonging to him. In the beginning

her readers may feel too small and hollow inside to be a palace for a King of so much majesty. But the Lord will enlarge the soul little by little and gradually give it an awareness of who dwells within. A kind of expansion of consciousness takes place so that what lies within seems to enclose inconceivably more than any palace or castle can. The soul has the capacity to be made large by the Lord, and will come to remain more easily within itself than outside, and discover there all that it can desire.

4. Teresa's method of recollection differs from other kinds of techniques of attentiveness, such as to one's breathing, to an abstract sound symbol or mantra, to a mandala, or to the flow of one's thoughts as they come and go. These techniques in their origins are means by which one may slip away from individual consciousness into the absolute consciousness of the One. What, then, is Teresa's method? She gives this definition of the recollection she is speaking of: "This prayer is called 'recollection' because the soul collects its faculties together and enters within itself to be with its God" (no. 4). The collecting of the faculties and the entering within are practices that would be useless for Teresa without what follows: "to be with its God." Here we have that essential element of Teresian prayer, "being with him who we know loves us" (L 8.5). For Teresa it has become easy to commune with either God the Father or God the Son; sometimes it is the Father she is speaking to (or of); sometimes the Son. There are many modes of relationship that can mark our "being with" or being present to: "...speak with him as with a father, or a brother, or a lord, or as with a spouse" (no. 3).

5. We might ask ourselves why if God is everywhere must we seek him within ourselves? In answer to this question Teresa would say that in addition to "being with" him, we must be "alone" with him. Entering within oneself is the equivalent of going into solitude. Furthermore, still lingering in her mind is a passage from St. Augustine of which she speaks in her *Life* (9.7–8). She tells of her fondness for St. Augustine and of her experience in reading his *Confessions.* Mentioning what Augustine says about finding God within, she very likely has the *Confessions* in mind: "Late have I loved you, O Beauty ever ancient, ever new, late have I loved you! You were within me, but I was outside, and it was there that I searched for you. In my unloveliness I plunged into the lovely things which you created. You were with me, but I was not with you. Created things kept me from you; yet if they had not been in you they would not have been at all. You called, you shouted, and you broke through my deafness. You flashed, you shone, and you dispelled my blindness. You breathed your fragrance on me; I drew in breath and now I pant for you. I have tasted you, now I hunger and thirst for more. You touched me, and I burned for your peace" (*Confessions* X.27).

6. As with Augustine, Teresa's readers, entering into this recollection, will come to hunger and thirst for more. "Those who by such a method can enclose themselves within this little heaven of our souls, where the Maker of heaven and earth is present...should believe they are following an excellent path and that they will not fail to drink water from the fount" (no. 5). She promises again the gift of contemplation (cf.17.7; 19.15; 25.4).

Of course the question arises, why is Teresa so sure of this if it is a gift from the Lord? First, it is not because of any physical, biological, or psychological laws of growth that she is certain. What impresses her are the invitation and promise of the Lord: "Let anyone who thirsts, come to me and drink" (Jn 7:27). "Come to me, all you who labor and are burdened, and I will give you rest" (Mt 11:28). In addition to the assurance these words of the Lord provide, she is certain because of God's self-manifestation to her. Being love, he is self-communication. "He doesn't desire anything else than to have those to whom to give" (VI.4.12). She invites us to look at her life and at what God did with her. It shows us that, magnanimous in his mercy, "he never tires of giving" (L 19.15). We make room in ourselves to receive what he wants to give by giving ourselves to him; that is how the recollection deepens, for there are degrees of recollection. God "doesn't give himself completely until we give ourselves completely" (12).

7. In a sense we are never alone with God in prayer. Teresa says, "His court attendants would never leave him alone." Not only that, "they beseech him on our behalf" (13). We belong to a community without number. Teresa at times in her prayer experienced the presence of the Blessed Virgin, angels, and saints. The communion of saints may intervene in prayer in an entirely personal manner. Our own parents, or a saint to whom we are particularly devoted, or a friend now dead may communicate with us through some word of the Scriptures, thereby encouraging or enlightening us.

QUESTIONS FOR DISCUSSION: 1. What does this prayer of recollection add to Teresa's understanding of mental prayer in general?

2. What are some of the things we must do in order to practice this prayer of recollection?

3. In what ways might the image of a palace help me in my prayer journey?

Chapter 29

Continues to present means for obtaining this prayer of recollection. How little it should matter to us whether or not we are favored by the bishop.

FOR THE LOVE OF GOD, daughters, don't bother about being favored by lords or prelates. Let each nun strive to do what she ought; if the bishop doesn't show gratitude for what she does, she can be sure that the Lord will repay and be grateful for it. Indeed, we have not come here to seek a reward in this life. Let us always direct our thoughts to what is lasting and pay no attention to things here below, for even though our lives are short these preferences do not last for us. Today the bishop will favor one Sister, and tomorrow he will favor you if he sees one virtue more in you; and if he doesn't favor you, it matters little. Give no room to these thoughts. Sometimes they begin in a small way, but they can become very disturbing to you. Cut them off with the thought that your kingdom is not here below and of how quickly all things come to an end.

2. But even this kind of remedy is a lowly one and not indicative of great perfection. It is better that this disfavor of your superior continue, that you be unappreciated and humbled, and that you accept this for the Lord who is with you. Turn your eyes inward and look within yourself, as has been said.[1] You will find your Master, for he will not fail you; rather, the less you have of exterior consolation the more he will favor you. He is very merciful, and he never fails persons who are afflicted

317

and despised if they trust in him alone. So, David says that the Lord is with the afflicted.[2] Either you believe this or you don't. If you believe it, then why are you killing yourselves?

3. O my Lord, if we truly knew you we wouldn't care at all about anything, for you give much to those who sincerely want to trust in you! Believe, my friends, that it is a great thing to have knowledge of this truth so that you can then see that all favors here below are a lie when they divert the soul somewhat from entering within itself. Oh, God help me, who will make you understand this! Certainly, not I; for I know that I, who more than anyone should understand, have not succeeded in understanding it as it should be understood.

4. Now to return to what I was saying.[3] I would like to know a way of explaining how this holy fellowship with our Companion, the Saint of saints, may be experienced without any hindrance to the solitude enjoyed between the soul and its Spouse when the soul desires to enter this paradise within itself to be with its God and close the door to all the world. I say "desires" because you must understand that this recollection is not something supernatural, but that it is something we can desire and achieve ourselves with the help of God — for without this help we can do nothing,[4] not even have a good thought. This recollection is not a silence of the faculties; it is an enclosure of the faculties within the soul.

5. The soul gains from this recollection in many ways as is written in some books [on mental prayer.[5] Since I'm speaking only of how vocal prayer should be recited well, there's no reason to say so much. What I'm trying to point out is that we should see and be present to the One with whom we speak without turning our backs on him, for I don't think speaking with God while thinking of a thousand other vanities would amount to anything else but turning our backs on him. All the harm comes from not truly understanding that he is near, but in

imagining him as far away. And indeed how far, if we go to
heaven to seek him! Now, is your face such, Lord, that we
would not look at it when you are so close to us? If people
aren't looking at us when we speak, it doesn't seem to us that
they are listening to what we say. And do we close our eyes to
avoid seeing that you, Lord, are looking at us? How will we
know whether you've heard what we're saying to you? This
alone is what I want to explain: that in order to acquire the
habit of easily recollecting our minds and understanding what
we are saying, and with whom we are speaking, it is necessary
that the exterior senses be recollected and that we give them
something with which to be occupied. For indeed we have
heaven within ourselves since the Lord of heaven is there.]

We must, then, disengage ourselves from everything so
as to approach God interiorly and even in the midst of occupations withdraw within ourselves. Although it may be for only
a moment that I remember I have that Company within myself, doing so is very beneficial. In sum, we must get used to
delighting in the fact that it isn't necessary to shout in order
to speak to him, for His Majesty will give the experience that
he is present.

6. With this method we shall pray vocally with much
calm, and any difficulty will be removed. For in the little
amount of time we take to force ourselves to be close to this
Lord, he will understand us as if through sign language. Thus
if we are about to say the Our Father many times, he will understand us after the first. He is very fond of taking away our
difficulty. Even though we may recite this prayer no more
than once in an hour, we can be aware that we are with him,
of what we are asking him, of his willingness to give to us, and
how eagerly he remains with us. If we have this awareness, he
doesn't want us to be breaking our heads trying to speak a
great deal to him. [Therefore, Sisters, out of love for the Lord,
get used to praying the Our Father with this recollection, and

you will see the benefit before long. This is a manner of praying that the soul gets so quickly used to that it doesn't go astray, nor do the faculties become restless, as time will tell. I only ask that you try this method, even though it may mean some struggle; everything involves struggle before the habit is acquired. But I assure you that before long it will be a great consolation for you to know that you can find this holy Father, whom you are beseeching, within you without tiring yourself in seeking where he is.]

7. May the Lord teach this recollection to those of you who don't know about it, for I confess that I never knew what it was to pray with satisfaction until the Lord taught me this method. And it is because I have always found so many benefits from this habit of recollection that I have enlarged so much upon it.

I conclude by saying that whoever wishes to acquire it — since, as I say, it lies within our power — should not tire of getting used to what has been explained. It involves a gradual increase of self-control and an end to vain wandering from the right path; it means conquering, which is a making use of one's senses for the sake of the inner life. If you speak, strive to remember that the One with whom you are speaking is present within. If you listen, remember that you are going to hear One who is very close to you when he speaks. In sum, bear in mind that you can, if you want, avoid ever withdrawing from such good company; and be sorry that for a long time you left your Father alone, of whom you are so much in need. If you can, practice this recollection often during the day; if not, do so a few times. As you become accustomed to it you will experience the benefit, either sooner or later. Once this recollection is given by the Lord, you will not exchange it for any treasure.

8. Since nothing is learned without a little effort, consider, Sisters, for the love of God, as well employed the attention

you give to this method of prayer. I know, if you try, that within a year, or perhaps half a year, you will acquire it, by the favor of God. See how little time it takes for a gain as great as is that of laying a good foundation. If then the Lord should desire to raise you to higher things he will discover in you the readiness, finding that you are close to him. May it please His Majesty that we not consent to withdrawing from his presence. Amen. [Perhaps all of you know what I've explained, but someone may come along who will not know it. For that reason don't be annoyed that I've mentioned it here. Now let us come to learn how our good Master continues and begins to petition his holy Father for us; it is good that we understand what he asks.]

MORE COUNSELS ON RECOLLECTION

In comparing the things of heaven to those of earth, Teresa was led into another digression, although brief, before presenting further practical advice about the prayer of recollection.

29.1–3: Don't bother about being favored by the prelate (bishop).

- Do what you ought and the Lord will repay you.

- Let us always direct our thoughts to what is lasting.

- Your kingdom is not here below; all things come to an end quickly.

- It is better that for the Lord you accept being unappreciated.

- Turn your eyes inward, and look within yourself, and find your Master.

- He never fails persons who are afflicted and despised if they trust in him.

- I, who more than anyone should understand, have not succeeded in doing so as required.

29.4: Teresa returns to her subject of recollection.

- It is not something supernatural.

- We can obtain it ourselves.

- It is not a silence of the faculties but an enclosure of them within the soul.

29.5–8: We should see and be present to the One with whom we speak.

- We should disengage ourselves from everything so as to approach God interiorly.

- Even in the midst of occupations withdraw within ourselves, though it be for only a moment.

- With this method we shall pray vocally with much calm.

- Even though we may recite this prayer no more than once in an hour, we can be aware that we are with him and how eagerly he remains with us.

- He doesn't want us to be breaking our heads to speak a great deal.

- I have found so many benfits from this habit of recollection that I have enlarged my treatment of it.

- If you can, practice this recollection often during the day; if not, do so a few times.

- If you try, within a year or a half year, you will acquire this habit of recollection.

INTERPRETIVE NOTES: 1. The first foundation of St. Teresa's was placed under the jurisdiction of its local bishop, not under the Carmelite Order. The bishop, Don Alvaro de Mendoza, supported Teresa's efforts and befriended the community. He seemingly paid more attention to some than to others. Teresa gives practical advice on how to deal with the resulting feelings of rejection. She shows a deep understanding of feelings like these and implies that she is as much in need of her own advice as anyone else. The counsel is typically Teresian: Cut off such thoughts with the thought that your kingdom is not here below and how quickly all things come to an end; turn your eyes inward and you will find your Master; if you truly knew him, you wouldn't care about all these things.

2. Making it clear that this recollection is not something supernatural, Teresa explains how we can achieve it by ourselves. For Teresa the term "supernatural prayer" is the equivalent of mystical or infused or passive prayer, or contemplation. In her *Life*, while discussing the second water (or degree of prayer), she describes a recollection that is infused (15.1); she does so again in a later work, *The Interior Castle.* In this latter she explains the prayer of infused recollecion through an exquisite comparison: "Like a good shepherd, with a whistle so gentle that even they themselves [the senses and faculties] almost fail to hear it, he makes them recognize his voice and stops them from going so far astray so that they will return to their dwelling place"(IV. 3.1–8). The gentle whistle of the shepherd that draws the faculties into recollection is not yet as perceptible as is the prayer of quiet. It is the first delicate summoning of the soul into passive prayer. But in the present work, the prayer of recollection is an acquired form of prayer. Yet, when Teresa speaks of this prayer that can be achieved through our own efforts, she adds "with

the help of God." She knew well that all prayer is a gift from God. The difference lies in the way in which the gift is given and received. These two forms of recollection are often referred to by Teresian authors as active recollection and passive recollection.

3. In mentioning books written about this recollection, Teresa must have had in mind particularly the book she spoke of in her *Life* (4.7), *The Third Spiritual Alphabet* by Francisco de Osuna. Teresa's copy of this book is still conserved at her monastery of St. Joseph's in Avila. One can see the many marginal signs made by her. One of the passages marked by her is the following: "The heart of the just is an earthly paradise to which the Lord comes for his pleasure, for it is said that his delights are to be with the children of men (Pr 8:31). And it is a paradise of delight for us as well, for we begin to taste the joy of paradise in our heart particularly when God dwells in it, and this delight far surpasses all earthly pleasure" (*Third Spiritual Alphabet* IV. 3).

4. "The words 'Our Father who art in heaven' ought to be understood in relation to the heart of the just in whom God dwells as in his temple. Thus the one who prays desires to see that the One who is invoked is residing within" (St. Augustine, *Serm. Dom.* 2.5.17)

QUESTIONS FOR DISCUSSION. 1. How would you describe the prayer of recollection?

2. Why is it compatible with vocal prayer?

3. How would we know that we have acquired the habit of this recollection?

Chapter 30

The importance of understanding what is being asked for in prayer. Deals with the next words of the Our Father: Sanctificetur nomen tuum, adveniat regnum tuum. *Applies these words to the prayer of quiet and begins to explain this kind of prayer.*

ARE THERE ANY AMONG US, however foolish, who when about to ask for something from an important person do not think over how to go about asking? We must find favor with this person and not seem rude. We think about what we should ask for and why we need it, especially if we are asking for something significant, which is what our good Jesus teaches us to ask for. There is something it seems to me that should be noted: Couldn't you, my Lord, have concluded the Our Father with the words: "Give us, Father, what is fitting for us"? It doesn't seem there would have been need to say anything else to One who understands everything so well.

2. O Eternal Wisdom! Between you and your Father these words would have sufficed. Your petition in the garden was like this. You manifested your own desire and fear, but you abandoned them to his will.[1] Yet, you know us, my Lord, that we are not as surrendered to the will of your Father as you were. You know that it was necessary for you to make those specific requests so that we might pause to consider if what we are seeking is good for us, so that if it isn't we won't ask for it. If we aren't given what we want, being what we are, with this free will we have, we might not accept what the Lord gives. For although what he gives is better, we don't think we'll ever become rich, since we don't at once see the money in our hand.

327

3. Oh, God help me! What a pity to have so unawakened a faith that we never come to understand fully the certainty of both punishment and reward! As a result it is good, daughters, that you understand what you are asking for in the Our Father so that if the Eternal Father should offer it to you, you will not scoff at it. And consider very carefully whether what you ask for is good for you; if it isn't, don't ask for it, but ask His Majesty to give you light. For we are blind and feel loathing for the food that will give us life; we want the food that will bring us death. And what a death! So dangerous and so everlasting!

4. Well, Jesus says that we may recite these words in which we ask for a kingdom like his to come within us: "Hallowed be your name, your kingdom come within us." [2]

Now behold, daughters, how great the wisdom of our Master is. I am reflecting here on what we are asking for when we ask for this kingdom, and it is good that we understand our request. But since His Majesty saw that we could neither hallow, nor praise, nor extol, nor glorify this holy name of the Eternal Father in a fitting way, because of the tiny amount we ourselves are capable of doing, he provided for us by giving us here on earth his kingdom. That is why Jesus put these two petitions next to each other. I want to tell you here, daughters, what I understand so that we may know what we are asking for and the importance of our begging persistently for it, and do as much as we can so as to please the One who is to give it to us. If I do not satisfy you, you can think up other reflections yourselves. Our Master will allow us to make these reflections provided that we submit in all things to what the church[3] holds, as I do [always. And I will not even give you this to read until learned persons have seen it. At least, if there is anything incorrect, the error will not be done through malice but for my not knowing any better.]

5. Now, then, the great good that it seems to me there will be in the kingdom of heaven, among many other blessings, is

that one will no longer take any account of earthly things, but have a calmness and glory within, rejoice in the fact that all are rejoicing, experience perpetual peace and a wonderful inner satisfaction that comes from seeing that everyone hallows and praises the Lord and blesses his name and that no one offends him. Everyone loves him there, and the soul itself doesn't think about anything else than loving him; nor can it cease loving him, because it knows him. And would that we could love him in this way here below, even though we may not be able to do so with such perfection or stability. But if we knew him we would love in a way very different from that in which we do love him.

6. It seems I'm saying that we would have to be angels in order to make this petition and recite well our vocal prayers. Our divine Master would truly desire this since he asks us to make so lofty a petition, and certainly he doesn't tell us to ask for impossible things. The above would be possible, through the favor of God, for a soul placed in this exile, but not with the perfection of those who have gone forth from this prison; for we are at sea and journeying along this way. But there are times when, tired from our travels, we experience that the Lord calms our faculties and quiets the soul. As though by signs, he gives us a clear foretaste of what will be given to those he brings to his kingdom. And to those to whom he gives here below the kingdom we ask for, he gives pledges so that through these they may have great hope of going to enjoy perpetually what here on earth is given only in sips.

7. If you wouldn't say that I'm treating of contemplation, this petition would provide a good opportunity for speaking a little about the beginning of pure contemplation; those who experience this prayer call it the prayer of quiet. But since, as I say, I'm dealing with vocal prayer, it may seem to anyone who doesn't know about the matter that vocal prayer doesn't go with contemplation; but I know that it does. Pardon me, but I

want to say this: I know there are many persons who while praying vocally, as has already been mentioned,[4] are raised by God to sublime contemplation [without their striving for anything or understanding how. It's because of this that I insist so much, daughters, upon your reciting vocal prayer well.] I know a person[5] who was never able to pray any way but vocally, and though she was tied to this form of prayer she experienced everything else. And if she didn't recite vocal prayer her mind wandered so much that she couldn't bear it. Would that our mental prayer were as good! She spent several hours reciting a certain number of Our Fathers, in memory of the times our Lord shed his blood, as well as a few other vocal prayers. Once she came to me very afflicted because she didn't know how to practice mental prayer nor could she contemplate; she could only pray vocally. I asked her how she was praying, and I saw that though she was tied to the Our Father she experienced pure contemplation and that the Lord was raising her up and joining her with himself in union. And from her deeds it seemed truly that she was receiving such great favors, for she was living a very good life. So I praised the Lord and envied her for her vocal prayer.

If this account is true, as it is, those of you who are the enemies of contemplatives should not think that you are free from being a contemplative if you recite your vocal prayers as they should be recited, with a pure conscience. [And so I will speak of this again. Whoever doesn't want to hear it may pass on.]

THE FIRST TWO PETITIONS OF THE OUR FATHER

After the sublime realities she discovered in the opening words of the Our Father, Teresa begins to examine the petitions.

30.1–3. A. If we are going to ask something of an important person, we think about how we are going to ask.

B. Couldn't the Lord have concluded with "Give us, Father, what is fitting for us?"

- She enters into a prayer to Eternal Wisdom.

  - The words would have sufficed for you.

  - We are not as surrendered as you.

  - You made specific requests that we might pause to consider if what we are seeking is good for us.

- Ask His Majesty to give you light about what to ask for.

- We are blind and feel loathing for the food that will give us life.

30.4: "Hallowed be your name, your kingdom come within us."

- We are incapable of hallowing the Father's name in a fitting way.

- He provided by giving us here on earth his kingdom.

- I am telling you what I understand of the words; you are free to think up other reflections if mine do not satisfy you.

- We can be free in our reflections provided we submit all to what the church holds.

30.5: Some blessings of the kingdom of heaven:

- One no longer takes account of earthly things;

- Calmness and glory within;

- Joy in the fact that all are rejoicing;

- Perpetual peace;

- Wonderful satisfaction to see that everyone hallows and praises the Lord and that no one offends him;

- The soul cannot cease loving him because it knows him.

30.6: The divine Master asks us to make so lofty a petition.

- There are times when we experience that the Lord calms our faculties and quiets the soul.

- As though by signs he gives us a clear foretaste of what will be given in his kingdom.

- He gives hope of enjoying perpetually what is here given only in sips.

- You may say I'm speaking about contemplation and that vocal prayer does not go with it.

- I know that it does.

- I have known many who while praying vocally are raised by God to sublime contemplation.

- She gives a striking example.

INTERPRETIVE NOTES: 1. The prayer of petition presents the problem of the appropriateness of what one prays for. Teresa has already lamented some of the things that her nuns are asked to pray for: "...that if God were to give them, we'd have one less soul in heaven" (1.7). Still the prayer of petition expresses a basic attitude before the mystery of God. We experience human need and believe that God loves us and therefore cares about our needs: "Ask and it will be given to you; seek and you will find; knock and the door will be opened to you.... If you then, who are wicked, know how to give good gifts to your children, how much more will your heavenly Father give good things to those who ask him" (Mt 7:7, 11). With the sending of the Holy Spirit, God's own desires and yearnings become a part of our own: "In the same way, the Spirit too comes to the aid of our weakness; for we do not know how to pray as we ought, but the Spirit itself intercedes with inexpressible groanings. And the one who searches hearts knows what is the intention of the Spirit, because it intercedes for the holy ones according to God's will" (Rom 8:26–27). Teresa looks on these petitions of the Our Father as sublime, specific expressions of Christ's own yearnings in the Spirit and as guides for us in knowing what to pray for.

2. She links the first two petitions, quoting them in Latin in the chapter heading and in Spanish in the body of the chapter. From her experience of contemplation she feels that God has given her a clear foretaste of the kingdom of heaven and of how his name is hallowed there. She touches on the wonderful satisfaction that comes from knowing that everyone loves, blesses, and praises the Lord. Teresa admits outright that her interpretation of these two petitions (that contemplation, the foretaste of God's kingdom, come on earth so that his name may be hallowed) is her own. She seemingly foresees the objections that could be made to her interpretation and averts them by telling her readers that if they don't like her reflections they can make their own, within the limits of what the church holds.

3. The subject of contemplation obliges Teresa once more to insist, as she did in chapters 24 and 25, that vocal prayer when combined with mental prayer, as it should be, does not in itself present an obstacle to the reception of the gift of contemplation. She appeals to her knowledge of the experience of many persons who while praying vocally are raised to "sublime" contemplation. The example about the elderly nun's prayer contains significant details: the practice was actually a popular form of devotion (the recitation of a certain number of Our Fathers in memory of the times Our Lord shed his blood); the nun thought she was unable to practice mental prayer or contemplate; if she didn't pray vocally her mind would wander unbearably; her devotional prayers could last several hours; she came

to Teresa very afflicted about her prayer. The pure contemplation that Teresa detected in her prayer was obviously not apparent to the nun herself. This incident brings to mind Teresa's pertinent words in her *Life:* "For it is one grace to receive the Lord's favor; another, to understand which favor and grace it is; and a third, to know how to describe and explain it. And although no more than the first grace seems necessary, it is a great advantage and a gift for the soul that it also understand the favor so as not to go about confused and afraid.... Each one of these graces is a reason for those who receive it to praise the Lord greatly and, also, for those who may not receive it to praise him because His Majesty gave it to one of the living so that that person might help the rest of us" (17.5). Finally, Teresa discerns the quality of the nun's prayer not only from whatever experiences were related to it but also from its effects. "And from her deeds it seemed truly that she was receiving such great favors." Who would say that the quality of this soul's prayer could not match that of the more notable contemplatives of the times? Teresa ends the account by praising the Lord confessing a holy envy of the nun's vocal prayer.

4. Contemplation is like an underground river. It may at times gush up into cool springs in undetermined places. It may reveal its presence only by the plants and flowers it waters from below. Its depth is difficult to measure, its quality hidden from sight. St. John of the Cross wrote of contemplation as being secret:

"Since the wisdom of this contemplation is the language of God to the soul, of Pure Spirit to pure spirit, all that is less than spirit, such as the sensory, fails to perceive it. Consequently this wisdom is secret to the senses; they have neither the knowledge nor ability to speak of it, nor do they even desire to do so because it is beyond words. We understand, then, why some persons who tread this road and desire to give an account of this experience to their director — for they are good and God-fearing — are unable to describe it. They feel great repugnance in speaking about it, especially when the contemplation is so simple that they are hardly aware of it" (*Night* 2.17.4–5).

QUESTIONS FOR DISCUSSION: 1. How will a foretaste of the kingdom of heaven here below help us to hallow God's name?

2. What are some of the blessings of the kingdom of heaven?

3. Is it essential to contemplative prayer that one experience spiritual delight?

Chapter 31

Continues on the same subject. Explains the nature of the prayer of quiet. Gives some advice for those who experience it. This chapter should be carefully noted.

WELL, DAUGHTERS, I NONETHELESS want to explain this prayer of quiet. I have heard talk about it, or the Lord has given me understanding of it, perhaps, that I might tell you of it [and that others may praise him; although since I have written about it elsewhere, as I said, I will not give lengthy explanations but just say something.] In this prayer it seems the Lord begins, as I have said,[1] to show that he hears our petition. He begins now to give us his kingdom here below so that we may truly praise and hallow his name and strive that all persons do so.

2. This prayer is something supernatural, something we cannot procure through our own efforts. In it the soul enters into peace or, better, the Lord puts it at peace by his presence, as he did to the just Simeon,[2] so that all the faculties are calmed. The soul understands in another way, very foreign to the way it understands through the exterior senses, that it is now close to its God and that not much more would be required for it to become one with him in union. This is not because it sees him with the eyes either of the body or of the soul. The just Simeon didn't see any more than the glorious, little, poor child. For by the way the child was clothed and by the few people that were in the procession, Simeon could have easily judged the babe to be the

son of poor people rather than the Son of our heavenly Father. But the child himself made Simeon understand. And this is how the soul understands here, although not with as much clarity. For the soul, likewise, fails to understand how it understands. But it sees it is in the kingdom, at least near the King who will give the kingdom to the soul. And seemingly the soul has so much reverence that it doesn't even dare ask for this. The state resembles an interior and exterior swoon; for the exterior part (or so that you will understand me better, I mean the body [for some simpleton will come along who won't know what "interior" and "exterior" means]) doesn't want any activity. But like those who have almost reached the end of their journey such persons want to rest so as to be better able to continue; in this rest their strength for the journey is doubled.

3. They feel the greatest delight in their body and a great satisfaction in their soul. They feel so happy merely with being close to the fount that they are satisfied even without drinking. It doesn't seem there is anything else for them to desire. The faculties are still; they wouldn't want to be busy; everything else seems to hinder them from loving. But they are not completely lost; they can think of who it is they are near, for two of them are free. The will is the one that is captive here. If there is some sorrow that can be experienced while in this state, that sorrow comes from a realization that the will must return to the state of being free. The intellect wouldn't want to understand more than one thing; nor would the memory want to be occupied with anything else. Persons in this prayer see that only this one thing is necessary, and everything else disturbs them. They don't want the body to move because it seems they would thereby lose that peace; thus they don't dare stir. It pains them to speak; in their saying "Our Father" just once, a whole hour passes. They are so close that they see they are understanding as though through signs. They are within the palace, near the King, and they see that he is beginning to give them here his

kingdom. It doesn't seem to them that they are in the world, nor would they want to see or hear about anything other than their God. Nothing pains them, nor does it seem anything ever will. In sum, while this prayer lasts they are so absorbed and engulfed with the satisfaction and delight they experience within themselves that they do not remember there is more to desire; they would eagerly say with St. Peter: "Lord, let us build three dwelling places here." [3]

4. Sometimes in this prayer of quiet the Lord grants another favor which is very difficult to understand if there is not a great deal of experience. But if there is some experience, the one who receives it will immediately understand. It will be a great consolation for you to know what it is, and I believe God often grants this favor together with the other one. When this quiet is great and lasts for a long while, it seems to me that the will wouldn't be able to remain so long in that peace if it weren't bound to something. For it may happen that we will go about with this satisfaction for a day or two and will not understand ourselves — I mean those who experience it — and they definitely see that they are not wholly in what they are doing, but that the best part is lacking, that is, the will. The will, in my opinion, is then united with its God, and leaves the other faculties free to be occupied in what is for his service — and they then have much more ability for this. But in worldly matters, these faculties are dull and at times as though in a stupor.

5. This is a great favor for those to whom the Lord grants it; the active and the contemplative lives are joined. The faculties all serve the Lord together: the will is occupied in its work and contemplation without knowing how; the other two faculties serve in the work of Martha. Thus Martha and Mary walk together.

I know someone whom the Lord often placed in this state. She didn't know what to make of it and asked a great contemplative. He answered that the experience was very possible, that it had happened to him.[4] Thus, I think that because the soul is so satisfied in this prayer of quiet the faculty of the will remains more continually united with him who alone can satisfy it.

6. I think it would be good here to give some counsels for those of you, Sisters, whom the Lord, solely through his goodness, has brought here, for I know there are some among you.

The first is that since they see themselves in that contentment and do not know how it came on them — at least they see they cannot obtain it by themselves — they experience this temptation: they think they'll be able to hold on to that satisfaction and they don't even dare take a breath. This is foolish, for just as there's nothing we can do to make the sun rise, there's little we can do to keep it from setting. This prayer is no longer our work, for it's something very supernatural and something very much beyond our power to acquire by ourselves. The best way to hold on to this favor is to understand clearly that we can neither bring it about nor remove it; we can only receive it with gratitude, as most unworthy of it; and this not with many words, but by raising our eyes to him, as the publican did.[5]

7. It is good to find more solitude so as to make room for the Lord and allow His Majesty to work as though with something belonging to him. At most, a gentle word from time to time is sufficient, as in the case of one who blows on a candle to enkindle it again when it begins to die out. But if the candle is burning, blowing on it will in my opinion serve no other purpose than to put it out. I say that the blowing should be gentle lest the will be distracted by an intellect busying itself with many words.

8. And note well, friends, this counsel that I now wish to give, for you'll often see that you'll be unable to manage these other two faculties.[6] It happens that the soul will be in the greatest

quiet and the intellect will be so distracted that it won't seem that the quiet is present in the intellect's house. It seems to the intellect, during that time, that it is nowhere else than in a stranger's house, as a guest, and seeking other dwelling places because the house it's in doesn't satisfy it and it knows little about how to remain stable. Perhaps it's only my intellect that's like this, and others' intellects are not. I am speaking about myself, for sometimes I want to die in that I cannot cure this wandering of the intellect. At other times I think it takes up residence in its own house and accompanies the will. It's a wonderful thing when all three faculties are in accord. It's like what happens between two married people: if they love each other, the one wants what the other wants. But if the husband is unhappily married, it's easy to see what disturbance he'll cause his wife. Thus when the will finds itself in this quiet [and note well this counsel, for the matter is important], it shouldn't pay any more attention to the intellect than it would to a madman. For should it want to keep the intellect near itself, it will necessarily have to be somewhat disturbed and disquieted. And in this state of prayer everything will then amount to working without any further gain but with a loss of what the Lord was giving the will without its own work.

9. And notice carefully this comparison [for the Lord put it in my mind while I was at prayer]; it seems to me very appropriate: the soul is like an infant that still nurses when at its mother's breast, and the mother without her babe's effort to suckle puts the milk in its mouth in order to give it delight. So it is here; for without effort of the intellect the will is loving, and the Lord desires that the will, without thinking about the matter, understand that it is with him and that it does no more than swallow the milk His Majesty places in its mouth, and enjoy that sweetness. For the will knows that it is the Lord who is granting that favor. And the will rejoices in its enjoyment. It doesn't desire to understand how it enjoys the favor

or what it enjoys; but it forgets itself during that time, for the One who is near it will not forget to observe what is fitting for it. If the will goes out to fight with the intellect so as to give a share of the experience, by drawing the intellect after itself, it cannot do so at all; it will be forced to let the milk fall from its mouth and lose that divine nourishment.

10. This is the way this prayer of quiet is different from that prayer in which the entire soul is united with God, for then the soul doesn't even go through the process of swallowing this divine food. Without its understanding how, the Lord places the milk within it. In this prayer of quiet it seems that he wants it to work a little, although so gently that it almost doesn't feel its effort. [Whoever experience this prayer will understand clearly what I'm saying if after having read this they reflect on it carefully; and let them consider how important the matter is. If they don't experience the prayer, this will seem like gibberish.] That which torments the will is the intellect. The intellect doesn't cause this torment when there is union of all three faculties, for he who created them suspends them. With the joy he gives them he keeps them all occupied without their knowing or understanding how. Thus, as I say, they feel this prayer within themselves, a quiet and great contentment of the will, without being able to discern what it is specifically. Yet the soul easily discerns that it is far different from earthly satisfactions and that ruling the world with all its delights wouldn't be enough to make the soul feel that delight within itself. The delight is in the interior of the will, for the other consolations of life, it seems to me, are enjoyed in the exterior of the will, as in the outer bark, we might say. When the will sees itself in this degree of prayer so sublime (for the prayer is, as I have already said,[7] very recognizably supernatural), it laughs at the intellect as at a fool when this intellect — or mind, to explain myself better — goes off to the more foolish things of the world. The will remains in its quietude, for the intellect will come and go. In

this prayer the will is the ruler and the powerful one. It will draw the intellect after itself without your being disturbed. And if the will should desire to draw the intellect by force of arms, the strength it has against the intellect will be lost. This strength comes from eating and receiving that divine food. And neither the will nor the intellect will gain anything, but both will lose. As the saying goes, whoever tries to grasp too much loses everything; this it seems to me is what will happen here. Experience will enable one to understand, for I wouldn't be surprised if to anyone who doesn't have this experience what I've said would seem very obscure and unnecessary. But I've already mentioned[8] that with a little experience one will understand it, be able to benefit from it, and will praise the Lord because he was pleased that I managed to explain it here.

11. Now, then, let's conclude by saying that to the soul placed in this prayer it seems the Eternal Father has already here below granted its petition for his kingdom. Oh, blessed request, in which, without realizing it, we ask for so much good! What a blessed way of asking! For this reason, Sisters, I want us to look at how we recite this prayer, the Our Father, and all other vocal prayers. For when this favor is granted by God, we shall forget the things of the world; when the Lord of the world arrives he casts out everything else. I don't say that all those who experience this prayer must by necessity be completely detached from the world. At least, I would like them to know what is lacking and that they humble themselves and try to go on detaching themselves from everything; if they don't, they will remain in this state. A soul to whom God gives such pledges has a sign that he wants to give it a great deal; if not impeded through its own fault, it will advance very far. But if the Lord sees that after he places the kingdom of heaven in the soul's house this soul turns to earthly things, he will not only fail to show it the secrets there are in his kingdom but will seldom grant it this favor, and then for just a short space of time.

12. Now it could be that I am mistaken in this matter, but I see and know that this is what happens, and in my opinion this is why there are not many more spiritual persons. When individuals do not respond by service that is in conformity with so great a favor, when they do not prepare themselves to receive it again, but take back their wills from the hands of the Lord who already possesses these wills as his own, and set them upon base things, the Lord goes in search of those who do love him so as to give more to them. Yet he doesn't take away entirely what he has given, when one lives with a pure conscience. But there are persons — and I have been one of them — who make themselves deaf when the Lord, taking pity on them, gives them holy inspirations and light concerning the nature of things, and, in sum, gives this kingdom and places them in this prayer of quiet. For they are so fond of speaking and reciting many vocal prayers very quickly, like one who wants to get a job done, since they oblige themselves to recite these every day, that even though, as I say, the Lord places his kingdom in their hands, they do not receive it. But with their vocal prayers they think they are doing better, and they distract themselves from the prayer of quiet.

13. Do not do this, Sisters, but be on your guard when the Lord grants you this favor. Consider that you are losing a great treasure and that you do much more by saying one word of the Our Father from time to time than by rushing through the entire prayer many times. You are very close to the One you petition; he will not fail to hear you. And believe that herein lies the true praise and hallowing of his name. For now, as one who is in his house, you glorify the Lord and praise him with more affection and desire; and it seems that you cannot fail to serve him. [Thus I counsel you to be very careful in this matter because it is extremely important.]

THE PRAYER OF QUIET

The first two petitions of the Our Father lead Teresa to a reflection on the prayer of quiet, a foretaste of the kingdom of heaven.

31.1: I want to explain this prayer of quiet.

- The Lord has given me understanding of it:

    - Perhaps that I might tell you about it;

    - That others may praise God.

- I have written about it elsewhere, so I'll say only something about it.

- In this prayer the Lord begins to show that he hears our petition.

- He begins to give us his kingdom here below so that we may truly praise and hallow his name and strive that all persons do so.

31.2–3: This prayer is something supernatural.

- In it the Lord gives the soul peace by his presence.

- The soul understands in another way, very foreign to the way it understands through the exterior senses:

    - That it is close to God;

    - That not much more would be required to become one with him in union.

    - The soul understands as Simeon understood who the child was.

- The soul sees that it is at least near the kingdom.

- The prayer gives delight to the body and satisfaction to the soul.

- The will is held captive.

- Persons in this prayer tend to think that the body must not stir lest they lose the peace.

- They say the Our Father slowly; maybe once in a whole hour.

- While absorbed in the satisfaction and delight, they do not remember there is more to desire.

31.4–5: Sometimes, the satisfaction may last for a day or two, and the will is not wholly in what one is doing.

- The active and contemplative lives are joined.

- The will is occupied in its contemplation without knowing how; the other two faculties serve in the work of Martha.

31.6–10: Counsels for those whom the Lord has brought here.

- We can neither bring this prayer about nor can we hold on to it so that it will last longer.

- It is good to find more solitude so as to allow the Lord to work.

- A gentle word from time to time is sufficient.

- When the will is in this quiet, it shouldn't pay any more attention to the intellect than to a madman.

- Teresa here compares God to a mother nursing her infant.

  - The prayer of recollection: the babe suckles;

  - The prayer of quiet: the mother puts milk into the child's mouth so as to give it delight, and the babe has only to swallow;

  - The prayer of union: without the child's knowing how, the Lord places the milk within it without its even having to swallow.

- In the prayer of quiet it seems the Lord wants it to work a little.

- In the prayer of union, the intellect doesn't cause disturbance, but all three faculties are suspended by God.

- In the prayer of quiet the intellect will come and go.

- If the will tries to force the intellect to be still, both will lose.

31.11: In this prayer it seems the Eternal Father has already granted the soul's petition for his kingdom.

- Those who experience this prayer should try to go on detaching themselves from everything.

- If they do, the Lord will give more.

- There are souls so fond of speaking and reciting many vocal prayers very quickly that they do not receive the kingdom when the Lord places it in their hands.

- You do much more by saying one word of the Our Father from time to time than rushing through it many times.

- Herein lies the true praise and hallowing of his name.

INTERPRETIVE NOTES: 1. Teresa calls the prayer of quiet the "beginning of pure contemplation." When speaking of contemplation, she is always referring to a prayer that is in her terminology "supernatural." It cannot be acquired, but is received. In her descriptions she draws largely from what her own experiences of this prayer were. Theologically speaking, God changes the way in which he communicates himself to the soul. "The Lord puts it at peace by his presence"(2). We have in this unadorned yet remarkable statement the simple intuition or awareness of the truth of God's presence and a tranquil repose in the object known, the fruition or possession of truth. The soul receives understanding that it is close to its God, the way Simeon understood that the babe in Mary's arms was the Christ child. But when Teresa explains that the soul fails to understand how it understands, an unforgettable passage in her *Life* comes to mind: "The will is fully occupied in loving, but it doesn't understand how it loves. The intellect, if it understands, doesn't understand how it understands; at least it can't comprehend anything of what it understands. It doesn't seem to me that it understands, because, as I say, it doesn't understand — I really can't understand this!" (18.14). Other biblical figures used to illumine her explanations are Peter on Tabor, Martha and Mary, and the publican praying in the temple.

2. Padre Tomás de Jesús, who made his profession as a discalced Carmelite in Valladolid in 1587, five years after the death of Teresa and five years before the death of St. John of the Cross, learned a method of prayer, taught in the discalced Carmelite novitiates at the time, that was divided into seven parts: preparation, reading, meditation, contemplation, thanksgiving, petition, and epilogue. The contemplation followed as the natural term of discursive meditation. Tomás de Jesús later named this contemplation "acquired contemplation." It is acquired through meditation and gradually becomes a habit. When one has the habit of this contemplation called acquired, one is disposed to be brought by the Lord to infused contemplation. This became the traditional teaching of the "Carmelite School" of prayer. During the first half of this twentieth century, a sometimes heated debate developed over the term "acquired contemplation." At the root of the debate was another one that reared its head through the teachings of Fr. Poulain, S.J., and those of Abbé Saudreau. Poulain asserted that an essential distinction lay between the ascetical and mystical life. The two do not constitute parts of one and the same way leading to perfection. Saudreau taught the opposite, that anyone journeying on the path to perfection would have to pass through both the ascetical and mystical life as two steps along one path. The Carmelites generally sided with Poulain and held that acquired contemplation was the term of the prayer of

one following the ascetical path and that perfection or union with God was reached when individuals had attained to complete conformity of their wills with God's will. Those journeying on the mystical path would experience the gift of infused contemplation and undergo the passive nights or purifications, as explained by St. John of the Cross, in preparation for the mystical union of the spiritual marriage. The Jesuits with various nuances tended to side with both Poulain and the Carmelites, whereas the Dominicans with their own nuances agreed with Saudreau. The Dominican Fr. Arintero complained that acquired contemplation was a dangerous novelty leading directly into quietism. In periodicals and congresses the Carmelites, with fiery passion, fought for the traditions of their school. As the controversy reached a standstill, authors such as Joseph De Guibert, S.J., and Gabriel of St. Mary Magdalen, O.C.D., looked in different ways for a middle ground. After the Second World War, Carmelite scholars began to turn their backs on the previous disputes to concentrate with greater care on the writings of their two founders, leaving aside concern for fitting them into any preconceived system or using them to shore up a position. The thought of the two saints transcended the limitations of the systems they were being used to support. Researchers, as well, brought to Teresa and John new questions which gave their teaching a wider appeal. As for Teresa, she was a genius whose writings cannot be made subservient to their interpreters. Part of the problem had been the reluctance of those trained in theology to think they could learn any theology from a woman untrained in the schools. In 1970, Paul VI gave Teresa's gifts of sanctity and wisdom their due and proclaimed her a Doctor of the Church, the first woman saint to be so recognized.

3. Generally, authors today do not use the term "contemplation" in Teresa's strict sense. The *Catechism of the Catholic Church* asserts that the Christian tradition has conserved three main expressions of the life of prayer: vocal prayer, meditation, and the prayer of contemplation. It admits with Teresa the importance in vocal prayer of presence to the one before whom we are praying and of vocal prayer's capacity to become contemplative. Meditation, it continues, makes use of the thinking powers and moves along in a discursive manner seeking understanding so as to respond. The *Catechism* then presents contemplation as a prayer more like Teresa's mental prayer or prayer of recollection, although it wouldn't be excluding infused contemplation either. Similarly, as another example, Hans Urs von Balthasar in his book entitled *Prayer* used the term "contemplation" in the broader sense that the *Catechism* now does. With respect to meditation, authors today, often through the influence of Eastern forms of meditation, will speak of Christian meditation in terms of practices that are non-discursive. Considerable confusion can arise from a lack of clarity about how these terms are being understood.

4. To return to Teresa's times, this chapter presented a problem already in the chapter heading given it. Although quietism had not yet come on the scene as an error to be condemned, the word "quiet" was suspect; it smacked of the *Alumbrados*. Teresa was still alive as

this book of hers was being prepared for publication. The word "quiet" was deleted from the heading so that it simply read "Explains the nature of prayer", which was the theme of chapter 22. Eventually, the archbishop of Evora, Don Teutonio Braganza, a friend of Teresa's, submitted her manuscript to the Inquisition of Lisbon. The end result was the suppression of the entire chapter. In 1583, shortly after Teresa's death, *The Way of Perfection* was published, but without this significant chapter. The work continued to be published with the omission until Fray Luis de León restored it in his edition of the works of St. Teresa published in Salamanca in 1588. This is the only chapter in the *Way* that deals with contemplation expressly and integrally. It plays an essential role in the entire thrust of the book.

5. In her first redaction, at the beginning of this chapter, Teresa intended to speak just a bit about contemplation. But on reviewing her first redaction (Escorial), she apparently thought that what she had written was insufficient and decided to add four pages to her manuscript as an appendix. These pages were then included in her definitive draft (Valladolid); they are the equivalent of nos. 8, 9 and 10 of this chapter 31. The image of the suckling child, which came to her in prayer and which formed a part of this addition, she again employed in *Meditations on the Song of Songs* (4.4–5) and in the *Interior Castle* (IV.3.10). It illustrated for her the intervention of God and the degrees of passivity in contemplative prayer. The image illustrating the part humans may play in this prayer is

that of one blowing gently on a candle to keep the flame alive as it begins to die out. A gentle blowing is the equivalent of a gentle word said from time to time in contrast to many busy words, tantamount to blowing too hard and putting out the flame.

6. Speaking of the trouble the wandering intellect caused her during the prayer of quiet, Teresa merely gathered from her own experience what she should call intellect. She had not studied the speculative psychology of the scholastics. As pointed out in note no. 6, Teresa wrote in the manuscript of Toledo a few times above her term "intellect" the words "or imagination," "or mind or imagination." In *The Interior Castle* (IV.1.8), she confessed: "A little more than four years ago I came to understand through experience that the mind (or imagination to put it more clearly) is not the intellect. I asked a learned man and he told me that this was so; which brought me no small consolation." This learned man could well have been St. John of the Cross. In St. John of the Cross's teaching, the intellect and will are spiritual faculties which receive the general loving knowledge of contemplation. It is the interior sense faculty of the imagination that wanders during the prayer of quiet. In the *Ascent of Mt. Carmel*, he writes: "The second sign [of contemplation] is an awareness of a disinclination to fix the imagination or sense faculties on other particular objects, exterior or interior. I am not affirming that the imagination will cease to come and go — even in deep recollection it usually wanders freely — but that the person does not want to fix it purposely on extraneous things" (2.13.3).

QUESTIONS FOR DISCUSSION: 1. What is meant by mystical understanding?

2. Does Teresa ever speak of "acquired" contemplation?

3. What must we do to cooperate with God's grace in the prayer of quiet?

4. Is it possible in my life for Martha and Mary to walk together?

Chapter 32

Discusses the words of the Our Father, Fiat voluntas tua sicut in caelo et in terra; *the great deal a person does in saying them with full determination; and how well the Lord repays this. [So I counsel you to be attentive because the matter is very important.]*

NOW THAT OUR GOOD MASTER has asked, and taught us to ask, for something so highly valuable that it includes everything we can desire here below and that he has granted us so wonderful a favor as to make us his brothers, let us see what he desires us to give his Father, and how he offers this gift for us and what he asks of us. For it is right that we somehow serve him in return for such great favors. O good Jesus! What you give on our behalf in return for what you requested for us is no small thing, although it really amounts to nothing when compared to the greatness of the Lord and what we owe him. But certainly, my Lord, you do not leave us empty-handed when we give you everything we can — I mean if we really give it, as we say we will.

2. "Your will be done on earth as it is in heaven." You did well, good Master of ours, to make this petition so that we might accomplish what you give on our behalf. For certainly, Lord, if you hadn't made the petition, the task would seem to me impossible. But when your Father does what you ask him by giving us his kingdom here on earth, I know that we shall make your words come true by giving what you give for us. For once the earth has become heaven, the possibility is there for your will to be done in me. But if the earth hasn't — and

earth as wretched and barren as mine — I don't know, Lord, how it will be possible. It is indeed a great thing, that which you offer!

3. When I think of this, I am amused by persons who don't dare ask for trials from the Lord, for they suppose that in doing so they will be given them at once. I'm not speaking of those who fail to do so out of humility, thinking they will be incapable of suffering them; although I myself hold that he, who gives these persons the love to ask for these means, which are so harsh, in order that they may show their love, will give them the capacity to suffer them. I would like to question those who fear to ask for trials, lest these be given them at once, about what they say when they beseech the Lord to do his will in them. Perhaps they say the words just to say what everyone else is saying but not so that his will be done. To do this, Sisters, would not be right. Consider that Jesus acts here as our ambassador and that he has desired to intervene between us and his Father, and at no small cost of his own. It would not be right for us to fail to do what he has offered on our behalf; if we don't want to do it we shouldn't say these words.

4. Now let me put it in another way. Look, daughters, his will must be done whether we like this or not, and it will be done in heaven and on earth. Believe me, take my advice, and make a virtue of necessity. O my Lord, what a great comfort this is for me, that you didn't want the fulfillment of your will to depend on a will as wretched as mine! May you be blessed forever, and may all things praise you! Your name be glorified forever! I'd be in a fine state, Lord, if it were up to me as to whether or not your will were to be done! Now I freely give mine to you, even though I do so at a time in which I'm not free of self-interest. For I have felt and have had great experience of the gain that comes from freely abandoning my will to yours. O friends, what a great gain there is here! Oh, what

a great loss there is when we do not carry out what we offer to the Lord in the Our Father!

5. Before I tell you about what is gained, I want to explain the great deal you offer so that afterward you won't take back what you gave, claiming that you hadn't understood. Don't be like some religious who do nothing but promise; and when we don't follow through, we make an excuse saying we didn't understand what we were promising. And this could be so, because to say that we abandon our will to another's will seems very easy until through experience we realize that this is the hardest thing one can do if one does it as it should be done. But superiors are not always strict in leading us since they see we are weak. And at times they lead both the weak and the strong in the same way. With the Lord, such is not the case; he knows what each one can suffer. He does not delay in doing his will in anyone he sees has strength.[1]

6. Well, I want to advise you and remind you what his will is. Don't fear that it means he will give you riches, or delights, or honors, or all these earthly things. His love for you is not that small, and he esteems highly what you give him. He wants to repay you well, for he gives you his kingdom while you are still alive. Do you want to know how he answers those who say these words to him sincerely? Ask his glorious Son, who said them while praying in the Garden.[2] Since they were said with such determination and complete willingness, see if the Father's will wasn't done fully in him through the trials, sorrows, injuries, and persecutions he suffered until his life came to an end through death on a cross.

7. Well, see here, daughters, what he gave to the one he loved most. By that we understand what his will is. For these are his gifts in this world. He gives according to the love he bears us: to those he loves more, he gives more of these gifts; to those he loves less, he gives less. And he gives according to

the courage he sees in each and the love each has for His Majesty. He will see that whoever loves him much will be able to suffer much for him; whoever loves him little will be capable of little. I myself hold that the measure for being able to bear a large or small cross is love. So, Sisters, if you love him, strive that what you say to the Lord may not amount to mere polite words; strive to suffer what His Majesty desires you to suffer. For, otherwise, when you give your will, it would be like showing a jewel to another, making a gesture to give it away, and asking that he take it; but when he extends his hand to accept it, you pull yours back and hold on tightly to the jewel.

8. This is no way to mock him who was the butt of so much mockery for our sakes. Even if there were no other reason, it would not be right to mock him so often; the number of times we say the Our Father is not small. Let's give him the jewel once and for all, no matter how many times we have tried to give it before. The truth is that he rewards us beforehand so that we might give it to him. [Oh, God help me, how obvious it is that my good Jesus knows us! For he doesn't say at the outset that we should give this will to the Lord, but first reveals that we will be well paid for this little service and that the Lord wants us to benefit a great deal by it. Even in this life he begins to reward us, as I shall now say.] Those in the world will be doing enough if they truly have the determination to do his will. You, daughters, will express this determination by both saying and doing, by both words and deeds, as indeed it seems we religious do. But at times we not only commit ourselves to giving the jewel but place it in his hand, only to take it back again. We are quick to be generous, but afterward so stingy that it would have been more fruitful, in part, if we had delayed in giving.

9. Because everything I have advised you about in this book is directed toward the complete gift of ourselves to the Creator, the surrender of our wills to his, and detachment

from creatures — and you have understood how important this is — I'm not going to say any more about the matter; but I will explain why our good Master teaches us to say the words mentioned above, as one who knows the many things we gain by rendering this service to his eternal Father. For we are preparing ourselves that we may quickly reach the end of our journey and drink the living water from the fount we mentioned.[3] Unless we give our wills entirely to the Lord so that in everything pertaining to us he might do what conforms with his will, we will never be allowed to drink from this fount. Drinking from it is perfect contemplation, that which you told me to write about.

10. In this contemplation, as I have already written,[4] we don't do anything ourselves. Neither do we labor, nor do we bargain, nor is anything else necessary — because everything else is an impediment and hindrance — than to say *fiat voluntas tua:* Your will, Lord, be done in me in every way and manner that you, my Lord, want. If you want it to be done with trials, strengthen me and let them come; if with persecutions, illnesses, dishonors, and a lack of life's necessities, here I am; I will not turn away, my Father, nor is it right that I turn my back on you. Since your Son gave you this will of mine in the name of all, there's no reason for any lack on my part. But grant me the favor of your kingdom that I may do your will, since he asked for this kingdom for me, and use me as you would your own possession, in conformity with your will.

11. O my Sisters, what strength lies in this gift! It does nothing less, when accompanied by the necessary determination, than draw the Almighty so that he becomes one with our lowliness, transforms us into himself, and effects a union of the Creator with the creature. Behold whether or not you are well paid and have a good Master; since he knows how the love of his Father can be obtained, he teaches us how and by what means we must serve him.

12. And the more our deeds show that these are not merely polite words, all the more does the Lord bring us to himself and raise the soul from itself and all earthly things so as to make it capable of receiving great favors, for he never finishes repaying this service in the present life. He esteems it so highly that we do not ourselves know how to ask for ourselves, and His Majesty never tires of giving. Not content with having made this soul one with himself, he begins to find his delight in it, reveal his secrets, and rejoice that it knows what it has gained and something of what he will give it. He makes it lose these exterior senses so that nothing will occupy it. This is rapture. And he begins to commune with the soul in so intimate a friendship that he not only gives it back its own will but gives it his. For in so great a friendship the Lord takes joy in putting the soul in command, as they say, and he does what it asks since it does his will. And he does this even better than the soul itself could, for he is powerful and does whatever he wants and never stops wanting this.

13. The poor soul cannot do what it desires even though it may want to; nor can it give anything save what is given. This is its greatest wealth: the more it serves, the more indebted it remains. It often grows weary seeing itself subject to so many difficulties, impediments, and fetters, which result from dwelling in the prison of this body. It would want to repay something of what it owes. To grow weary is quite foolish; for even though one does what's in one's power, what can those of us repay who, as I say, don't have anything save what we have received? All we can do is know ourselves and what we are capable of, which is to give our will, and give it completely. Everything else encumbers the soul brought here by the Lord and causes it harm rather than benefit. Only humility can do something, a humility not acquired by the intellect, but by a clear perception that comprehends in a moment the truth one would be unable to grasp in a long time through the work of the imagination about what a trifle we are and how very great God is.

14. I give you one counsel: that you don't think that through your own strength or efforts you can arrive, for reaching this stage is beyond our power; if you try to reach it, the devotion you have will grow cold. But with simplicity and humility, which will achieve everything, say: *fiat voluntas tua.*

UNION WITH GOD

The next petition of the Our Father ("Your will be done on earth as it is in heaven") stirs Teresa to speak of conformity with God's will and of the prayer of union.

32.1–3: A. Our Master has asked for and taught us to ask for something so valuable that it includes everything we can desire here below. Now we turn to both the gift he offers for us and what he asks of us.

- She speaks in a prayer to Jesus about what he requested for us and what he gives to us.

  - If you hadn't made the petition on our behalf, the task would be impossible.

  - When the Father gives what you ask for, the possibility is there for his will to be done.

- We must not make this petition just to say what everyone else is saying.

32.4: His will must be done whether we like it or not; make a virtue out of necessity. She begins again to pray to the Lord:

- What a comfort to me that you didn't want the fulfillment of your will to depend on my wretched will.

- I'd be in a fine state if this were up to me.

- Now I give mine to you even though I'm not free of self-interest.

- I have felt the gain that comes from freely abandoning my will to yours.

32.5: She speaks to her readers wanting to explain what is offered.

- To abandon our will to another is the hardest thing we can do if we do it as it should be done.

- Superiors see that we are weak and lead the strong and the weak in the same way, as though leading only the weak.

- The Lord knows what each can suffer.

32.6–8: I want to advise you about what his will is.

- His love for you is not small.

- He esteems highly what you give him.

- If you want to know what his will is, ask his Son.

- See what he gave to the one he loved most.

- To those he loves more, he gives more of what he gave his Son.

- Strive to suffer what the Lord desires you to suffer.

- To take back what we give him in the Our Father would be to mock him.

- The truth is that he rewards us beforehand so that we might give our will to him.

32.9: Everything I have advised you about in this book is directed toward the complete gift of ourselves to the Creator.

- We are preparing ourselves that we may quickly reach the end of our journey and drink the living water from this fount.

- Unless we give our wills entirely to the Lord, we will never be allowed to drink from this fount.

- Drinking from it is perfect contemplation.

32.10: In perfect contemplation we don't do anything ourselves other than say "Your will be done" in every way that you want.

- Grant me the favor of your kingdom that I may do your will.

- Use me as you would your own possession.

32.11–12: This gift draws the Almighty to become one with our lowliness.

- Our Master knows how the love of His Father can be obtained.

- The more our deeds show that our words are not merely polite ones, the more the Lord brings us to himself.

  - He never finishes repaying this service in our present life.

  - He begins to find his delight in the soul and reveal his secrets.

– He makes it lose its exterior senses so that nothing will occupy it.

– He begins to commune with the soul in so intimate a friendship that he gives it back its own will and gives it his.

– The Lord takes joy in putting the soul in command.

– He does what it asks.

32.13: The soul would want to repay something of what it owes.

• Only humility can do something: a clear perception of the truth about what a trifle we are and how very great God is.

• Reaching this stage is beyond our powers.

– If you try to reach it through your own strength, your devotion will grow cold.

– But with simplicity and humility say: "Your will be done."

INTERPRETIVE NOTES: 1. Jesus in his prayer in Gethsemane is the model for us and of how we must give God the gift of ourselves through conformity with his will. Offering God the gift of ourselves disposes us for God's full gift of himself to us in perfect contemplation. From chapter 19, we know that perfect contemplation corresponds to reaching the fount of living water. By having asked in this prayer for God's kingdom

CONCUPISENCE : to desire
ardently : covet ; strong
desires ego sexual desires

366   *The Way of Perfection: Study Edition*

to come, Jesus indicated the means by which both the Father's name will be hallowed and we will be made capable of making a gift of ourselves. Once we begin to experience a foretaste of the kingdom (when "earth has become heaven"), the possibility is there for God's will to be done. The focus of God's will is not on riches, delights, and honors, the objects of greed, concupiscence, and pride, but a life configured to Jesus' life.

2. Conformity with God's will bears on more than a mere act of the will. It demands the gift of yourself from the bottom-most depth of your being, as Teresa expresses in her spontaneous prayer (10). The struggle against concupiscence, greed, and pride matches the struggle for the virtues (love, detachment, and humility) that must necessarily accompany the life of prayer. Aware of her own self-interest as she recited this prayer, Teresa insists on the need for the favor of God's kingdom as a help to the poor soul that cannot do what it desires. Finally, she turns to humility and says only humility can do something. As it drew the King from heaven to the Virgin Mary's womb, so it will draw him to our souls (16.2). Here she describes humility as a clear perception of the truth about what a trifle we are and how very great God is. Blaise Pascal wrote in his *Pensées:* "There is nothing so perilous as what pleases God and man. For those states, which please God and man, have one property which pleases God, and another which pleases men; as the greatness of Saint Teresa. What pleased God was her deep humility in the midst of her revelations; what pleased men was her light. And so we torment ourselves to imitate her discourses, thinking to

imitate her conditions, and not so much to love what God loves, and to put ourselves in the state which God loves" (no. 499).

3. Doing God's will, making a complete gift of oneself, does not imply a suppression of human nature. Teresa sets down a note of caution in her *Interior Castle:* "Don't think the matter lies in my being so conformed to the will of God that if my father or brother dies I don't feel it, or that if there are trials or sicknesses I suffer them happily" (V.3.7).

4. This work takes the reader as far as the prayer of union or perfect contemplation. But mention is none-theless made that God, "who never tires of giving," will begin to reveal his secrets and find his delight in the soul, and even make it lose the exterior senses so that nothing will occupy it. These additional graces re-ceive lengthy treatment in her *Life;* she will turn to them again, with further developments, in the *Interior Castle.* Another important aspect of Teresa's teaching about this union is that God returns the soul's will to it and, in addition, gives it his own so that in its prayer of petition he does whatever it asks. "And whatever you ask in my name, I will do, so that the Father may be glorified in the Son" (Jn 14:13). The unerring character of this prayer has its base in the work and prayer of Christ. You must pray in his name (with his disposition and intention) and he himself will see to the fulfillment of the prayer (Jn 15:16). He knows that the Father always hears him (Jn 11:42). From this knowledge he can shape the prayer of those who are his, and take it up into his own prayer (Jn 17:9).

368 *The Way of Perfection: Study Edition*

5. How are we to know what God's will is? For Teresa's nuns it was a matter of practicing the virtues outlined here and following the style of life she set down in her constitutions. This union with God's will does not demand extraordinary exploits but the daily fulfillment of one's responsibilities. Cardinal Newman saw it this way: "By perfect we mean that which has no flaw in it, that which is complete, that which is consistent, that which is sound—we mean the opposite to imperfect. As we know well what imperfection in religious service means, we know by the contrast what is meant by perfection. He, then, is perfect who does the work of the day perfectly, and we need not go beyond this to seek for perfection. You need not go out of the *round* of the day. I insist on this because I think it will simplify our views, and fix our assertions on a definite aim. If you ask me what you are to do in order to be perfect, I say, first—Do not lie in bed beyond the due time of rising; give your first thoughts to God; make a good visit to the Blessed Sacrament; say the Angelus devoutly; eat and drink to God's glory; say the Rosary well; be recollected; keep out bad thoughts; make your evening meditation well; examine yourself daily; go to bed in good time, and you are already perfect" (*Meditations and Devotions*).

QUESTIONS FOR DISCUSSION: 1. What is the main characteristic of union?

2. What is this whole book directed toward?

3. How can perfect contemplation help us toward this goal?

4. How does perfect contemplation differ from the prayer of quiet?

Chapter 33

Deals with the great need we have that the Lord give us what we ask for in these words of the Our Father: Panem nostrum quotidianum da nobis hodie.

A S I HAVE SAID,[1] Jesus understands what a difficult thing it is he offers for us. He knows our weakness, that we often show we do not understand what the Lord's will is. We are weak and he is merciful. He knows that a means was necessary. He saw it would not be in any way to our benefit if we failed to give what he gave, because all our gain lies in giving this. He saw that doing the Father's will was difficult. If we tell a rich man living in luxury that it is God's will that he be careful and use moderation at table so that others might at least have bread to eat, for they are dying of hunger, he will bring up a thousand reasons for not understanding this save in accordance with his own selfish purposes. If we tell backbiters that it is God's will that they love their neighbor as themselves, they will become impatient and no reason will suffice to make them understand. We can tell religious who have grown accustomed to freedom and comfort that they should remember their obligation to give good example and should keep in mind that when they say these words they should do more than just say words; they should put them into practice since they have promised them under vow. And we can tell them they should remember that it is God's will that they be faithful to their vows, and that they should note that if they give scandal they are acting very contrary to them, even though they may not be breaking them entirely; and that since they promised poverty, they should observe it without subterfuge, for this is what the Lord wills. But it is just useless to insist nowadays with some of them. What would happen if the Lord had not provided for us with the remedy he gave? There would have been only a very few who would have carried out these words he spoke for us to the Father, *fiat voluntas tua.*

Now then, once Jesus saw the need, he sought out a wonderful means by which to show the extreme of his love for us, and in his own name and in that of his brothers he made the following petition: "Give us this day, Lord, our daily bread."

Let us understand, Sisters, for the love of God, what our good Master is asking for; it is a matter of life and death not to pass over these words hastily. Consider what you have given as very little since you will receive so much.

2. Now I think — unless one has a better opinion — that Jesus observed what he had given for us, how important it was that we in turn give this, and the great difficulty there is in our doing so, as was said,[2] since we are the way we are: inclined to base things and with so little love and courage that it was necessary for us to see his love and courage in order to be awakened — and not just once but every day. After he saw all this, he must have resolved to remain with us here below. Since to do this was something so serious and important, he desired that it come from the hand of the Eternal Father. For even though they are one and he knew that what he did on earth God would do in heaven and consider good — since his will and that of his Father were one — the humility of Jesus was such that he wanted, as it were, to ask permission. He already knew that his Father loved him and took his delight in him.[3] He well understood that he was asking for more in this request than he was in the others, for he knew beforehand the death

they would make him die and the dishonors and insults he would suffer.

3. Well, what father could there be, Lord, who in having given us his son, and a son like this who receives such treatment, would consent that he remain among us every day to suffer? Certainly no father, Lord, but yours. You well know whom you are petitioning.

Oh, God help me, what great love from the Son and what great love from the Father! Yet I am not so surprised about Jesus, for since he had already said, *fiat voluntas tua*, he had to do that will, being who he is. Yes, for he is not like us! Since, then, he knows that he does it by loving us as himself, he went about looking for ways of doing it with greater perfection, even though his fulfillment of this commandment was at a cost to himself. But you, Eternal Father, how is it that you consented? Why do you desire to see your Son every day in such wretched hands? Since you have already desired to see him in these hands and given your consent, you have seen how they treated him. How can you in your compassion now see him insulted day after day? And how many insults will be committed today against this Most Blessed Sacrament! In how many enemies' hands must the Father see him! How much irreverence from these heretics!

4. O eternal Lord! Why do you accept such a petition? Why do you consent to it? Don't look at his love for us, because in exchange for doing your will perfectly, and doing it for us, he allows himself to be crushed to pieces each day. It is for you, my Lord, to look after him, since he will let nothing deter him. Why must all our good come at his expense? Why does he remain silent before all and not know how to speak for himself, but only for us? Well, shouldn't there be someone to speak for this most loving Lamb? [Allow me, Lord, to speak — since you have willed to leave him to our power —

and to beseech you since he so truly obeyed you and with so much love gave himself to us.] I have noticed how in this petition alone he repeats the words: first he says and asks the Father to give us this daily bread, and then repeats, "give it to us this day, Lord," invoking the Father again.[4] It's as though Jesus tells the Father that he is now ours since the Father has given him to us to die for us; and asks that the Father not take him from us until the end of the world; that he allow him to serve each day. May this move your hearts, my daughters, to love your Spouse, for there is no slave who would willingly say he is a slave, and yet it seems that Jesus is honored to be one.

5. O Eternal Father! How much this humility deserves! What treasure do we have that could buy your Son? The sale of him, we already know, was for thirty pieces of silver.[5] But to buy him, no price is sufficient. Since by sharing in our nature he has become one with us here below — and as Lord of his own will — he reminds the Father that because he belongs to him the Father in turn can give him to us. And so he says, "our bread." He doesn't make any difference between himself and us, but we make one by not giving ourselves up each day for His Majesty.

JESUS WITH US IN THE EUCHARIST

Teresa turns to the next petition: "Give us this day our daily bread." Giving some examples of the difficulty people have in doing God's will, she marvels at how the Lord has provided for us through the Eucharist.

33.1: Jesus saw that doing the Father's will was difficult.

- Examples of the difficulty: the rich man living in luxury, the backbiters, the religious accustomed to freedom.

- Jesus sought a wonderful means to show the extreme of his love for us through this petition for our daily bread.

33.2: We have so little love and courage that it was necessary for us to see these in Jesus for us to be awakened.

- He must have resolved to remain with us here below.

- Although he and the Father are one, Jesus in his humility, as it were, wanted to ask permission.

33.3–5: A. What father, having given us his son, would consent that he remain among us every day to suffer? This thought leads Teresa into prayer.

- What great love from the Son and what great love from the Father!

- Jesus does the Father's will by loving us, and went about looking for ways to love us with greater perfection.

- You, Eternal Father, why do you desire to see your Son every day in such wretched hands?

- How many insults will be committed today against the Most Blessed Sacrament!

- O eternal Lord! Why do you accept such a petition?

- It is for you, my Lord, to look after him.

- Why does he remain silent? He speaks not for himself but only for us.

- In this petition he asks the Father not to take him away from us until the end of the world.

B. She addresses her daughters with the hope that their hearts may be moved to love their Spouse.

C. She returns to her prayer to the Father.

- What treasure can buy your Son?

- He reminds the Father that he belongs to him and therefore the Father can give him to us.

- He says "our bread," making no difference between himself and us.

- But we make a difference by not giving ourselves.

INTERPRETIVE NOTES: 1. Teresa at once interprets the words of this petition as referring to the Eucharist. She sees in the Eucharist a means chosen by Jesus to show the extent of his love for us. The Eucharist is, in fact and above all, the sacrament of God's love for us, a love without conditions. By noting Jesus' love and courage we can be awakened. Why courage? Because, as Teresa poignantly observes, for Christ to remain present with us and for us in the Eucharist, he must suffer every day. As at the very beginning of the Our Father, Teresa is now carried aloft in prayer. What she cannot understand is how the Father would consent to the petition made by Jesus for us in the Our Father. Then in her love she begs the Father for Jesus' sake. He pleads for us, shouldn't there be someone to plead for him? It strikes us as strange that she would take on the role of pleading to the Father for the release, as it were, of Jesus. In her *Life*, Teresa tells of a prayer in which the soul is immersed in a sea of love but not to the extent that it cannot function. In this love it "speaks folly in a thousand holy ways" (16.2). But not everything said in her prayer is folly. Teresa understands that the self-giving of Jesus to his own and to the world reveals the self-giving of the Father who out of love for us gives what is most precious to himself, his Son. If we find folly in her words, it lies only in her pleading. The eucharistic gesture itself of Jesus' distribution of himself to his own and through them to the world is an irreversible gesture lasting till the end of time. There can be no talk to the Father—making allowances, however, for the folly of love—of taking back what the Son has definitively given.

2. We gather that Teresa has no doubt that by remaining with us in the Eucharist Jesus continues to suffer. This perception is what stirs her so deeply. Five years after she wrote this work, she was once undergoing the

"great suffering" she sometimes had to bear "of being separated from God." After she had endured three days of this, the Lord appeared and broke the bread Teresa was about to force herself to eat — because of her illness — and said: "Eat, daughter, and bear up as best you can. What you suffer grieves me, but it suits you now." Teresa then adds: "The words 'grieves me' made me stop to think because it doesn't seem to me he can be sorrowful over anything any more" (ST 22). The glorified body of the Lord still bears the wounds; the crucified One is the risen One and never becomes past or mere remembrance. By continuing to remain present among us as self-gift, Jesus shows his commitment to us in love. Could a love that would be untouched by our rejection of it or our coldness or by our sufferings be called love?

QUESTIONS FOR DISCUSSION: 1. How can the Eucharist help us to do the Father's will?

2. In what ways might I benefit from Teresa's prayer in this chapter?

Chapter 34

Continues on the same subject. The matter is very helpful with regard to the time immediately following reception of the most Blessed Sacrament.

IN THIS PETITION THE WORD "DAILY" seems to mean forever. Reflecting upon why after the word "daily" the Lord said "give us this day, Lord," that is, be ours every day, I've come to think that it is because here on earth we possess him and also in heaven we will possess him if we profit well by his company.[1] He, in fact, doesn't remain with us for any other reason than to help, encourage, and sustain us in doing this will that we have prayed might be done in us.

2. In saying "this day," it seems to me, he is referring to one day: that which lasts as long as the world and no longer. And one day indeed! With regard to the unfortunate ones who will be condemned (who will not enjoy him in the next life), it will not be the Lord's fault if they let themselves be conquered.[2] He doesn't stop encouraging them until the battle is over. They will have no excuse or complaint to make to the Father for taking him away when they most need him. So the Son tells his Father that because there is no more than one day the Father should let him pass it in servitude. Since the Father has already given us his Son and, just because he wanted to, sent him into the world, the Son, just because he wants to, desires not to abandon us but to remain here with us, to the greater glory of his friends and the affliction of his

enemies. He asks again for no more than to be with us this day only, because it is a fact that he has given us this most sacred bread forever. His Majesty gave us, as I have said, the manna and nourishment of his humanity that we might find him at will and not die of hunger,[3] save through our own fault. In no matter how many ways the soul may desire to eat, it will find delight and consolation in the most Blessed Sacrament. [I don't want to think the Lord had in mind the other bread that is used for our bodily needs and nourishment; nor would I want you to have that in mind. The Lord was in the most sublime contemplation (for whoever has reached such a stage has no more remembrance that he is in the world than if he were not, however much there may be to eat), and would he have placed so much emphasis on the petition that he as well as ourselves eat? It wouldn't make sense to me. He is teaching us to set our wills on heavenly things and to ask that we might begin enjoying him from here below; and would he get us involved in something so base as asking to eat? As if he didn't know us! For once we start worrying about bodily needs, those of the soul will be forgotten! Well, we are such temperate people that we are satisfied by little and ask for little! On the contrary, the more he gives us the more we think we are lacking everything, even water. Let those, my daughters, who want more than is necessary ask for this material bread.] There is no need or trial or persecution that is not easy to suffer if we begin to enjoy the delight and consolation of this sacred bread.

3. Ask the Father, daughters, together with the Lord, to give you your Spouse "this day" so that you will not be seen in this world without him. To temper such great happiness it's sufficient that he remain disguised in these accidents of bread and wine. This is torment enough for anyone who has no other love than him nor any other consolation. Beg him not to fail you, and to give you the dispositions to receive him worthily.

4. Don't worry about the other bread, those of you who have sincerely surrendered yourselves to the will of God. I mean during these times of prayer when you should be dealing with more important things; there are other times for working and for earning your bread. [Have no fear that you will be in want of bread if you are not wanting in what you have said about the surrender of yourselves to God's will. And indeed, daughters, I say for myself, if I should maliciously fail in this surrender, as I have many other times, I would not beg that he give me this bread or anything else to eat. Let me die of hunger; why should I want life if with it I am daily gaining more of eternal death?] Carefully avoid wasting your thoughts at any time on what you will eat. Let the body work, for it is good that you work to sustain yourselves; let your soul be at rest. Leave this care, as has been amply pointed out,[4] to your Spouse; he will care for you always.

5. Your attitude should be like that of servants when they begin to serve. Their care is about pleasing their master in everything. But the master is obliged to provide his servants with food as long as they are in the house and serve him, unless the master is so poor that he doesn't have enough either for himself or for his servants. In our case this isn't so; the Master always is, and will be, rich and powerful. Well, it wouldn't be right for the servants to go about asking for food when they know that the master of the house takes care of providing it for them, and must do so. The master would rightly tell his servants to be occupied in serving and seeking ways to please the master, for the servants, by worrying about what isn't their business, would be doing everything wrong.

Thus, Sisters, let whoever so wants be concerned with asking for this bread. As for ourselves, let us ask the Eternal Father that we might merit to receive our heavenly bread in such a way that the Lord may reveal himself to the eyes of our soul and make himself thereby known since our bodily eyes cannot delight in beholding him, because he is so hidden. Such knowledge is another kind of satisfying and delightful sustenance that maintains life. [In order to sustain life we will be desiring that other bread more often than we want and asking for it even without realizing we're doing so. There's no need to stir ourselves to ask for it; for our wretched tendency toward base things will awaken us, as I say, more often than we may desire. But let us watch so that we don't advertently place our care on anything other than begging the Lord for what I have mentioned; in having this, we will have everything.]

6. Do you think this heavenly food fails to provide sustenance, even for these bodies, that it is not a great medicine even for bodily ills? I know that it is. I know a person[5] with serious illnesses, who often experiences great pain, who through this bread had them taken away as though by a gesture of the hand and was made completely well. This is a common experience, and the illnesses are very recognizable, for I don't think they could be feigned. And because the wonders this most sacred bread effects in those who worthily receive it are well known, I will not mention many that could be mentioned regarding this person I've spoken of. I was able to know of them, and I know that this is no lie. But the Lord had given her such living faith that when she heard some persons saying they would have liked to have lived at the time Christ our Good walked in the world, she used to laugh to herself. She wondered what more they wanted since in the most Blessed Sacrament they had him just as truly present as he was then.

7. But I know that for many years, when she received Communion, this person, though she was not very perfect, strove to strengthen her faith so that in receiving her Lord it was as if, with her bodily eyes, she saw him enter her house. Since she believed that this Lord truly entered her poor home, she freed herself from all exterior things when it was possible

and entered to be with him. She strove to recollect the senses so that all of them would take notice of so great a good, I mean that they would not impede the soul from recognizing it. She considered she was at his feet and wept with the Magdalene, no more nor less than if she were seeing him with her bodily eyes in the house of the Pharisee.[6] And even though she didn't feel devotion, faith told her that he was indeed there.

8. If we don't want to be fools and blind the intellect there's no reason for doubt. Receiving Communion is not like picturing with the imagination, as when we reflect upon the Lord on the cross or in other episodes of the Passion, when we picture within ourselves how things happened to him in the past. In Communion the event is happening now, and it is entirely true. There's no reason to go looking for him in some other place farther away. Since we know that Jesus is with us as long as the natural heat doesn't consume the accidents of bread, we should approach him. Now, then, if when he went about in the world the mere touch of his robes cured the sick,[7] why doubt, if we have faith, that miracles will be worked while he is within us and that he will give what we ask of him, since he is in our house? His Majesty is not accustomed to paying poorly for his lodging if the hospitality is good.

9. If it pains you not to see him with your bodily eyes, consider that seeing him so is not fitting for us. To see him in his glorified state is different from seeing him as he was when he walked through this world. On account of our natural weakness there is no person capable of enduring such a glorious sight, nor would anyone in the world want to continue in it. In seeing this Eternal Truth one would see that all the things we pay attention to here below are lies and jokes. And in beholding such great Majesty, how would a little sinner like myself who has so much offended him remain so close to him? Beneath that bread he is easy to deal with. If a king were disguised it wouldn't matter to us at all if we conversed with

him without so many gestures of awe and respect. It seems he would be obliged to put up with this lack since he is the one who disguised himself. Who would otherwise dare approach so unworthily, with so much lukewarmness, and with so many imperfections!

10. Oh, how we fail to know what we are asking for;[8] and how his wisdom provided in a better way! He reveals himself to those who he sees will benefit by his presence. Even though they fail to see him with their bodily eyes, he has many methods of showing himself to the soul, through great interior feelings and through other different ways. Be with him willingly; don't lose so good an occasion for conversing with him as is the hour after having received Communion.[9] If obedience should command something, Sisters, strive to leave your soul with the Lord. If you immediately turn your thoughts to other things, if you pay no attention and take no account of the fact that he is within you, how will he be able to reveal himself to you? This, then, is a good time for our Master to teach us, and for us to listen to him, kiss his feet because he wanted to teach us, and beg him not to leave.[10]

11. If you have to pray to him by looking at his picture, it would seem to me foolish. You would be leaving the Person himself in order to look at a picture of him. Wouldn't it be silly if a person we love very much and of whom we have a portrait came to see us and we stopped speaking with him so as to carry on a conversation with the portrait? Do you want to know when it is very good to have a picture of Christ and when it is a thing in which I find much delight? When he himself is absent, or when by means of a great dryness he wants to make us feel he is absent. It is then a wonderful comfort to see an image of One whom we have so much reason to love.[11] Wherever I turn my eyes, I would want to see his image. With what better or more pleasing thing can our eyes be occupied than with One who loves so much and who has in himself all

goods. Unfortunate are those heretics who through their own fault have lost this consolation among others.

12. But after having received the Lord, since you have the Person himself present, strive to close the eyes of the body and open those of the soul and look into your own heart. For I tell you, and tell you again, and would like to tell you many times that you should acquire the habit of doing this every time you receive Communion and strive to have such a conscience that you will be allowed to enjoy this blessing frequently. Although he comes disguised, the disguise, as I have said,[12] does not prevent him from being recognized in many ways, in conformity with the desire we have to see him. And you can desire to see him so much that he will reveal himself to you entirely.

13. On the other hand, if we pay no attention to him but after receiving him leave him and go seeking after other base things, what is there for him to do? Must he force us to see him, since he wants to reveal himself to us? No, for they didn't treat him so well when he let himself be seen openly by all and told them clearly who he was; very few were those who believed him. So His Majesty is being merciful enough to all of us who love him, by letting us know that it is he who is present in the most Blessed Sacrament. He doesn't want to show himself openly, communicate his grandeurs, and give his treasures except to those who he knows desire him greatly; these are his true friends. I tell you that whoever is not his true friend and does not draw near to receive him as such, by doing what lies in her power, will never trouble him with requests that he reveal himself. Such a person will hardly have fulfilled what the church requires when she will leave and quickly forget what took place. Thus, such a person hurries on as soon as she can to other business affairs, occupations, and worldly impediments so that the Lord of the house may not occupy it.

EUCHARISTIC EXPERIENCE

Teresa now more particularly interprets the petition of the Our Father from a Eucharistic perspective. She reveals her own experience of the Eucharist out of which she draws counsels for her readers.

34.1–2: This day refers to one day, the day that lasts as long as the world.

- The Son desires not to abandon us during this day.

- His Majesty gave us the manna and nourishment of his humanity that we might find him at will and not die of hunger.

  - He is teaching us to set our wills on heavenly things.

  - He wants us to begin enjoying him here on earth.

  - He doesn't want us to get involved in worrying about bodily needs.

  - The more he gives us of material things the more we think we are lacking everything.

  - Let those who want more than is necessary ask for this material bread.

- Need or trial are easy to suffer if we begin to enjoy the delight and consolation of this sacred bread.

34.3: Ask the Father to give you your Spouse "this day" so that you will not be without him.

- To temper you happiness it's sufficient that he remain disguised.

- The disguise is the accidents of bread and wine.

34.4–5: Don't worry about the other bread.

- Work to sustain yourselves and let your soul be at rest.

- As servants, leave the care for earthly sustenance to your Master.

- As for us, let us ask for our heavenly bread in such a way that the Lord may reveal himself to the eyes of our soul.

34.6–7: A. Teresa now speaks from her experience that this heavenly food is a great medicine even for bodily ills.

- Through this bread she had the great bodily pains of an illness taken away.

- The illnesses were very recognizable and couldn't have been feigned.

B. This person strove to strengthen her faith so that she received the Lord as though he were entering into her house.

34.8: Why doubt that he will give us what we ask of him, since he is in our house?

34.9: On account of our natural weakness no one in the world could endure seeing him in his glorified state.

- Beneath that bread, he is present in a way that is easier for us to deal with.

- He reveals himself to those who will benefit by his presence, even though they do not see him with bodily eyes.

34.10–13: He has many methods of showing himself to the soul through great interior feelings, and through other different ways.

- If you take no account of his presence within you, how will he be able to reveal himself to you?

- This is a good time for our Master to teach us, and for us to listen.

- Do not leave the Person himself in order to look at his picture.

- There are other times when it is good to have a picture of Christ.

- After receiving the Lord, since you have the Person present, close the eyes of your body, open those of your soul, and look into your heart.

- Despite his disguise, he is recognized in conformity with one's desire.

- He gives his treasures to those who he knows desire him greatly.

- Those who are not his true friends will hurry on as soon as possible to other business affairs and occupations.

INTERPRETIVE NOTES: 1. When we pray this petition today, we can remember the physical hunger suffered by large numbers of people. The drama of world hunger calls Christians, especially when they recite this prayer, to be effectively concerned with providing bread to the hungry. In Teresa's situation, the nuns themselves had to learn poverty of spirit and trust in the Lord that he would provide them with their daily bread and other material needs. She had dealt with the topic in Chapter 2 of this work. Now, since her readers asked her to write about prayer and contemplation, she focuses on the spiritual meaning of the words, seeing in them a request for the bread of life. This bread, the Blessed Sacrament, is the manna which will provide not only nourishment but delight and consolation. It will make need, trial, and persecution easier to bear.

2. The Greek word *epiousios,* usually translated as "daily," is not found in any Greek literature, only in the Lord's Prayer. St. Jerome translated it as "supersubstantial," above the essence or substance. In this interpretation, the bread would be living, superessential bread taken for the sustenance of immortal life, Christ himself; this is the bread that should be sought first of all: "Seek first the kingdom of God and his righteousness, and all these things will be given you besides" (Mt 6:33).

3. The section within brackets in no. 2 was crossed out with large strokes by the censor in Teresa's first draft where she asserts that the Lord couldn't have been asking for the bread that is used for bodily needs, but

that he was teaching us to set our wills on heavenly things. The censor wrote in the margin: "Christ our Lord asked for everything that pertained to the sustenance of both body and soul, material bread and the Eucharist. And this is what the church asks for in the litany."

4. Teresa puzzles over the expression "this day" and concludes that it refers to time that will continue until the end of the world. In the unrolling of the plan of God an event has come in relation to which everything is defined as "before" or "after." The time of Jesus is the fullness of time; he has introduced the definitive element. His time is not only in the middle of earthly duration; it completely dominates times. Jesus' time is the acceptable time, the "now," the day of salvation put within reach of all. It is the today of God during which we are called to conversion and to be attentive to the voice of the Lord (2 Cor 6:1–2; Heb 3:7). For this day, Teresa notes, Jesus does not stop encouraging us until the battle is over.

5. In paragraphs 6–7 she begins to speak from the perspective of her own experience of the Eucharist. She observes that the heavenly food provides sustenance even for the body, providing a medicine for bodily ills. The person she refers to as having very serious illnesses and pain is herself, and these were sometimes taken away when she received the Eucharist.

6. The next more important reality in her experience was the intensity of her faith in the Lord's presence. When receiving Communion she felt as though the

Lord were entering her house as he did the house Martha and Mary. It is the personal aspects of the Eucharist that at once draw her: Jesus himself, his presence, friendship, intimacy, communion with him. She entered within with him, remaining at his feet in the prayer of recollection, thus interiorizing the presence, communing with the Lord as really as did Martha or Mary or Lazarus or some of the other biblical persons who knew him.

7. The "accidents" was a scholastic term used to refer to the appearances of bread and wine under which the Lord is present. Teresa urges her readers to realize that he is just as much present as he would be if they saw him with their bodily eyes; they should look at him in faith with the eyes of their souls. She marvels at how good it is that the Lord comes to us "disguised"; we would, indeed, be unable to endure the vision of his glory. In her *Life* she had written: "When I approached to receive Communion and recalled that extraordinary majesty I had seen and considered that it was present in the Blessed Sacrament (the Lord often desires that I behold it in the host), my hair stood on end; the whole experience seemed to annihilate me. O my Lord! If you did not hide your grandeur, who would approach so often a union of something so dirty and miserable with such great majesty! May the angels and all creatures praise you, for you so measure things in accordance with our weakness that when we rejoice in your sovereign favors your great power does not so frighten us that, as weak and wretched people, we would not dare enjoy them" (38.19).

8. In the Eucharist, the Lord assumes this "disguised" presence, subject to the limits of the sacramental symbol, so as to commune with us and be more approachable in consideration of our human condition. It is easier to speak with a king if he is disguised. "Beneath that bread, he is easy to deal with" (9). On account of the presence, Teresa prizes the time after Communion as a privileged time for the prayer of recollection. "He has many methods of showing himself to the soul, through great interior feelings and through other different ways" (10).

QUESTIONS FOR DISCUSSION: 1. What are some of the blessings offered to us in the mystery of the Eucharist?

2. How does Teresa relate the prayer of recollection to the reception of the Eucharist?

3. Why is the hour after Communion a good time for prayer, and what might we do if we are not free for prayer at that time?

Chapter 35

With a prayerful exclamation to the Eternal Father concludes the subject that was begun.

BECAUSE THIS MATTER is so important I have greatly enlarged upon it, even though in discussing the prayer of recollection I spoke of the significance of entering within ourselves to be alone with God. When you do not receive Communion, daughters, but hear Mass, you can make a spiritual communion. Spiritual communion is highly beneficial; through it you can recollect yourselves in the same way after Mass, for the love of this Lord is thereby deeply impressed on the soul. If we prepare ourselves to receive him, he never fails to give, in many ways which we do not understand. It is like approaching a fire; even though the fire may be a large one, it will not be able to warm you well if you turn away and hide your hands, though you will still get more heat than you would if you were in a place without one. But it is something else if we desire to approach him. If the soul is disposed (I mean, if it wants to get warm), and if it remains there for a while, it will stay warm for many hours.

2. Now then, Sisters, consider that if in the beginning you do not fare well (for it could be that the devil will make you feel afflicted and constrained in heart since he knows the great damage that will be caused him by this recollection), the devil will make you think you find more devotion in other things

and less in this recollection after Communion. Do not abandon this practice; the Lord will see in it how much you love him.
Remember that there are few souls who accompany him and
follow him in trials. Let us suffer something for him; His Majesty will repay you for it. Remember also how many persons
there are who not only refuse to remain with him but rudely
reject him. Well, we have to suffer something that he may understand we desire to see him. And since he suffers and will
suffer everything in order to find even one soul that will receive him and lovingly keep him within, let your desire be to
do this. If there isn't anyone who will do it, the Eternal Father
will rightly refuse to let him remain with us. But the Father is
so fond of friends and so much the Lord of his servants that in
seeing the will of his good Son he doesn't want to hinder this
excellent work; in it the Son's love for him is fully demonstrat-
ed [by the invention of this admirable means in which he shows
how much he loves us and helps us suffer our trials].

3. Well, holy Father in heaven, since you desire and accept this work, and it is clear that you will not deny us anything that is good for us, there has to be someone, as I said in
the beginning,[1] who will speak for your Son since he never
looks out for himself. Let us be the ones, daughters, even
though the thought is a bold one, we being who we are. But
obeying and trusting in the Lord's command to us that we ask,[2]
let us beseech His Majesty in the name of Jesus that, since nothing remained for him to do and he left sinners a gift as great
as this one, he might in his compassion desire and be pleased
to provide a remedy that his Son may not be this badly treated. Let us beseech him that, since his Son provided a means
so good that we may offer him many times in sacrifice, this precious gift may avail; that there'll be no advance made in the
very great evil and disrespect committed and shown in places
where this most Blessed Sacrament is present among those
Lutherans, where churches are destroyed, so many priests lost,
and the sacraments taken away.[3]

4. Well, what is this, my Lord and my God! Either bring the world to an end or provide a remedy for these very serious evils. There is no heart that can suffer them, not even among those of us who are wretched. I beseech you, Eternal Father, that you suffer them no longer. Stop this fire, Lord, for if you will you can. Behold that your Son is still in the world. Through his reverence may all these ugly and abominable and filthy things cease. In his beauty and purity he doesn't deserve to be in a house where there are things of this sort. Do not answer for our sakes, Lord; we do not deserve it. Do it for your Son's sake. We don't dare beseech you that he be not present with us; what would become of us? For if something appeases you, it is having a loved one like this here below. Since some means must be had, my Lord, may Your Majesty provide it.

5. O my God, would that I might have begged you much and served you diligently so as to be able to ask for this great favor in payment for my services, since you don't leave anyone without pay! But I have not done so, Lord; rather, perhaps I am the one who has angered you so that my sins have caused these many evils to come about. Well, what is there for me to do, my Creator, but offer this most blessed bread to you, and even though you have given it to us, return it to you and beg you through the merits of your Son to grant me this favor since in so many ways he has merited that you do so? Now, Lord, now; make the sea calm! May this ship, which is the church, not always have to journey in a tempest like this. Save us, Lord, for we are perishing.[4]

EUCHARISTIC PRAYER

After some words about spiritual communion, Teresa concludes with a spontaneous Eucharistic prayer.

35.1–2: The prayer of recollection after Communion may also be practiced through spiritual communion.

- The love of the Lord is thereby deeply impressed.

- He never fails to give in many ways.

- A large fire cannot warm you if you turn away from it.

- If the soul wants to get warm and remains near the fire for a while, it will stay warm for many hours.

- Do not abandon this practice; the Lord will see in it how much you love him.

- Let your desire be to lovingly keep him within, since he will suffer everything in order to find one soul that will receive him.

35.3–5: She begins her Eucharistic prayer: Obeying and trusting in the Lord's command, let us beseech His Majesty in the name of Jesus:

- that since nothing remained for him to do,

- and he left sinners a gift as great as this,

- that in his compassion he might be pleased to provide a remedy that his Son may not be this badly treated.

- Let us beseech him that since his Son provided the means by which we may offer him many times in sacrifice that there'll be no advance in the disrespect now shown among those Lutherans.

- Eternal Father stop this fire; through your Son's reverence make these evil things cease.

- Answer our prayer for your Son's sake.

- What would become of us if he were not present with us?

- Perhaps I am the one who has angered you that my sins have caused these many evils to come about.

- What is there for me to do but offer you this most blessed bread and beg you through the merits of your Son to make the sea calm?

- May your ship, which is the church, not have to journey in a tempest like this.

INTERPRETIVE NOTES: 1. Making no specific command about the frequency of the reception of the Eucharist, the Lord is seen to have compared it to manna which was the daily fare of the Jews wandering in the desert (Jn 6:49–50). In apostolic times the Eucharist was probably received every week at "the breaking of the bread." In the 2nd and 3rd centuries it was probably not uncommon for Christians to receive Communion daily. In the 4th and 5th century Christians normally communicated every day. From the 6th century to the 12th, a general decline in the practice of frequent reception took place. The Fourth Lateran Council (1215) had to demand that all Christians communicate yearly to remain in good standing as members of the church. The Council of Trent expressed the desire that all Christians be so disposed (by confessing grave sins) that they could receive Communion at every Mass they attended. Despite the teaching of the Council of Trent, the return to frequent Communion developed slowly. In recent times, the mitigation of the eucharistic fast and emphasis on the Mass as a sacrificial meal have led to an increase in the practice of frequent Communion. Spiritual communion is a communion in desire when actual Communion is not possible. Those wishing to partake spiritually in the body of Christ are now advised to prepare themselves as if they were attending Mass so that the link between Communion and the Mass is not ignored.

2. In view of the above facts, frequent Communion was not customary in Teresa's day. She tells how her Dominican confessor got her to return to the practice of prayer and says that "he had me receive Communion every 15 days" (L 7.17). Though St. Ignatius of Loyola encouraged daily Communion, Jesuit theologians of Teresa's century allowed only weekly reception. Teresa attempted to counteract this whole situation by recommending spiritual Communion to her nuns. In her own case, when her directors told her their conclusion that her experiences originated with the devil, they also warned her not to receive Communion so often (L 25.14). But Teresa's longings to receive were often vehement, and she eventually obtained permission to receive Communion daily. In her *Life*, she gives us an

example of what these longings could become: "On occasion there come over me such ardent desires to receive Communion that I don't think they could be exaggerated. They came upon me one morning when it was raining so hard it seemed impossible to leave the house. When I was outside the house, I was already so outside myself with the desire for Communion that even should lances have been held to my heart I think I'd have gone into their midst; how much more into the midst of rain" (39.22).

3. The section ending these chapters on the Eucharist resemble a eucharistic prayer: "Obeying and trusting in the Lord's command...let us beseech His Majesty in the name of Jesus that, since nothing remained for him to do and he left sinners a gift as great as this one.... Let us beseech him that, since his Son provided a means so good that we may offer him many times in sacrifice, this precious gift may avail.... I beseech you, Eternal Father.... Behold that your Son is still in the world. Through his reverence may all these ugly and abominable and filthy things cease.... Do not answer for our sakes, Lord.... Do it for your Son's sake.... If something appeases you, it is having a loved one like this here below.... O my God, would that I might have begged you much and served you diligently.... Well, what is there for me to do, my Creator, but offer this most blessed bread to you...and beg you through the merits of your Son to grant me this favor.... Now, Lord.... May this ship, which is the church, not always have to journey in a tempest like this. Save us, Lord, for we are perishing" (3–5).

QUESTIONS FOR DISCUSSION: 1. What is a spiritual communion, and when might be a good time to make a spiritual communion?

2. What are some of the characteristics of Teresa's Eucharistic prayer?

Chapter 36

Discusses these words of the Our Father: Dimitte nobis debita nostra.

SINCE OUR GOOD MASTER SAW that with this heavenly bread everything is easy for us, save through our own fault, and that we can carry out very well what we have said about the Father's will being done in us, he now tells the Father to forgive us our debts since we ourselves forgive. Thus, he says, going on with the prayer he teaches us, "And forgive us, Lord, our debts as we forgive our debtors."[1]

2. Let us observe, Sisters, that he doesn't say "as we will forgive." We can thereby understand that whoever asks for a gift as great as the one last mentioned and whoever has already surrendered his will to God's will should have already forgiven. So, he says, "as we forgive." Thus, whoever may have said sincerely to the Lord *fiat voluntas tua* should have done that will entirely; at least have had the resolve to.

You see here why the saints were pleased with the wrongs and persecutions they suffered; they then had something to offer the Lord when they prayed to him. What will someone as poor as I do, who has had so little to pardon and so much to be pardoned for?

This is a matter, Sisters, that we should reflect upon very much: that something so serious and important, as that our

Lord forgive us our faults, which deserve eternal fire, be done by means of something so lowly as our forgiving others. And I have so little opportunity to offer even this lowly thing, that the Lord has to pardon me for nothing. [What can be said against someone like myself, or what wrong can be done to her who has deserved to be always mistreated by the demons? If the world were to treat me very badly, such mistreatment would be just. In sum, my Lord, I have nothing as a result to give you by means of which I may ask you to forgive my debts. May your Son pardon me; no one has done me an injustice, and so I have nothing to pardon for your sake, unless, Lord, you accept my desire. It seems to me that anything I might forgive I would forgive in order that you would forgive me, or to do your will unconditionally. Yet I don't know what I would do actually if I were condemned without fault. Now I see myself so deserving of blame in your presence that everyone falls short with respect to blaming me; although those who do not know what I am, as you know, think they are offending me.] Here your mercy fits in well. May you be blessed for putting up with one so poor as I. What your Son says in the name of all has to exclude me because of what I am and because I am so penniless.

3. But, my Lord, are there some persons in my company who have not understood this? If there are, I beg them in your name to remember this and pay no attention to the little things they call wrongs. It seems that, like children, we are making houses out of straw with these ceremonious little rules of etiquette. Oh, God help me, Sisters, if we knew what honor is and what losing honor consists in! Now I am not speaking of ourselves, for it would be quite bad for us not to have understood this yet, but of myself at the time when I prized honor without understanding what it was. I was following the crowd [through what I heard.] Oh, by how many things was I offended! I am ashamed now. Yet, I wasn't at that time one of those

who pay close attention to these little rules of etiquette. But neither was I careful about the main rule, because I didn't consider or pay any heed to the honor that is beneficial; that is, the honor that benefits the soul. And how well it was said by whoever said it that honor and profit don't go together; although I don't know if it was said with this purpose in mind. But it is right to the point because the soul's profit and what the world calls honor can never go together. It's a frightful thing; the world moves in the opposite direction. Blessed be the Lord who drew us out of it. [May it please His Majesty that such a concept of honor always be as far from this house as it is now. God deliver us from monasteries where they pay attention to these ceremonious little rules. He is never much honored in such monasteries. God help me, what great foolishness, that religious seek honor in such trifles; I am astonished! You don't know about this, Sisters, but I want to tell you about it so that you will guard yourselves against it.]

4. But consider, Sisters, that the devil hasn't forgotten us. He also invents his own honors in monasteries and establishes his own laws. There, people ascend and descend in rank just as in the world. Those with degrees must follow in order, according to their academic titles. Why? I don't know. The one who has managed to become professor of theology must not descend to professor of philosophy, for it is a point of honor that he must ascend and not descend. Even if obedience should command, he would consider the change an affront. And there will always be someone standing by to defend him and tell him that it's an insult; then the devil at once discloses reasons why even according to God's law this thinking seems right. Well, now, among ourselves: the one who has been prioress must remain ineligible for any lower office; a preoccupation about who the senior is — for we never forget this — and we even think at times we gain merit by such concern because the order commands it.

5. One doesn't know whether to laugh or to cry; the latter would be more fitting. The order doesn't command us to lack humility. It commands that there be a balanced arrangement of things, but I don't have to be so careful about this arrangement when it comes to matters of self-esteem that I am as concerned about these little ceremonious rules as about other practices that perhaps we observe imperfectly. All of our perfection doesn't consist in the observance of what has to do with our honor. Others will look after me if I forget about myself. The fact is that since we are inclined to ascend — even though we will not ascend to heaven by such an inclination — there must be no descending. O Lord, Lord! Are you our Model and Master? Yes, indeed! Well then, what did your honor consist of, you who honored us? Didn't you indeed lose it in being humiliated unto death? No, Lord, but you won it for all.

6. Oh, for the love of God, Sisters, how we get lost on the road because we start out wrong from the beginning.[2] Please God no soul will be lost because it keeps these miserable little rules of etiquette without understanding what honor consists in. And then we shall reach the point of thinking that we have done a great deal if we pardon one of these little things that was neither an offense, nor an injury, nor anything. Like someone who has accomplished something, we shall think that the Lord pardons us because we have pardoned others. Help us understand, my God, that we do not know ourselves and that we come to you with empty hands; and pardon us through your mercy. [Indeed, you are always the wronged and the offended one.] Truly, Lord, since all things come to an end, but the punishment is without end, I don't see anything that would give us a reason to remind you to grant us so great a favor; unless you would grant it because of your Son who asks it of you.

7. But yet, how the Lord must esteem this love we have for one another! Indeed, Jesus could have put other virtues

first and said: forgive us, Lord, because we do a great deal of penance or because we pray much and fast or because we have left all for you and love you very much. He didn't say forgive us because we would give up our lives for you, or, as I say, because of other possible things. But he said only, "forgive us because we forgive." Perhaps he said the prayer and offered it on our behalf because he knows we are so fond of this miserable honor and that to be forgiving is a virtue difficult for us to attain by ourselves but most pleasing to his Father.

8. Well, consider carefully, Sisters, that he says, "as we forgive," as though it were something already being done, as I have mentioned.[3] And pay very close attention, for when among the favors God grants in the prayer of perfect contemplation that I mentioned[4] there doesn't arise in the soul a very resolute desire to pardon any injury however grave it may be and to pardon it in deed when the occasion arises, do not trust much in that soul's prayer. And I don't refer to these nothings that they call injuries. For the soul God brings to himself in so sublime a contemplation is not touched by these wrongs nor does it care at all whether it is esteemed or not. I didn't say this well, "nor does it care at all," for it is much more afflicted by honor than by dishonor and by a lot of ease and rest than by trials. For when truly the Lord has given his kingdom here below, the soul no longer desires honor in this world. And so as to reign more sublimely it understands that the above-mentioned way is the true way; it has already seen through experience the great gain and progress that comes to it by suffering for God. Very seldom does God give such great gifts, save to persons who have willingly undergone many trials for him. As I have said in another part of this book,[5] the trials of contemplatives are great, and so the Lord looks for contemplatives among people who have been tested.

9. Now then, Sisters, realize that since these contemplatives already know what everything is worth, they are not long

delayed by a passing thing. If at first a great affront or trial causes pain, their reason comes to their rescue, before the pain is fully felt, with another consideration as if to raise the banner and almost annihilate the pain by means of joy. This joy comes from their seeing that the Lord has placed in their hands something by which they will gain more graces and perpetual favors from His Majesty than they would in ten years through trials they might wish to undertake on their own. This is very common from what I understand, for I have dealt with many contemplatives and am certain that this is what happens. Just as others prize gold and jewels, they prize trials and desire them; they know that these latter are what will make them rich.

10. Self-esteem is far removed from these persons. They like others to know about their sins and like to tell about them when they see themselves esteemed. The same is true in matters concerning their lineage. They already know that in the kingdom without end they will have nothing to gain from this. If they should happen to be pleased to be of good descent, it's when this would be necessary in order to serve God. When it isn't, it grieves them to be taken for more than what they are; and without any grief at all but gladly they disillusion others. So it is with those to whom God grants the grace of this humility and great love for himself. In what amounts to his greater service, they are already so forgetful of self that they can't even believe that others feel some things and consider them an affront.

11. These effects I just mentioned are found in persons who are closer to perfection and whom the Lord very habitually favors by bringing to himself through perfect contemplation. But of the first effect, which is the resolve to suffer wrongs and suffer them even though this may be painful, I say that it will soon be possessed by anyone who has from the Lord this

favor of the prayer of union. If one doesn't experience these effects and come away from prayer fortified in them, one may believe that the favor was not from God but an illusion, or the devil's gift bestowed so that we might consider ourselves more honored.

12. It can happen that in the beginning when the Lord grants these favors the soul will not immediately experience this fortitude. But I say that in a short while if he continues to grant them, it will have fortitude in this virtue of forgiving others even though it may not have fortitude in other virtues. I cannot believe that a soul that comes so close to Mercy itself, where it realizes what it is and the great deal God has pardoned it of, would fail to pardon its offender immediately, in complete ease, and with a readiness to remain on very good terms with that person. Such a soul is mindful of the gift and favor granted by God, by which it saw signs of great love; and it rejoices that an opportunity is offered whereby it can show the Lord some love.

13. I repeat that I know many persons whom the Lord has favored by raising to supernatural things, giving them this prayer or contemplation that was mentioned, and even though I see other faults and imperfections in them, I have never seen any of them with this one; nor do I believe that such a fault will be present if the favors are from God, as I have said.[6] Those who receive greater favors should observe whether these effects are increasing within them. If they don't see any increase, they should be afraid and refuse to believe that these gifts are from God, as I have said. For God's favor always enriches the soul it reaches. This is certain. Although the favor and gift passes quickly, it is gradually recognized through the benefits the soul receives. Since Jesus knows this well, he says resolutely to his holy Father that "we pardon our debtors."

FORGIVENESS

The Eucharist provides for us so that we may do the Father's will. Now more specifically it facilitates what we need for our next petition in which we ask for divine forgiveness.

36.1–6: A. The Lord doesn't say "forgive us our debts as we will forgive."

- Those who have surrendered their wills to God will at least have had the resolve to forgive.

- In my case, I have little opportunity to forgive since, considering who I am, no one has offended me.

- Pay no attention to the little things that some call wrongs.

- How many times was I offended when I prized honor.

  - I wasn't one of those who pay close attention to little rules of etiquette.

  - Yet, I didn't pay any heed to the honor that benefits the soul.

  - The soul's profit and what the world calls honor don't go together.

  - The devil also invents his own honors in monasteries.

  - Since we are inclined to ascend, there is no descending in rank.

 – We shall come to think we are doing a great
   deal if we pardon one of these little things,
   which was no real offense.

B. Teresa turns to the Lord in a prayer:

 • We do not know ourselves and that we come to
   you with empty hands.

 • Pardon us through your mercy.

 • You are always the wronged and offended one.

36.7–10: A. How the Lord must esteem this love we
have for one another.

 • He did not pray, "forgive us because we do a
   great deal of penance, pray, and fast."

 • He did not say "because we would give up our
   lives for you."

B. Some effects of perfect contemplation:

 • The soul that God brings to perfect contemplation is not touched by any injury however grave.

 • Such a soul will pardon an offense when the
   occasion arises.

 • It is much more afflicted by honor than by dishonor.

 • When the Lord has given it his kingdom here
   below, the soul no longer desires honor in this
   world.

- The Lord looks for contemplatives among people who have been tested since their trials are great.

- If at first an affront causes great pain, their reason comes to the rescue.

- Joy comes on seeing that the Lord has given them something by which they will receive more graces.

- Self-esteem is far removed from these persons; they like others to know their sins.

- The same is true in matters of their lineage.

- They are already so forgetful of self that they can't believe that others feel some things to be an affront.

36.11: Anyone receiving the prayer of union will have at least the resolve to suffer wrongs even though painful.

INTERPRETIVE NOTES: 1. The Eucharist is the means by which we are enabled to respond positively to the petition "your will be done." The will of God as seen here is principally the practice of forgiving those who offend us. Forgiveness flows from the Eucharist. As a result, chapters 32 to 36 bear resemblance to a triptych, with its center piece dedicated to the Eucharist.

2. In Teresa's confession to us, she explains her need to approach God somewhat differently. Profoundly

heedful of her own wretchedness without God, she was unable to think that anyone had offended or mistreated her. "What your Son says in the name of all has to exclude me" (2). She reasoned that the Lord would have to pardon her for nothing since she had nothing to offer him. What else could she do but rely on his mercy? She was penniless. As anyone might expect, the censor recoiled from these reflections and crossed them out with large strokes (the passage in brackets in no. 2). In a marginal note he attempts to give the passage a more "realistic" touch: "The injuries and offenses done to us by others are real, even though we may be the greatest of sinners; but they must be forgiven because God forgives us our offenses." Teresa, conversely, wanted her readers to know that they go to God with empty hands and are pardoned through his mercy (7).

3. In chapters 12 and 13, she had written about detachment from honors. Here Teresa turns again to this topic and laments the fact that religious, though drawn out of the world, go about setting up a whole new system of honors in their communities with the result that they take offense over trifles ("miserable little rules of etiquette"). They were often failing to forgive not only serious wrongs but even slight infractions of proper decorum in matters of rank. Teresa is clear: what the world calls honor and what is good for the soul are incompatible. Those who have come to know great love of God can't bring themselves to believe that others feel some things and consider them an affront. All of this leads to the teaching of the present

chapter. The prayer of union bears with it a clear sign or effect: the desire and ability to forgive an offender immediately and with complete ease, and the readiness to remain on very good terms with others, even those who have given offense. Those individuals who have come so close to Divine Mercy have a keen cognizance of the extent to which God has forgiven them.

4. To the question of Peter about how often forgiveness is to be meted out, Jesus answered that it is to be given without measure (seventy times seven times) (Mt 18:22). And Paul taught that love "does not brood over injuries" (1 Cor 13:5). There can be offenses that strike at the heart and destroy something that may have taken years to build. In cases like this, even though pardon is bestowed, there remains the impossibility of freeing the heart of the bitterness caused by the offense. Then you can offer patiently the pain of heart and, through sentiments of love, try not to feed positively the feelings of rancor that persist. But Teresa adds that you can help annihilate the pain with the joy of of "seeing that the Lord has placed in your hands something by which you will gain more graces and perpetual favors from His Majesty than you would in ten years through trials you might wish to undertake" (9). Fortitude for such efforts is given through the Eucharist. Jesus gives explicit counsels in this regard: "Love your enemies, do good to them, and lend expecting nothing back; then your reward will be great and you will be children of the Most High, for he himself is kind to the ungrateful and the wicked. Be merciful, just as your Father is merciful" (Lk 6:35).

QUESTIONS FOR DISCUSSION: 1. What are some of the things people worry about in our times comparable to what was called honor in Teresa's day?

2. Why would the failure to forgive be incompatible with the prayer of union?

3. How might we deal with strong feelings of resentment over injury?

Chapter 37

Speaks of the excellence of this prayer, the Our Father, and of how we shall in many ways find consolation in it.

WE OUGHT TO GIVE GREAT PRAISE to the Lord for the sublime perfection of this evangelical prayer. Each of us, daughters, can apply the prayer to her own needs since it was composed by such a good Master. I marvel to see that in so few words everything about contemplation and perfection is included; it seems we need to study no other book than this one. Up to now the Lord has taught us the whole way of prayer and of high contemplation, from the beginning stages to mental prayer, to the prayer of quiet, and to that of union; so much so that, if I knew how to explain the matter, a large book on prayer could be written based on this genuine foundation.[1] From here on, the Lord begins to teach us about the effects of his favors, as you have seen.

2. I have wondered why His Majesty did not explain more about these sublime and obscure things that we might all know about them. It has seemed to me that since this prayer was intended for general use so that each of us could petition according to our own intention, be consoled, and think that we have a good understanding of the prayer, the Lord left it in this obscure form. Contemplatives and persons already very much committed to God, who no longer desire earthly things, ask for the heavenly favors that can, through God's goodness,

be given on earth. Those who still live on earth, and it is good that they live in conformity with their state in life, may ask also for bread. They must be sustained and must sustain their households. Such a petition is very just and holy, and so also is their petition for other things according to their needs.

3. But both should consider that two of the things mentioned pertain to all: giving him our will and forgiving others. True, there is a more and a less in the degree to which this is done, as has been said.[2] The perfect will give their will in the way perfect souls do and forgive with that perfection that was mentioned. We, Sisters, will do what we can; the Lord receives everything.[3] It seems that on our behalf he makes a kind of pact with his Eternal Father, like one who says: "You do this, Lord, and my brothers will do that." Well, surely he doesn't fail to do his part. Oh, oh, how well he pays! And he pays without measure!

4. We can say this prayer only once in such a way that the Lord will enrich us since he sees that we do so sincerely and are determined to do what we say. He likes us to be truthful with him. If we speak plainly and clearly so that we don't say one thing and then act differently, he always gives more than what we ask of him.

Our good Master knows this well. He knows that those who ask with perfection will be filled with such favors from his Father that they will reach a high state. In fact, those who are already perfect or those who are approaching it are not afraid of anything, nor should they be, since they have trampled the world underfoot, as the saying goes. The Lord of the world is pleased with them, and they have the greatest hope of this in the effects of the favors he grants them. Absorbed in these delights they don't want to remember even that there is a world or that they have enemies.

5. O Eternal Wisdom! O good Teacher! What a wonderful thing it is, daughters, to have a wise and cautious teacher who foresees the dangers. This is the entire good that a spiritual soul can desire here below because it provides great security. One could not exaggerate the importance of this. Thus since the Lord sees that it is necessary to awaken and remind us that we have enemies, that it is very dangerous to be negligent with regard to these enemies, and that we need much more help from the Eternal Father because our fall will be from a higher place, and so that we do not go about mistaken and without self-knowledge, he makes the following petitions so necessary for all as long as we live in this exile: "And lead us not, Lord, into temptation; but deliver us from evil."

A PERFECT PRAYER

By way of parenthesis, Teresa cannot resist telling us of her surprise: the entire path of prayer may be found in these few words of the Our Father.

37.1–2: Praise the Lord for the sublime perfection of the Our Father.

- In so few words we find everything about contemplation and perfection.

- A large book on prayer could be written with this prayer as its basis.

- The Lord left it in an obscure form so that each one of us could find in it what we need.

37.3: Two things, though, pertain to all of us: giving him our will; forgiving others.

- Any difference lies in the degree to which each is carried out.

- We do what we can; the Lord receives everything.

- He pays well and without measure.

37.4: If we speak plainly and don't then act differently, he always gives more than what we ask of him.

37.5: In the next petition, the Lord reminds us that we have enemies so that we do not leave self-knowledge behind.

INTERPRETIVE NOTES: 1. From the earliest centuries in both the Eastern and Western liturgies, the Lord's Prayer was an integral part of the Eucharist. Its simplicity and forceful condensation of Jesus' spirit and message make it the unequaled expression of Christian prayer. St. Cyprian teaches that the few words of the Our Father impart great spiritual strength and comprise a summary of divine teachings that includes all of our prayers and petitions (*Treatise on the Lord's Prayer*, nos. 8–9). St. Augustine believes that we can search through all the prayers contained in the Scriptures and will not find anything that is not included in the Our Father. He also holds that if we pray rightly and fittingly, we can say nothing else but what is contained in this prayer of Our Lord (Ep 130.12.22). St. Thomas Aquinas points out that in the Lord's Prayer "not only do we ask for all that we may rightly desire, but we ask also in the order wherein we ought to desire, so this prayer not only teaches us to ask, but also directs all our affections" (*Summa Theologiae* II–II 83.9). St. John of the Cross taught that the seven petitions of the Our Father include all our temporal and spiritual needs (*Ascent* 3.44.4). Suddenly at this point in her reflections, Teresa, too, feels the need to praise the Lord for the "sublime perfection" of this prayer. She marvels at all that the prayer contains, even about contemplation and perfection. She admits the various meanings that people will find in it but also holds that contemplatives totally committed to God will discover in it meanings that would never occur to others. However, the petitions concerned with doing God's will and forgiving others are clear in their meaning to everyone.

2. Teresa has already agreed that those opposing the practice of mental prayer are correct when they say that "the Our Father and the Hail Mary are sufficient" (21.2).

She envisions the Our Father as a book no one can take away from her nuns. It is a book that will bring more recollection than other profound, deftly written ones. But now she reaches the further realization that a large book on prayer could be written based on the Our Father. Reciting the prayer well, and even only once, can so enrich us and lead the Lord to bestow such favors on us that she recognizes the need for the next petition as a necessary precaution.

QUESTIONS FOR DISCUSSION: 1. What makes the Our Father so perfect a prayer?

2. Which parts of the Our Father are obscure and which clear and why?

3. Why doesn't everyone find in these words what Teresa finds in them?

Chapter 38

Deals with the great need we have to beseech the Eternal Father to grant us what we ask for in the words, Et ne nos inducas in tentationem, sed libera nos a malo; *and explains some temptations. The subject matter is important.*

W E HAVE GREAT THINGS to think about and understand here, Sisters, because these things are what we are asking for. Now see, I am certain that those who reach perfection do not ask the Lord to free them from trials or temptations or persecutions or struggles. This is another very great and certain effect of the contemplation and the favors His Majesty gives, and of the Lord's Spirit rather than of an illusion. On the contrary, as I have said a little while ago,[1] these persons desire, ask for, and love trials. They are like soldiers who are happier when there are more wars because they then hope to earn more. If there is no war, they receive their wages but realize they won't get rich.

2. Believe, Sisters, that the soldiers of Christ, those who experience contemplation and engage in prayer, are eager to fight. They never fear public enemies very much; they already recognize them and know that these enemies have no power against the strength the Lord gives and that they themselves always come out the victors and with much gain. They never turn from these enemies. Those whom they fear — and it is right they fear and always ask the Lord to be freed from them — are the traitorous enemies, the devils who transfigure themselves into angels of light,[2] who come disguised. Not until they

419

have done much harm to the soul do they allow themselves
to be recognized. They suck away our blood and destroy our
virtues, and we about in the midst of the same temptation
but do not know it. With regard to these enemies, daughters,
let us ask and often beg the Lord in the Our Father to free us
and not let us walk into temptation, so that they will not draw
us into error or hide the light and truth from us, that the poison will be discovered. Oh, how rightly does our good Master
ask this for us and teach us to ask for it.

3. Consider, daughters, the many ways these enemies can
cause harm. Don't think they do so only by making us suppose
that the delights and consolations they can feign in us are from
God. This seems to me the least harm — in part — they can
cause; rather, it could be that by means of this they will make
one advance more quickly. For, in being fed on that delight,
such persons will spend more hours in prayer. Since they don't
know that the delight is from the devil and since they see they
are unworthy of those consolations, they don't stop thanking
God. They will feel greater obligation to serve him and, thinking the favors come from the hand of the Lord, they will strive
to dispose themselves so that God will grant them more.

4. Strive always, Sisters, for humility and to see that you
are unworthy of these favors; do not seek them. I hold that
the devil loses many souls who strive for this humility. He
thinks he is going to bring them to perdition, but the Lord
draws good from the evil the devil aims at. His Majesty looks
at our intention, which is to please and serve him and remain
with him in prayer; and the Lord is faithful.[3] It's good to be
on one's guard lest there be a break in humility, or some vainglory emerge. If you beseech the Lord to free you from this,
do not fear, daughters, that His Majesty will allow you to be
favored very much by anyone other than himself.

5. The way the devil can do a great deal of harm, without our realizing it, is to make us believe we have virtues when we do not. This is a pestilence.[4] In regard to the delights and consolations, it seems merely that we are receiving and that we have the greater obligation to serve. In regard to our thinking we are virtuous, it seems we are serving and giving and that the Lord is obliged to pay. Thus little by little this latter notion does great harm. On the one hand it weakens humility, and on the other hand we grow careless about acquiring that virtue we think we have already acquired. Well, what is the remedy, Sisters? That which seems best to me is what our Master teaches us: prayer and supplication to the Eternal Father not to let us enter into temptation.[5]

6. I also want to tell you something else. If it seems the Lord has already given us virtue, let us understand that actually it has been received and that he can take it away, as in fact often happens, but not without his wonderful providence. Haven't you ever seen this for yourselves, Sisters? I have. Sometimes I think I am very detached; and as a matter of fact when put to the test, I am. At another time I will find myself so attached, and perhaps to things that the day before I would have made fun of, that I almost don't know myself. At other times I think I have great courage and that I wouldn't turn from anything of service to God; and when put to the test, I do have this courage for some things. Another day will come in which I won't find the courage in me to kill even an ant for God if in doing so I'd meet with any opposition. In like manner it seems to me that I don't care at all about things or gossip said of me; and when I'm put to the test this is at times true — indeed I am pleased about what they say. Then there come days in which one word alone distresses me, and I would want to leave the world because it seems everything is a bother to me. And I am not alone in this. I have noticed it in many persons better than I, and know that it so happens.

7. Now since this is true, who will be able to say of themselves that they are virtuous or rich? For at the very moment when there is need of virtue one finds oneself poor. No, Sisters; but let us always think we are poor, and not go into debt when we do not have the means with which to repay. The treasure will have to come from elsewhere, and we do not know when the Lord will want to leave us in the prison of our misery without giving us anything. And if others in thinking that we are good, bestow favor and honor on us — which is the borrowing I mentioned — both they and we ourselves will have been fooled. True, if we serve with humility, the Lord in the end will succor us in our needs; but if this poverty of spirit is not genuinely present at every step, as they say, the Lord will abandon us. And this abandonment by the Lord is one of his greatest favors, for he does it so that we might be humble and understand in truth that we have nothing we haven't received.

8. Now, then, take note of some other advice: the devil makes us think we have a virtue, let's say of patience because we resolve and make very frequent acts of willingness to suffer much for God, and it seems to us as a matter of fact that we would suffer much; so we are very satisfied, for the devil helps us to believe this. I advise you not to pay any attention to these virtues; let us neither think we know them other than by name nor, until we see the proof, think the Lord has given them to us. For it will happen that with one displeasing word spoken to you, your patience will go tumbling to the ground. When you suffer often, praise God that he is beginning to teach you this virtue of patience and strive to endure, for the suffering is a sign that in this way he wants you to pay for the virtue. He gives it to you, and you do not possess it save as though on deposit, as has already been said.[6]

9. The devil brings about another temptation. We think we are very poor in spirit and have the habit of saying that we don't desire anything or that we couldn't care less about

anything. But hardly does the occasion arise to receive a gift — even if it would be more than we need — than our poverty of spirit is completely ruined. So often do we say we have this virtue that we end up believing we have it.

Great is the importance of always being careful to understand this temptation, both in the things I have mentioned as well as in many others. For when the Lord truly gives one of these solid virtues, it seems it carries all the others in its wake. This is something felt very clearly. But I again warn you that even though it seems you possess it, you should fear lest you be mistaken. The truly humble always walks in doubt about their own virtues, and usually those they see in their neighbors seem more certain and more valuable.

TEMPTATIONS OF CONTEMPLATIVES

The two final petitions of the Our Father inspire Teresa to write about the temptations that come not to beginners but to those who have passed beyond the stage of beginners.

38.1-4: Those who have reached perfection in the spiritual life do not ask the Lord to free them from temptations, struggles, and persecutions.

- On the contrary, these persons love trials.

- Their enemies (trials and persecutions) have no power over the strength given them by the Lord.

- They fear the devils who transform themselves into angels of light.

  - Devils do not harm us by making us think that the consolations feigned by them are from God.

  - In receiving these, we will thank God over and over, feel obliged to serve him better, and dispose ourselves so that he will grant more.

  - We should have a humble attitude: not seeking God's favors but considering ourselves unworthy of them.

38.5: The way the devil can do us harm, by making us believe we have virtues when we do not.

- In regard to consolations, it seems we are receiving and so more obliged.

- In regard to thinking we're virtuous, it seems we are giving and that the Lord is obliged to pay.

- We then grow careless about the virtue we think we have.

- The remedy: prayer to the Eternal Father not to let us enter into temptation.

38.6: A. If the Lord has given us a virtue, let us understand two things: it has been received; it can be taken away.

B. Teresa now gives examples from her own experience:

- She thinks one day she is detached, and on another feels so attached she doesn't recognize herself.

- She thinks one day she has great courage, and on another she doesn't have the courage to kill an ant.

- She doesn't care one day about gossip said of her, and on another she's greatly distressed by one word.

38.7-8: Let us always think we are poor.

- If we serve humbly, the Lord will succor us in our needs.

- When you suffer, praise God that he is beginning to teach you the virtue of patience; he wants you to pay for the virtue he gives you.

38.9: When the Lord gives one of these solid virtues, it seems to carry all the others in its wake; but the humble walk in doubt about their own virtues; virtues possessed by their neighbors seem more certain.

INTERPRETIVE NOTES. 1. At the beginning of this book Teresa set out to do some ground work explaining to the nuns that they must live in peace if they are going to be contemplatives and that three practices would bring them that peace: charity, detachment, and humility. Progressing through her work, we gradually discovered that, though we can make every effort to obtain these virtues, they come, in the end, as the true fruit of prayer. Charity, detachment, and humility are experienced as God's gifts; they are the effects of his graces given in prayer, especially when you drink directly from the fount.

2. What is humility? This may be the place to ask. Those who have done some reading in spirituality know that the answer given as Teresa's is that humility is truth. Here is what Teresa says: "Once I was pondering why our Lord was so fond of this virtue of humility, and this thought came to me — in my opinion not as a result of reflection but suddenly: It is because God is supreme Truth; and to be humble is to walk in truth, for it is a very deep truth that of ourselves we have nothing good but only misery and nothingness" (IC VI.10.7). That humility is truth needs some further clarification, which Teresa supplied and which is seldom mentioned. The deep truth is that by ourselves we have nothing good. In her *Life*, she gives the same thought somewhat differently: "For a soul surrendered into God's hands doesn't care whether they say good or evil about it. It

thoroughly understands — since the Lord desires to grant it the favor of understanding this — that of itself it has nothing" (31.16). The positive side of that clear understanding is that every good comes to us from God (IC VI.1.4); every blessing, through Jesus Christ (L 22.4.6-7).

3. St. Thérése of Lisieux, who provides a clear example of the humility and spiritual poverty fostered by Teresa, inspires us to reflection with these words: "There is only one way to force God not to judge us at all, and that is to appear before him with empty hands."

4. Another Discalced Carmelite nun, Jessica Powers, echoes Teresa and Thérèse in these lovely words:

"If You Have Nothing"

The gesture of a gift is adequate.
If you have nothing: laurel leaf or bay,
No flower, no seed, no apple gathered late,
do not in desperation lay
the beauty of your tears upon the clay.
No gift is proper to a Deity;
no fruit is worthy for such power to bless.
If you have nothing, gather back your sigh,
and with your hands held high,
   your heart held high,
lift up your emptiness!

(*The Selected Poetry of Jessica Powers,* ed. Regina Siegfried and Robert Morneau [Washington, D.C.: ICS Publications, 1999], 91.)

QUESTIONS FOR DISCUSSION: 1. What should our attitude be toward the favors God grants us?

2. What is the temptation I should be wary of and why?

3. What does Teresa mean when she says "let us always think we are poor"?

Chapter 39

Continues the same subject, gives advice about some different kinds of temptations, and sets down two remedies by which to free oneself from them.

NOW BE ALSO ON YOUR GUARD, daughters, against types of humility given by the devil in which great disquiet is felt about the gravity of our sins. This disturbance can afflict in many ways even to the point of making one give up receiving Communion and practicing private prayer.[1] These things are given up because the devil makes one feel unworthy. And when such persons approach the Blessed Sacrament, the time they used to spend in receiving favors is now spent in wondering whether or not they are well prepared. The situation gets so bad that the soul thinks God has abandoned it because of what it is; it almost doubts his mercy. Everything it deals with seems dangerous, and what it uses, however good, seems fruitless. It feels such distrust of itself that it folds its arms and remains idle; what is good in others seems evil when the soul sees it within its own self.

2. Consider carefully, daughters, the matter I'm going to speak to you about, for sometimes it will be through humility and virtue that you hold yourselves to be so wretched, and at other times it will be a gross temptation. I know of this because I have gone through it. Humility does not disturb or disquiet. or agitate, however great it may be; it comes with peace, delight, and calm. Even though a soul upon seeing itself so wretched

understands clearly that it merits to be in hell, suffers affliction, thinks everyone should in justice abhor it, and almost doesn't dare ask for mercy, its pain, if the humility is genuine, comes with a sweetness in itself and a satisfaction that it wouldn't want to be without. The pain doesn't agitate or afflict the soul; rather, this humility expands it and enables it to serve God more. The other type of pain disturbs everything, agitates everything, afflicts the entire soul, and is very painful. I think the devil's aim is to make us think we are humble and, in turn, if possible, make us lose confidence in God.

3. When you find yourselves in this condition, stop thinking about your misery, insofar as possible, and turn your thoughts to the mercy of God, to how he loves us and suffered for us. And if you are undergoing a temptation, you will not even be able to do this, for the devil will not let you quiet your mind or concentrate on anything unless so as to tire you all the more. It will be enough if you recognize that this is a temptation.[2]

Likewise he tempts us in regard to excessive penances so that we might think we are more penitential than others and are doing something. If you hide them from your confessor or prioress, or if when told to stop you do not do so, you are clearly undergoing a temptation. Strive to obey, even if this may be more painful for you, since the greatest perfection lies in obedience.

4. The devil sets up another dangerous temptation: self assurance in the thought that we will in no way return to our past faults and worldly pleasures: "For now I have understood the world and know that all things come to an end and that the things of God give me greater delight." If this self-assurance is present in beginners, it is very dangerous because with it a person doesn't take care against entering once more into the occasions of sin, and falls flat; please God the relapse will not bring about something much worse. For since the devil sees

that he is dealing with a soul that can do him harm and bring profit to others, he uses all his power so that it might not rise. Thus, however many delights and pledges of love the Lord gives you, never proceed with such self-assurance that you stop fearing lest you fall again; and be on guard against the occasions of sin.

5. Strive, without hiding anything, to discuss these favors and consolations with someone who will enlighten you. And take care about this: however sublime the contemplation, let your prayer always begin and end with self-knowledge. And if the favor is from God, even though you may not want to follow the advice, you will still follow it most of the time because God's favor brings humility and always leaves greater light that we may understand the little that we are.

I don't want to enlarge on this any more, for you will find many books with such advice. I have said what I did because I have experienced it and found myself in trouble at times. All that we say, however much it is, cannot give us complete security.

6. Thus, Eternal Father, what can we do but have recourse to you and pray that these enemies of ours not lead us into temptation? Let public enemies come, for by your favor we will be more easily freed. But these other treacheries; who will understand them, my God? We always need to pray to you for a remedy. Instruct us, Lord, so that we may understand ourselves and be secure. You already know that few take this path; but if they have to travel it with so many fears, many fewer will take it.

7. What a strange thing! It's as though the devil tempts only those who take the path of prayer. And everyone is more surprised by a mistake of one of those who are nearing perfection than by the public mistakes and sins of a hundred thousand

others. With these latter mistakes there is no need to consider whether they are good or bad, for from a thousand-leagues distance one recognizes that they come from Satan.

As a matter of fact people are right in being surprised, for among those who recite the Our Father as was explained there are so very few deceived by the devil that as something new and unusual their mistake causes surprise. It is something very common among mortals that they pass over easily what they continually see, and wonder about what seldom or almost never happens. And the devil himself causes them to be surprised, for this surprise is to his advantage; he loses many souls through one who reaches perfection. [And I say that this is so surprising I do not marvel that others are surprised. Unless it is very much due to their own fault, souls who practice prayer walk so much more securely than those who take another road. They are like those in the stands watching the bull in comparison with one who is right in front of its horns. I have heard this comparison, and it seems to me true to the letter.

Do not fear, Sisters, to travel these paths, for in prayer there are many. Some souls profit by one path, and others by another, as I have said. Prayer is a safe road; you will be more quickly freed from temptation when close to the Lord than when far. Beseech him and ask him to deliver you from evil as you do so often each day in the Our Father.]

TEMPTATIONS OF CONTEMPLATIVES (CONTINUED)

She gives some signs for discerning true humility from false and turns her attention to some other temptations from which prayer can free us.

39.1: A false humility given by the devil: disquiet over the gravity of one's sins.

- It can even make one give up Communion.

- The soul thinks God has abandoned it, and almost doubts his mercy.

- Everything it deals with seems dangerous.

- It feels distrust of itself.

39.2–4: A. True humility does not disturb.

- It comes with peace, delight, and calm.

- Where humility is genuine, the thought of one's sins doesn't agitate or afflict.

- When you find yourselves agitated and afflicted, turn your thoughts to the mercy of God and stop thinking about your misery.

B. Another temptation is toward excessive penances; submit them to your confessor or superior.

C. A further temptation is self-assurance that we will never regress.

- Self-assurance in beginners is very dangerous.

- They can enter the occasion of sin and fall flat.

39.5: God's favor brings humility, leaving greater light for us to understand the little that we are.

39.6: Here Teresa turns in prayer to the Eternal Father and prays for help against our treacherous enemies, not the public ones.

39.7: Everyone is rightly more surprised by a mistake of one nearing perfection than by the public mistakes and sins of a hundred thousand others.

- Prayer is a safe road.

- You will be more quickly freed when close to the Lord.

INTERPRETIVE NOTES: 1. Three temptations are set before us: affliction and agitation over one's sins; excessive bodily penance; and self-assurance against falling back into past faults (covered in the previous chapter). The first goes patently counter to the peace and calm experienced in God's gift of humility. Compunction is a basic sentiment that runs through all of Teresa's writings. An unwary reader will think her outpourings of compunction amount to exaggerated guilt feelings. In her *Life* (30.9), she explains in greater detail the way true humility may be distinguished from an unhealthy affliction over our sins. She admits that we can have exaggerated thoughts about our wickedness and that they are felt, but accompanying these feelings is a humility that consoles one quietly, gently, and with light. The false humility carries with it agitation, disturbance, and darkness.

Another feature of true humility is that the soul "grieves for its offenses against God; yet, on the other hand, his mercy lifts its spirits." The devil, by contrast, attacks the soul, representing God's justice in such a way that it cannot be consoled by the thought of his mercy.

2. The next temptation is a puzzling one. How could anyone be tempted to excessive bodily penance? In her *Life*, Teresa tells about the huge fire of love that always needs something to burn so as not to go out. One kind of wood is penance (30.20). In an account of her spiritual life written in 1563, she states: "The impulses to do penance that come upon me sometimes, and have come upon me, are great. And if I do penance, I feel so little, on account of that strong desire, that sometimes it seems to me — or almost always — that penance is a special favor; although I don't do much since I am very sickly" (ST 3.5). This coincides with what she teaches about the effects of the prayer of union and of ecstasy: among them are great desires to do penance (IC V.2.7,14; VI.4.15). It is where these desires are present that the devil may tempt one, as she explained in chapter 19.9, "to perform indiscreet penances so that one's health will be lost." Teresa preferred that her nuns concentrate on charity and humility, "for you already know that I am rather strict when there is question of your doing too many penances" (15.3). The prudent procedure in this matter, she teaches, is supervision. The nuns needed permission from the prioress to perform extra penances (IC I.2.16); Teresa herself sought permission from her confessors.

One day while thinking about Catalina de Cardona's extraordinarily severe penances, she began to lament the fact that her confessors had not given her permission for more penances. The Lord interrupted her thoughts and spoke these words: "Do you see all the penance she does? I value your obedience more" (ST 19).

3. In time the scriptural understanding of "conversion" was reduced to "penance" which is a turning away from sin and atonement for it. The practice of penance was often identified with mortification as a means of atoning for sin, works of penance being seen as self-purification and self-punishment. In the measure that you grow in the spiritual life, you grow in sensitivity to sin, an awareness of your own sins and of others' sins and also of the evil present in society. In the first centuries, Christians moved away from the multitude of worries filling their lives with noise and confusion, toward simplicity, frugality, and quiet. They took the most fundamental and self-centered drives of human nature, eating, sleeping, and possessing, and made them instruments of attentiveness to God and neighbor through fasting, vigils, and almsgiving. Other forms of bodily penance that later came into use as a means of punishing the body (1 Cor 9:27) were the discipline (a knotted rope used as a whip), the hairshirt, and sharp chains. In addition to being seen as ascetical means to gain freedom from bodily passions and appetites, these practices were also seen as a means of joining Christ in his passion and atoning for sin. Pope Paul VI's postconciliar reform of penitential practices, and especially of the disciplines of fasting and

abstinence, reaffirmed the necessity of penitence, but also asserted the need to "seek beyond fast and abstinence new expressions more suitable for the realization, according to the character of various epochs, of the precise goal of penitence." He pointed out that to make reparation for sin it is necessary to reestablish friendship with God and also restore those values damaged with respect to the sinner and the human community (*On Indulgences,* 2–3; *On Fast and Abstinence,* II). As a result, an effort is being made today to link penance with social responsibility and the work for peace and justice in our world. For example, besides providing the poor with money saved by abstinence from food, fasting forms a bond of sympathy with starving people by sharing in their suffering to some degree; it places one on the same level with the suffering neighbor; and it stengthens one's desire to help the poor by restructuring the distribution of this world's goods.

4. Self-assurance runs along the same lines as the temptation discussed in the previous chapter. In urging humility, Teresa does not want her readers to deny the favors and blessings given them by God. That would be contrary to the truth that is so essential to humility. Throughout her *Life* she speaks of God's favors to her so as to make known his mercy and press readers not to abandon prayer, the means by which God shares his life with us and makes us happy: "Before I grew tired of offending him, His Majesty began to pardon me. He never tires of giving, nor can he exhaust his mercies. Let us not tire of receiving" (L 19.15).

QUESTIONS FOR DISCUSSION: 1. How can we discern true from false humility in our lives?

2. What are some other temptations the devil might bother us with?

3. How can we help ourselves deal with such temptations?

Chapter 40

Tells how by striving always to walk in the love and the fear of God we will proceed safely among so many temptations.

NOW THEN, GOOD MASTER, teach us how to live without any sudden assault in so dangerous a war. What we can have, daughters, and what His Majesty gave us are love and fear. Love will quicken our steps; fear will make us watch our steps to avoid falling along the way. On this way there are many stumbling blocks for all of us who are alive and continue our journey. With this fear we will be secure against being deceived.

2. You will ask me how you can tell if you have these two virtues which are so great; and you are right in doing so, for you cannot be very certain and definite about them. If we possess love, we are certainly in the state of grace. But reflect, Sisters, that there are some signs that even the blind, it seems, see. They are manifest signs, though you may not want to recognize them. They cry out loudly, for not many possess them perfectly; and hence these signs are more obvious. Love and fear of God: what more could you ask for! They are like two fortified castles from which one can wage war on the world and the devils.

3. Those who truly love God, love every good, desire every good, favor every good, praise every good. They always join, favor, and defend good people. They have no love for

anything but truth and whatever is worthy of love. Do you think it is possible for those who really love God to love vanities? No, indeed, they cannot; nor can they love riches, or worldly things, or delights, or honors, or strife, or envy. All of this is so because they seek only to please the Beloved. These persons go about dying so that their Beloved might love them, and thus they dedicate their lives to learning how they might please him more. Hide itself? Oh, with regard to the love of God — if it is genuine love — this is impossible. If you don't think so, look at St. Paul or the Magdalene. Within three days the one began to realize that he was sick with love; that was St. Paul. The Magdalene knew from the first day; and how well she knew! Love has this characteristic: it can be greater or lesser in degree. Thus, the love makes itself known according to its intensity. When slight, it shows itself but slightly; when strong, it shows itself strongly. But where there is love of God, whether little or great, it is always recognized.

4. However, the things with which we are now dealing more specifically, the deceptions and illusions the devil brings on contemplatives, are not few. With contemplatives there is always much love, or they wouldn't be contemplatives; and so their love is clearly recognized and in many ways. It is a great fire; it cannot but shine brightly. And if this splendor is not present, they should walk with serious misgivings; they should believe that they indeed have many reasons for fear; they should strive to understand these; they should pray, walk with humility, and beseech the Lord not to lead them into temptation. For certainly if this sign isn't present, I fear we may walk into temptation. But if one proceeds with humility, strives to know the truth, is subject to a confessor, and communicates with him openly and truthfully, it will come about, as has been said,[1] that the things by which the devil intends to cause death will cause life, however many the haunting illusions he wants to scare you with.

5. But if you feel this love of God I've mentioned and the fear I shall now speak of,[2] rejoice and be at peace. In order to disturb your soul so that you will not enjoy these wonderful blessings the devil will set a thousand false fears before you and strive that others do so. Since he cannot win us over, he can at least try to make us lose something. He may strive to make souls lose when they might have gained a great deal by thinking that his favors are from God and are bestowed on creatures as wretched as themselves and that it is possible for God to grant favors — for it seems sometimes we have forgotten about the Lord's ancient mercies.[3]

6. Do you think it matters little to the devil to set up these fears? No, it matters a great deal, for he causes two kinds of harm. First, those who listen to him are struck with a terror of approaching prayer, for they think they will be deceived. Second, if it were not for these fears many more would come closer to God in seeing that he is so good, as I have said,[4] and that it is possible for him now to communicate so much with sinners. They covet these favors. And they are right, for I know some persons who were encouraged by such favors and began prayer; and in a short while the favors became authentic, and the Lord granted them great ones.

7. So, Sisters, when you see among yourselves someone to whom the Lord gives favors, praise the Lord very much but don't think she is for this reason safe; rather help her with more prayer. No one can be safe while living and engulfed in the dangers of this tempestuous sea.

You will not fail to recognize this love where it is present, nor do I know how it can be concealed.[5] If we love creatures here on earth, it's impossible, we are told, to hide this, and the more we do to hide it the more it is revealed (and it is something so lowly that it doesn't merit the name "love," for it is grounded on nothing). And could one conceal a love that is so strong and just that it always increases and sees no reason to stop since its foundation is made from the cement of being repaid by another love? This other love can no longer be doubted since it was shown so openly and with so many sufferings and trials, and with the shedding of blood even to the point of death in order that we might have no doubt about it. Oh, God help me, how different must the love of God be from the love of creatures for whoever has experienced the former!

8. May it please His Majesty to give us his love before he takes us out of this life, for it will be a great thing at the hour of death to see that we are going to be judged by the One whom we have loved above all things. We shall be able to proceed securely with the judgment concerning our debts. It will not be like going to a foreign country but like going to our own, because it is the country of one whom we love so much and who loves us. [In this love — besides everything else — there is greater security than with earthly loves; in loving God we are certain that he loves us.] Remember here, my daughters, the gain there is in this love, and the loss in not having it. Such a loss puts us in the hands of the enemy, in hands so cruel, hands so hostile toward everything good, and so fond of everything bad.

9. What will become of the poor soul that, after being freed from the sufferings and trials of death, falls immediately into these hands? What terrible rest it receives! How mangled as it goes to hell! What a multitude of different kinds of serpents! What a terrifying place! What a wretched inn! If it is hard for a self-indulgent person (for such are the ones who will be more likely to go there) to spend one night in a bad inn, what do you think that sad soul will feel at being in this kind of inn forever, without end?

Let us not desire delights, daughters; we are well-off here; the bad inn lasts for only a night. Let us praise God; let us force ourselves to do penance in this life. How sweet will be the death of the soul that has done penance for all its sins, of one who won't have to go to purgatory! Even from here below you can begin to enjoy glory! You will find no fear within yourself but complete peace.

10. As long as we have not reached this state, Sisters, let us beseech God that if therefore we are to receive sufferings, they will be received here below. For, with the hope of being freed from them, we can bear them here willingly, and we will not lose his friendship and grace. Let us beseech him to give us his grace in this life so that we will not walk unawares into temptation.[6]

THE LOVE OF GOD

Teresa now presents to her readers the image of two fortified castles that will protect the soul from temptation.

40.1–3: Love and fear of God are like two fortified castles from which we can wage war.

- If we possess love, we are certainly in the state of grace.

- Those who truly love God:

  - Desire, favor, and praise every good.

  - Defend good people.

  - Have no love for anything but truth and whatever is worthy of love.

  - Cannot love vanities, riches, worldly things, honors, strife, or envy.

  - Dedicate their lives to learning how they might please their Beloved.

  - Like St. Paul and the Magdalene, cannot hide their love.

- Love makes itself known according to its intensity.

40.4–7: The contemplative's love cannot but shine brightly.

- If you feel this love of God and the fear I shall now speak of, rejoice and be at peace.

- The devil causes two kinds of harm:

- Those who listen to him fear they will be deceived by prayer.

- They will think it is impossible for God to communicate so much with sinners.

• Love cannot be concealed, and it is repaid by another love that was shown openly through suffering and the shedding of blood.

40.8–10: At the hour of our death we will see that we are going to be judged by the One whom we have loved above all things.

• What a wretched inn hell is.

• The bad inn of this life lasts only a night.

• How sweet the death of one who will not have to go to purgatory.

• Even from here below you can begin to enjoy glory.

• You will find no fear within yourself but complete peace.

• Let us beseech God that if we are to receive sufferings, they will be received here below.

INTERPRETIVE NOTES. 1. To the first of the last two petitions of the Our Father, Teresa devoted four chapters. The first (38) dealt with the most basic temptation, the second (39), with some temptations in detail. In these last two chapters she concentrated on two remedies: love and fear of God. We recall that at the beginning of her book Teresa asserted she would deal with only three things necessary for following the way of prayer. The first of these was love for one another (4.4); the other two, detachment and humility, then followed. The latter "are two inseparable sisters" (3.10). Now, at the end, she has two virtues ("fortified castles") belonging to those who are genuine contemplatives (in her lexicon), those who have completed a long part of the journey. These two virtues are the fruit of prayer.

2. Great love is always present in contemplatives, and it cannot be concealed. This love responds positively to everything in life that is good and true; it is a great fire, a safeguard against temptations. When Teresa asserted that if we possess love, we are certain of being in the state of grace, an anonymous censor wrote of such certitude in the margin: "which is impossible save by a special privilege." He was reacting to Teresa's words from within the climate of the Council of Trent. It had declared that "no one can know with the certitude of faith whether he is in grace or not." But just before, Teresa had said that you cannot be very certain or definite about whether you have these two virtues or not. Nonetheless, she insists that love will show itself and be clearly recognized. The Council of Trent was responding negatively to the claim that it is necessary for the sinner to have an inner certitude of being justified in order to be justified. As to whether one can be certain of being in grace, the Council wanted to deny explicitly only a certitude of infallible faith. It left to the investigation of theologians what other kinds of

certitude might be possible. They came to agree that certain signs could indicate the presence of grace: a willingness to serve Christ, to be with him in prayer. This doesn't necessarily require consolation. It would imply turning away from sin and avoiding the occasions of sin. The resulting certitude is called moral certitude. You cannot, however, have a certitude with regard to the future. And so for Teresa, manifest love must still be accompanied by fear of God.

3. In regard to the foregoing, Teresa asserted the same view in her *Life:* "Through extensive conjecturing the soul feels within itself that it truly loves him; in those who reach this state love isn't disguised as in the beginning stages, but it operates with such powerful impulses and desires to see God, as I shall say afterward or have already said, that everything tires, everything wearies, everything torments. If it is not with God or for God, there is no rest that doesn't weary it; so this love is something very clear and, as I say, doesn't pass by in disguise" (26.1). Such love in a way increased her fear of being separated from God: "If my intellect busies itself with this wisdom, my will complains. It wouldn't want anything to hinder it from loving you, because the intellect cannot reach the sublime grandeurs of its God. And my will desires to enjoy him, but it doesn't see how it can since it is placed in a prison as painful as is this mortality. Everything hinders my will, although it was helped by the consideration of your grandeurs, by which my countless miseries are better revealed.

"Why have I said this, my God? To whom am I complaining? Who hears me but you, my Father and Creator? That you might hear of my sorrow, what need have I to speak, for I so clearly see that you are within me? This is foolish to me. But, alas, my God, how can I know for certain I'm not separated from you? O my life, how can you live with such little assurance of something so important? Who will desire you, since the gain one can acquire or hope for from you, that is, to please God in all, is so uncertain and full of dangers?" (S 1.2–3).

QUESTIONS FOR DISCUSSION: 1. How can I know whether or not I truly love God?

2. What are some ways in which we can favor good?

3. What are some of Teresa's thoughts about the hour of our death?

Chapter 41

Speaks of the fear of God and of how we must be on guard against venial sins.

HOW LENGTHY I HAVE BEEN! But not as lengthy as I wanted to be, for it is a delight to speak about the love of God. What will it be like to possess it? May the Lord give it to me because of who His Majesty is. [Let me not leave this life, O my Lord, until I no longer desire anything in it; neither let me know any love outside of you, Lord, nor let me succeed in using this term "love" for anyone else. Everything is false since the foundation is false, and so the edifice doesn't last. I don't know why we are surprised. I laugh to myself when I hear it said: "That person repaid me badly." "This other one doesn't love me." What does anyone have to repay you for, or why should anyone love you? This experience will show you what the world is, for your very love for it will afterward punish you. And this is what wears you down: you realize you have let your affection become involved like children in their games.][1]

Now let us deal with the fear of God.[2] This trait is also something easily recognized by the person who has it as well as by those who approach him. But I want you to understand that in the beginning it is not so developed, unless in some persons to whom, as I have said,[3] the Lord grants great favors, for in a short time he makes them rich in virtue. Hence this fear isn't discernible in everyone — at the outset, I mean. It goes on increasing in strength each day. But it is soon recognized because in the beginning one starts to turn away from sin and its occasions and from bad companions; and other signs as well are seen. But once the soul has reached contemplation — which is what we are now dealing with most — the fear of God also, as with love, becomes very manifest; it doesn't disguise itself even exteriorly. Despite the fact that you may watch these persons very carefully, you will not see them become careless. For no matter how long we observe them, the Lord keeps them in such a way that even if a thing very much to their own interest comes along, they will not advertently commit a venial sin; mortal sins they fear like fire. And illusions involving sin are the ones I would want us, Sisters, to be very much afraid of. Let us beseech God always that the temptation may not be so strong as to make us offend him, that its strength might not outweigh the fortitude he gives us to conquer it. This fear is what is important; it is what I desire may never be taken from us, for it is what will help us.

2. Oh, what a great thing it is to have resisted offending the Lord so that his slaves and servants in hell may be bound; for in the end all must serve him despite themselves. But those in hell do so by force, whereas we do so willingly. Therefore, if we please the Lord, those in hell will be kept bound; they will not do anything that may be harmful to us however much they might draw us into temptation and set secret snares for us.

3. Be careful and attentive — this is very important — until you see that you are strongly determined not to offend the Lord, that you would lose a thousand lives rather than commit a mortal sin, and that you are most careful not to commit venial sins — that is, advertently; for otherwise, who can go without committing many? But there is an advertence that is very deliberate; another that comes so quickly that committing the venial sin and adverting to it happen almost together

in such a way that we don't first realize what we are doing. But from any very deliberate sin, however small it be, may God deliver us. [I don't know how we could be so bold as to go against such a great Lord, even though it be in something very small.] What's more, there is nothing small if it goes against his immense Majesty and we see he is looking at us. It seems to me a sin is very deliberate when, for example, one says: "Lord, although this grieves you, I will do it; I'm already aware that you see it, and I know you do not want it, and I understand this; but I want to follow my whim and appetite more than your will." It doesn't seem to me possible that something like this can be called little, however light the fault; but it's serious, very serious. [For the love of God, daughters, never become careless in this regard; now — glory be to the Lord — you are not.]

4. Consider, Sisters, for the love of God, if you want to gain this fear of the Lord, that it is very helpful to understand the seriousness of an offense against God and to reflect on this frequently in your thoughts; for it is worth our life and much more to have this virtue rooted in our souls. And until you have it, you must always proceed carefully and turn from every occasion and companion who does not help you come closer to God. We should take great care in everything we do to bend our will, and take care that our speech be edifying; we must flee those places where conversations are not of God.

It's very necessary that this fear be deeply impressed within the soul. Such fear is easy to obtain if there is true love together with a great inner determination, as I have said,[4] not to commit an offense against God for any created thing, even though afterward the soul may sometimes fall because we are weak and have no reason to trust ourselves. When we are more determined we are less confident of ourselves, for confidence must be placed in God. When we understand this that I said about ourselves, there will be no need to go about so tense and constrained; the Lord will protect us, and the habit acquired will now be a help against offending him. The need instead will be to go about with a holy freedom, conversing with those who are good even though they may be somewhat worldly. For those who, before you possessed this authentic fear of God, were a poison and a means of killing the soul will afterward often be a help to your loving and praising God more because he has freed you from that which you recognize as a glaring danger. If previously you played a part in contributing to their weaknesses, now by your mere presence you contribute to their restraint; this happens without their having any idea of paying you honor.

5. I often praise the Lord, thinking how it comes about that often a servant of God, without uttering a word, prevents things from being said against God. This must happen for the same reason that something similar happens here below: there is always some restraint so as not to offend an absent person in the presence of someone known to be a friend. So it is with servants of God: their friendship with God wins them respect no matter how lowly their status, and others avoid afflicting them in a matter they so well realize would grieve them; that is, others avoid offending God in their presence. The fact is that I don't know the reason for this, but I do know that it's a common occurrence. So do not be tense, for if you begin to feel constrained, such a feeling will be very harmful to everything good, and at times you will end up being scrupulous and become incapable of doing anything for yourself or for others. And if you don't end up being scrupulous, this constraint will be good for you but it will not bring many souls to God, because they will see so much repression and tenseness. Our nature is such that this constraint is frightening and oppressive to others, and they flee from following the road that you are taking, even though they know clearly that it is the more virtuous path.

6. Another harm derives from this attitude; it is that of judging others. There are those who advance with greater holiness and in order to be of benefit speak to their neighbor freely and without this constraint; but since they do not journey by your path they at once seem to you to be imperfect. If they have a holy joy, it will seem to be dissipation, especially to those of us who have no learning or knowledge of what one can speak about without sinning. This constraint is a very dangerous thing; it means going about in continual temptation and it bears ill effects; it is detrimental to your neighbor. To think that if all do not proceed as you do, in this constrained way, they are not proceeding well is extremely wrong.

And there is another harm: in some things of which you must speak, and it is right that you speak, you don't dare do so for fear of going to extremes; rather, perhaps, you speak well of something that it would be very good for you to abhor.

7. So, Sisters, strive as much as you can, without offense to God, to be affable and understanding in such a way that everyone you talk to will love your conversation and desire your manner of living and acting, and not be frightened and intimidated by virtue. This is very important for religious; the holier they are the more sociable they are with their Sisters. And even though you may feel very distressed if all your Sisters' conversations do not go as you would like them to, never turn away from them if you want to help your Sisters and be loved. This is what we must strive for earnestly, to be affable, agreeable, and pleasing to persons with whom we deal, especially our Sisters.

8. Thus, my daughters, strive to think rightly about God, for he doesn't look at trifles as much as you think, and don't lose your courage or allow your soul to be constrained, for many blessings could be lost. Have the right intention, a resolute will, as I have said,[5] not to offend God. Don't let your soul

withdraw into a corner, for instead of obtaining sanctity you will obtain many imperfections that the devil in other ways will place before you; and, as I have said,[6] you will not be of as much benefit to yourself or to others as you could have been.

9. Here you see how, with these two virtues — love and fear of God — you can advance on this road calmly and quietly, but not carelessly since fear must always take the lead. As long as we live, we will never have complete security; that would be a great danger. And this is what our Teacher understood when at the end of this prayer he spoke these words to his Father as one who well understood they were necessary.[7]

THE FEAR OF GOD

She considers the second of the two fortified castles.

41.1–5: A. She begins with a prayer that she will know no other love outside of her Lord.

B. She turns to her sisters: The world will punish you for any love you have for it.

C. She takes up the subject of the fear of God.

- This trait is also something easily recognized, within oneself or within others.

- Once a person has reached contemplation, the fear of God, as with love, becomes very manifest.

  - Persons with this fear will not become careless.

  - They will not advertently commit a venial sin; mortal sins they fear like fire.

    - There is an advertence that is very deliberate.

    - There is an advertence that comes so quickly along with the venial sin that we don't first realize what we are doing.

  - Nothing is small if we see it goes against his immense Majesty and we are very deliberate.

  - To gain this fear of the Lord, it is very helpful to understand the seriousness of an offense against God and to reflect on this frequently.

  - Our confidence must be placed in God, not in ourselves, for we are weak.

– People who prior to your gaining this fear were a danger now are an occasion for your loving and praising God because he freed you from the glaring danger of sin.

41.5–8: A. Often a servant of God without uttering a word prevents things from being said against God.

B. Do not be tense; constraint will be harmful to everything good.

- Constraint will not bring many souls to God.

- Constraint is frightening and oppressive to others and they flee from the road you are taking.

C. Another harm deriving from constraint is that of judging others for being joyful and free in their speech.

D. Another harm: you don't speak for fear of going to extremes, when in fact you should speak.

E. Strive to be affable and understanding.

- The holier you are the more sociable you will be.

- We must strive to be affable, agreeable, and pleasing to others.

F. God doesn't look at trifles as much as you think.

- Have the right intention and you will not offend God.

- Don't withdraw into a corner.

41.9: With these two virtues (love and fear of God) you can advance on this road (or way of perfection) calmly and quietly, but not carelessly.

- As long as we live we will never have complete security.

- Our Teacher understood this when he spoke these words at the end of his prayer.

INTERPRETIVE NOTES: 1. The fear of offending God through sin is the fear that Teresa wants us to have always. This is a fear that while undeveloped in the beginning grows as one grows in divine love. One of the fears that Teresa felt and which motivated her when she entered the religious life was the fear that she would go to hell if she didn't enter. She calls this fear "servile fear" (L 3.5–6). Many were the other fears Teresa endured herself and saw in others: fear of mental prayer, fear of vainglory, fear of illusions, fear of the devil, fear of trials, fear of dead bodies, fears before taking possesion of a new foundation, fear of oneself and one's weaknesses. Probably her worst experience of fear was of being deceived by the devil in the favors the Lord was granting her. Her directors contributed to this fear. A group of "five or six of them" came to the decision that her experience of God's favors was from the devil. She became "extremely fearful." "I was alone then without any person in whom I could find some support, unable to pray vocally or read, but terrified by so much tribulation and fear as to whether the devil would deceive me" (L 25.17).

While in this affliction she heard the Lord speak: "Do not fear, daughter; for I am, and I will not abandon you; do not fear" (18). These words brought about in her calm, courage, and security. In a short while she saw that she was another person. She wrote: "May it please His Majesty that we fear him whom we ought to fear and understand that more harm can come to us from one venial sin than from all hell together — for this is so" (20). As Teresa's love for God grew, all her other fears lost their power to affect her, and she remained with the one fear that always grew greater: the fear of offending God. Her mystical experience of his Majesty intensified her understanding of what an offense against God was and so also her fear of offending him. Of her experience of ecstasy, she wrote: "There is revealed a majesty about the One who can do this that makes a person's hair stand on edge, and there remains a strong fear of offending so awesome a God. Yet such fear is accompanied by great love for him, which grows ever deeper" (L 20.7).

2. It would be easy to think this fear of offending God involves much constraint. But constraint comes from a lack of confidence in God. It can be a sign we are trusting in ourselves. The first redaction of the *Way of Perfection* ended this chapter after number 6. In her second redaction Teresa added the wonderful exhortations in numbers 7–9. With further warnings against this constraint, she points out that God doesn't look at trifles as much as we think. As for the rest, Teresa herself was a congenial example of the affable, sociable, and pleasant bearing she highly recommends.

QUESTIONS FOR DISCUSSION: 1. How does the fear of God differ from all our other fears?

2. Why is fear of God so closely linked to love of God?

3. What are your reflections on Teresa's words that the holier you are the more sociable you will be?

4. How might this image of the two fortified castles help me in my spiritual life?

Chapter 42

Discusses these last words of the Our Father: Sed libera nos a malo. Amen. *But deliver us from evil. Amen.*

IT SEEMS TO ME JESUS WAS RIGHT to include himself in this petition, for we already see how tired he was of this life when he said to his Apostles at the last supper: *I have greatly desired to eat this supper with you.*[1] Here we see how weary he must have been of living. Nowadays people don't tire of living even if they go on to be a hundred, but always want to live longer. True, we don't suffer in life as much evil and as many trials as His Majesty suffered, nor such poverty. What was his whole life if not a continual death, in which he always saw beforehand that most cruel death they were going to inflict on him? And this was the least of his sufferings; but how many offenses committed against his Father and what a multitude of souls that were lost! If one who possesses charity here on earth finds all this a great torment, what must have been the Lord's torment, with his boundless and immeasurable charity? And what a good reason he had to beseech the Father to free him finally from so many evils and trials and bring him to rest forever in the Father's kingdom, since he was its true inheritor!

2. *Amen.* By the "amen" I understand that since with this word all things come to an end, the Lord asks likewise that we be freed from all evil forever. [It is useless, Sisters, to think

461

that while we live we can be free of many temptations and imperfections and even sins, for it is said that the soul that thinks
it is without sin deceives itself[2] — and this is true. Now, if we
turn to bodily ailments and hardships, who is without very
many and in many ways? Nor is it good that we ask to be without them.

Well, then, let us understand what we are asking for here
since it seems impossible to say "from all evil," whether of the
body or, as I have said, of imperfections and faults in the service of God. I am not speaking about the saints-they can do
everything in Christ, as St. Paul said[3] — but sinners like myself. I see myself closed in by weakness, lukewarmness, and a
lack of mortification, and many other things. I see that it behooves me to ask the Lord for a remedy. You, daughters, ask
according to what you think. I do not find this remedy while
living, and so I ask the Lord to deliver me from all evil forever. What good do we find in this life, Sisters, since we lack
so much good and are absent from him?

Deliver me, Lord, from this shadow of death, deliver me
from so many trials, deliver me from so many sufferings, deliver me from so many changes, from so many compliments that
we are forced to receive while still living, from so many, many,
many things that tire and weary me, that would tire anyone
reading this if I mentioned them all. There's no longer anyone who can bear to live. This weariness must come to me because I have lived so badly, and from seeing that the way I live
now is still not the way I should live since I owe so much.]
Thus I beseech the Lord to deliver me from all evil forever since
I do not make up for what I owe; it could be that perhaps each
day I become more indebted. And what is unendurable, Lord,
is not to know for certain that I love you or that my desires
are acceptable before you. O my Lord and my God, deliver me
now from all evil and be pleased to bring me to the place where
all blessings are. What do they still hope for here, those to whom

you have given knowledge of what the world is, and those who have a living faith concerning what the Eternal Father has kept for them?

3. To ask for these blessings with great desire and complete determination is a clear sign for contemplatives that the favors they receive in prayer are from God. Thus those who have this sign should esteem their prayer highly. In the case of my asking for these things the same is not true; I mean that it shouldn't be interpreted as a sign of divine favors; but since I have lived so badly, I fear living still longer; and so many trials weary me. It is no surprise that those who have a share in the consolations of God desire to be there where they will enjoy them more than in mere sips, that they do not want to remain in a life where there are these many obstacles to the enjoyment of so much good, and that they desire to be where the Sun of justice[4] does not set. Everything they afterward see here below will be completely dark to them, and I marvel at how they live. They cannot live with any contentment if they have received and already begun to enjoy the Lord's kingdom here below. And such persons must not live for their own will but for the will of their King.

4. Oh, how different this life would have to be in order for one not to desire death! How our will deviates in its inclination from that which is the will of God. He wants us to love truth; we love the lie. He wants us to desire the eternal; we, here below, lean toward what comes to an end. He wants us to desire sublime and great things; we, here below, desire base and earthly things. He would want us to desire only what is secure; we, here below, love the dubious. Everything is a mockery, my daughters, except beseeching God to free us from these dangers forever and draw us at last away from every evil. Even though our desire may not be perfect, let us force ourselves to make the request. What does it cost us to ask for a great deal? We are asking it of One who is powerful. But in

order to be right, let us leave the giving to his will since we have already given him our own. His name be forever hallowed in heaven and on earth, and may his will be always done in me. Amen.

[Here you see, friends, what it means to pray vocally with perfection. It means that you be aware of and understand whom you are asking, who it is that is asking, and what you are asking for. When they tell you that it isn't good to practice any other kind of prayer than vocal prayer, do not be distressed. Read this very carefully, and what you do not understand about prayer, beseech the Lord to teach you. For no one can take vocal prayer from you or make you recite the Our Father hastily and without understanding it. If some person should take it from you or counsel you to give it up, do not believe him. Believe that he is a false prophet and consider that in these times of ours you don't have to believe everybody. Even though there is nothing to fear from those who can counsel you now, we don't know what will come in the future.

I have also thought of saying something to you about how to recite the Hail Mary. But I have been so lengthy that I have to let it go. It is enough for you to have understood how to recite the Our Father well in order to know how to recite all the vocal prayers you must recite.]

5. Now see, Sisters, how the Lord by giving me understanding of the great deal we ask for when reciting this evangelical prayer has removed the difficulty involved in my teaching you and myself the path that I began to explain to you. May he be blessed forever! Certainly, it never entered my mind that this prayer contained so many deep secrets; for now you have seen the entire spiritual way contained in it, from the beginning stages until God engulfs the soul and gives it to drink abundantly from the fount of living water, which he said was to be found at the end of the way.[5] [And having come

out of it — I mean of this prayer — I don't know how to go any further.]

It seems the Lord has desired to give us understanding, Sisters, of the great consolation contained in this prayer. It is highly beneficial to persons who don't know how to read. If they understand this prayer, they can draw a lot of doctrine from it and find consolation there. [And when books are taken away from us, this book cannot be taken away, for it comes from the mouth of Truth itself, who cannot err. And since, as I have said, we recite the Our Father so many times in a day, let us delight in it and strive to learn from so excellent a Master the humility with which he prays and all the other things that were mentioned.]

6. Sisters, beg this good Master to pardon me, for I have been bold to speak of such sublime things. His Majesty knows well that my intellect would not have been capable of it if he had not taught me what I have said. Be grateful to him, Sisters, for he must have done so because of the humility with which you asked me and desired to be taught by someone so miserable.

[Well, Sisters, it now seems the Lord doesn't want me to say any more, for I don't know what to say; although I thought of going on. The Lord has taught you and me the path that I have described in the book I said I wrote,[6] how one reaches this fount of living water, what the soul feels there, how God satisfies it, takes away thirst for earthly things, and makes it grow in the things pertaining to the service of God. Those who have reached this fount will find that book very beneficial and receive much light from it. You may get it from Father Domingo Báñez, a *presentado* of the Order of St. Dominic, who as I said is my confessor and the one to whom I'll give this book. If this one is all right for you to see and he gives it to you, he'll also give you that other one.]

7. If he thinks this book will be helpful and gives it to you, I will be consoled that you are consoled. If it should be such that no one may see it, you can accept my good will, for by this work I have obeyed your command. I consider myself well paid for the trouble involved in writing it, for there has been no trouble at all in thinking out what I have said. May the Lord be blessed and praised; from him comes every good we speak of, think about, and do. Amen.

THE FINAL PETITION AND CONCLUSION

Teresa brings her book to a close with a prayerful reflection on the final petition of the Our Father and some concluding remarks.

42.1: We see in his words at the Last Supper how weary Jesus must have been of living(Lk 22:15).

- Nowadays people don't tire of living, but always want to live longer.

- We don't suffer as much as His Majesty.

- What good reason he had to beseech the Father to free him finally from so many evils and trials.

42.2–3: By the "amen" I understand that with this word all things come to an end, that we be freed from evil forever.

- It is useless to think we can be free of temptations, imperfections, sins, and bodily ailments.

- I see myself closed in by weakness and that it behooves me to ask the Lord for a remedy.

  - I don't find the remedy while living.

  - So I ask the Lord to deliver me from all evil forever.

  - This weariness must come to me because I have lived so badly.

- Speaking to the Lord she observes, "what is unendurable, Lord, is not to know for certain that

I love you or that my desires are acceptable before you."

- To ask for the blessings the Father has kept for them is a clear sign to contemplatives that the favors they receive in prayer are from God.

  - They want to be where they will enjoy the consolations of God more than in mere sips.

  - They cannot live with any contentment if they have received and already begun to enjoy the Lord's kingdom.

42.4: A. How our will deviates in its inclination from that which is the will of God.

- From truth to the lie, from the eternal to what comes to an end, from sublime things to base things, from the secure to the dubious.

- Everything is a mockery except beseeching God to free us from these evils and to draw us away at last from every evil.

B. Here you see what it means to pray vocally with perfection.

- No one can take vocal prayer from you or make you recite the Our Father hastily.

- If some person should counsel you to give up the Our Father, don't believe him.

- In these times of ours you don't have to believe everybody.

42.5: See how the Lord by giving me understanding has removed the difficulty involved in my teaching you and myself the path I began to explain.

- It never entered my mind that this prayer contained so many deep secrets.

- Now you have seen the entire spiritual way contained in it.

    - When books are taken away from us, this book cannot be taken away: it comes from the mouth of Truth itself.

    - Let us find our delight in it.

42.6: A. His Majesty has taught me what I have said.

B. Those who have reached this fount will find that other book (her *Life*) beneficial and enlightening.

- If Father Domingo Báñez gives you this book, he'll also give you the other one.

- If he thinks this book will be helpful and gives it to you, I will be consoled that you are consoled.

- If it is such that no one may see it, you can accept my good will.

- I consider the trouble of thinking out what I said well paid, for it was no trouble at all.

C. Concludes with a doxology.

INTERPRETIVE NOTES: 1. The anonymous censor for some reason took exception to Teresa's thoughts about Jesus being tired and wearied of life. Teresa proceeds in a meditative mood awakened by this last petition in which she manifests her longing to be free of all the evils she suffers in her earthly condition. She doesn't find a remedy in this life; in it she suffers from the lack of so much good and the absence of Christ. This all leads into her stirring prayer for deliverance. For Teresa, being delivered from all evil is equivalent to being brought to the place where all blessings are. Longing and asking for these blessings are the results of the favors of contemplative prayer, she asserts.

2. In this final chapter she once more returns to the defense of mental prayer and of how vocal prayer if it is to be genuine cannot be separated from mental prayer. If her readers understand how to recite the Our Father well, they will know how to recite well all the other vocal prayers they must recite. Alhough books may be taken from them, no one can take the Our Father from them, which is itself a book, coming from the mouth of Truth. They shouldn't believe anyone who counsels them to give it up.

3. The final numbers of this chapter constitute a kind of epilogue in which Teresa again expresses her amazement at all the deep secrets about the spiritual journey or way of perfection contained in the Our Father. Those who have reached the fount of living waters will find in her other book, *The Book of Her Life*, further beneficial teaching. But whether they are allowed to read this *Way of Perfection* or the other book depends on the

censor who she thought would be Domingo Báñez. As things turned out he was not one of the censors for this book, nor did he allow the nuns to read Teresa's *Life*. But today we can all freely read that other book about God's remarkable mercies. As for Teresa, she feels well repaid for the understanding given her by the Lord while writing this present book. She marvelled at the deep secrets contained in the Our Father; with Christians through the centuries, we marvel too at what she found there; her little book of counsels about prayer and the way of perfection has become a classic.

QUESTIONS FOR DISCUSSION: 1. Why was Teresa tired of her life on this earth?

2. What do you think of her interpretation of Christ's words at the Last Supper?

3. Do people nowadays always want to live longer on this earth? Do I?

4. Now that we have reached the end, are there any thoughts from Teresa that especially touched you and remained with you?

Notes

INTRODUCTION

1. See *The Collected Works of St. Teresa of Avila*, trans. Kieran Kavanaugh and Otilio Rodriguez, vol. 1 (Washington, D.C.: ICS Publications, 1976), 17-19.
2. See L epilogue.2.
3. See W 42.6.
4. Ibid., prologue.1.
5. See ibid., 16.3-6; 24.1-2; 30.7.
6. Ibid., prologue.1.
7. Ibid., 15.1.
8. Ibid., 42.6.
9. Ibid.
10. Ibid., prologue.1.
11. See *Camino de Perfección, Reproducción en facsímil del autógrafo de Valladolid*, ed. Tomás de la Cruz et al., vol. 2 (Rome: Tipografia Poliglotta Vaticana, 1965), 15–30.
12. See ibid.
13. Ibid., 16.6.
14. See L 39.22.
15. Ibid., 38.6.
16. See ibid., 20.13.
17. W 1.2.
18. Cf. ibid., 1.2, 5; 3.1, 8; 35.3.
19. L 25.12.
20. Ibid., 25.13.
21. ST 3.13.
22. Cf. W 21.10; 30.4.

473

23. Ibid., 3.9.
24. Ibid., 1.2.
25. Ibid., 3.1.
26. Ibid., 1.2.
27. Ibid. For further details about Teresa and the church, seeTomás de la Cruz, "Santa Teresa de Avila Hija de la Iglesia," *Ephemerides Carmeliticae* 17 (1966): 305-367.
28. For further information about these times, see my introduction to the *Life* in *The Collected Works of St. Teresa of Avila*, vol.1, pp. 6-22.
29. Francisco de Osuna, *Norte de Estados* (Seville, 1591), as quoted by Daniel de Pablo Maroto in *Dinámica de la Oración* (Madrid: Editorial de Espiritualidad, 1973), 109.
30. See *Biblioteca Mística Carmelitana*, ed. Silverio de Santa Teresa, vol. 18 (Burgos: El Monte Carmelo 1934), 10.
31. *Obras Completas de Santa Teresa de Jesús*, ed., Efrén de la Madre de Dios and Otger Steggink (Madrid: Biblioteca de Autores Cristianos, 1967), 190.
32. W 3.7.
33. See J. Ignacio Tellechea Idígoras, "Textos Inéditos sobre El Fenomeno de los Alumbrados," *Ephemerides Carmeliticae* 13 (1962): 768-774.
34. See P. Tommaso della Croce, "Santa Teresa E I Movimenti Spirituali Del Suo Tempo," *Santa Teresa Maestra De Orazione* (Rome: Teresianum, 1963), 30-36. Cf. D. de Pablo Maroto, *Dinámica De La Oración*, 106.
35. See L 26.5.
36. See D. de Pablo Maroto, *Dinámica De La Oración*, 107.
37. W 21.2
38. Ibid., 22.2.
39. Ibid., 21.8.
40. *Camino de Perfección, Reproducción en facsímil del autógrafo de Valladolid*, vol. 2, 76.
41. W 3.7
42. See ibid.
43. See ibid., 11.4.
44. Cf. *Rule of St. Albert*, eds. H. Clarke and B. Edwards (Aylesford: Carmelite Priory, 1973).
45. W 13.6.
46. Ibid., 4.9.

47. For a glimpse of life at the Incarnation, see P. Tomás Alvarez, "La visita del padre Rubeo a las carmelitas de La Encarnación de Avila (1567)," *Monte Carmelo* 86 (1978): 5-25. Cf. also D. de Pablo Maroto, "Camino De Perfección," *Introducción A La Lectura De Santa Teresa* (Madrid: Editorial de Espiritualidad, 1978): 285-288.
48. W 27.6.
49. Ibid., 2.8.
50. Ibid., 2.6.
51. Ibid., 4.7.
52. See ibid., 1.2.
53. See ibid., 4.1-2.
54. See ibid., 4.4.
55. Ibid., prologue.2.
56. See ibid., 4.12, note 8.
57. Ibid., 41.5.
58. Ibid., 2.8, note 4.
59. Ibid., 7.5.
60. Ibid., 10.2.
61. See ibid., 11.3.
62. Ibid., 12.5.
63. Ibid., 13.5, note 2.
64. Ibid., 10.3.
65. Ibid., 16.2.
66. Ibid., 39.2.
67. Ibid., 38.7.
68. Ibid., 19.1.
69. Ibid., 19.2.
70. Ibid.
71. Ibid., 28.4.
72. Ibid., 29.5.
73. Ibid., 26.3.
74. Ibid., 29.5.
75. Ibid., 26.3.
76. See ibid., 29.4.
77. Ibid., 28.7.
78. Ibid., 28.4.
79. Ibid., 29.7.
80. Ibid., 29.6.

81. See ibid., 26.4, 5, 8.
82. Ibid., 30.6-7.
83. Ibid., 31.6.
84. Ibid., 42.5.
85. Ibid., 21.2.

FOREWORD

1. Although St. Joseph's in Avila was founded by Teresa, she was not the first prioress. The first prioress was an older nun from the Incarnation, Ana de San Juan (Dávila), who was severe with Teresa, mortifying and humiliating her. After a short while this nun returned to the Incarnation because of bad health, and Teresa, near the beginning of March, 1563, was appointed prioress. She remained so until 1568, and certainly held office while writing this book.
2. This declaration of submission to the Roman Church was written later by Teresa in the copy of Toledo, which was sent for publication in 1579 to Don Teutonio de Braganza, archbishop of Evora.

PROLOGUE

1. An academic title, the equivalent of licentiate.
2. According to Teresa, Fr. Báñez was her confessor for six years, approximately from 1562 to 1568 (see ST 58.8).
3. A reference to her *Life*, the second redaction of which was finished at St. Joseph's in Avila toward the end of 1565, before she started *The Way of Perfection*.

CHAPTER 2

1. Allusion to Lk 21:33.
2. Here Teresa alludes to the social attitude in sixteenth-century Spain in which honor was reserved for people of the upper class or nobility. According to Philip II's *Pragmática*, titles were to be used only by the nobility. Poor people had no right to titles, and so were not honored or esteemed.

3. Teresa might have read such words, attributed to St. Clare, in St. Bonaventure's *Leyenda mayor de S. Francisco y S. Clara* (Toledo, 1526).

4. In the first redaction she wrote more emphatically: "...may such a building fall to the ground and kill you all the day you desire one. Moreover, I say this without remorse, and I'll beg it of God."

5. In the mind of Teresa the number of nuns in each community should be small. In 1561 she thought of fifteen (see *Letters*, to Lorenzo de Cepeda, 12 December 1561). Later she spoke of thirteen (see L 32.13), that is, twelve nuns, representing the number of apostles, and the prioress, standing in the place of Christ. Initially, the monastery of the Incarnation at Avila was to have only fourteen nuns, twelve for the apostles, and two others for our Lord and our Lady. When Teresa, following that early tradition of the Incarnation, added the fifteenth, it was to recall St. Joseph. In 1576, Fr. Gratian, as the apostolic commissary, established in accord with Teresa that there be thirteen or fourteen nuns, excluding the lay Sisters, in houses founded in poverty and twenty in those having an income. See *Biblioteca Mística Carmelitana*, ed. P. Silverio de Santa Teresa, O.C.D., 20 vols. (Burgos: El Monte Carmelo, 1915-1935), 6:525 (hereafter cited as BMC).

CHAPTER 3

1. Namely, the two mentioned in the preceding paragraph, wherein is contained the apostolic element of the Teresian charism.

2. This paragraph was deleted in the first redaction by Fr. García de Toledo, who thought it was too daring for the attitude toward women that was characteristic of the times. Teresa complied and omitted the passage in the second redaction. Nevertheless, it is a stirring statement in favor of women and of what they can contribute to the church and the world.

3. Lk 9:58.

4. A reference to the Bishop of Avila, Don Alvaro de Mendoza (see L 33.16). In the Toledo manuscript she added in her own hand: "...and this order of the Blessed Virgin, and all the other orders."

CHAPTER 4

1. In the autograph (Valladolid) this chapter was divided so that a new chapter began after no. 4. Teresa decided to join them when preparing the copy of Toledo for printing. The chapter heading consists of what originally had been two different headings.
2. The rule states: "Each one of you is to stay in his own cell or nearby, pondering the Lord's law day and night and keeping watch at his prayers unless attending to some other duty." See *The Rule of St. Albert*, eds. H. Clarke, O. Carm. and B. Edwards, O.C.D. (Aylesford: Carmelite Priory, 1973), 83.
3. See ch. 2, note 5.
4. This strong expression is a kind of Teresian anathema indicating a serious and contagious moral evil. See no. 8.
5. Biblical allusion to 1 Pt 1:18-19.
6. See note 2.
7. Jn 13:34.
8. Teresa was not satisfied with the way she wrote in her first redaction about this second type of love; in her second redaction she rewrote this part. But then she tore out the whole sheet and wrote what is contained in no. 13. The following is what she wrote in her first redaction: "…the other is spiritual and mixed with it our own sensuality and weakness. The important thing is that these two kinds of love are unaffected by any passion, for where passion is present the good order is thrown into complete disorder. And if we love discreetly and moderately with the love I mentioned, all will be meritorious, for what seems to us to be sensuality will be converted into virtue. But the sensuality is so intermingled with the spiritual love that at times there is no one who understands this love, especially if it is for some confessor. For if persons who practice prayer see that he is holy and understands their mode of procedure, they will get to love him deeply. And here the devil batters one with scruples that disturb the soul very much, which is what the devil wants to do. If, especially, the confessor is leading the soul to higher perfection, the devil afflicts it so much that it abandons the confessor. And neither if it goes to another confessor nor again to another does the devil cease to torment it with that temptation.

   What souls can do in this situation is to try not to think about whether they love the confessor or don't love him; but if they do love him, let them love him. For since we experience love for one who takes care of our bodies, shouldn't we also love one who always strives and works to care for our souls? Rather, I hold that a great principle for making much progress is to love the confessor, if he is holy and spiritual and if I see that he is diligent about my soul's progress. For our weakness is such that sometimes this love helps us very much to perform great deeds in the service of God. If the love is not of this kind, as I have said, there is danger; and the mere fact that he knows he is loved can do very serious harm, and in houses where there is a great deal of enclosure much more than in others. Because it is difficult to know which confessor is so good, there is need for much caution and prudence. The best advice is that the confessor not know that there is such affection and that no one tell him there is. But The devil so urges the soul to tell the confessor about this love that such advice becomes useless. It seems to the soul that all it has to confess is this affection and that it is obliged to confess it. For this reason I would like the Sisters to realize that this love doesn't amount to anything and pay no attention to it.

Let them take this counsel: if they know that the confessor directs all his words to the profit of their souls and they do not see or know of any other vanity (for this is soon understood by anyone who doesn't want to become a fool), and they know that he is God-fearing, they should not weary themselves over any temptation they may have about their great attachment; when the devil is worn out he will go away. But if they should become aware that the confessor is turning toward some vanity in what he says to them, they should be suspicious about it all and in no way carry on conversations with him even though these may concern prayer or God; but they should make their confession briefly and bring it to a conclusion. And it would be best to tell the Mother prioress that your soul doesn't get on well with him and change confessors. That would be the most proper thing to do, if there is the opportunity to do so, and I hope in God there will be. And you should do what you can to avoid speaking with him — even suffer death."

9. In no. 14.

CHAPTER 5

1. It is worth noting that this Teresian teaching on freedom for cloistered nuns with regard to confessors was later accepted by church law.

2. The first redaction has a somewhat different slant: "Let her always try to speak to someone with learning; and her nuns should do so as well. May God deliver them from being ruled in everything by the confessor if he is not learned, no matter how spiritual he may seem to be or in fact is."

3. In her *Life* Teresa mentions several instances in which she received bad counsel: 4.7; 5.3; 6.4; 8.11; 26.3.

4. The first redaction continues: "And do not take away their freedom to confess at times with learned men and to discuss their prayer with them even though there are confessors. For many reasons I know that this is fitting and that the harm that might arise is nothing in comparison with the deception and great harm, almost without remedy, so to speak, that comes with the opposite practice. For what happens in monasteries is that good soon suffers a decline if it is not preserved with great care, and evil once it gets started is extremely difficult to get rid of because very quickly the custom becomes a habit and imperfections become natural."

5. In Teresa's time the vicar of a cloistered monastery of nuns was a priest appointed by the local bishop or provincial with special instructions concerning the government of the monastery.

6. The first redaction continues, with insistence: "For as I have said, after everything was considered, grave reasons were found for deciding that this was the best course of action, that is: that the chaplain, if there be one, serve as the ordinary confessor and that when a soul feels the need, confession may be made to persons like the ones mentioned. These may be named by the bishop, or if the Mother prioress is such that the bishop entrusts this task to her, she may name them on her own. Since there are few nuns, they will take little of anyone's time. This practice was decided upon after much prayer by many persons including myself — although wretched — and among many persons of great learning, intelligence, and prayer. So I hope in the Lord it is the most fitting thing to do."

7. The reason the first monastery founded by Teresa was subject to the jurisdiction of the local bishop of Avila can be found in her *Life*, 33.16. See also the original petition to the Holy See in the latter part of 1561 as well as the brief "ex parte vestra" (7 February 1562) in *Monumenta Historica Carmeli Teresiani*, ed. Institutum Historicum Teresianum, vol. 1 (Rome: Teresianum, 1973–), 5, 10.

CHAPTER 6

1. See ch. 4, no. 12. She intended to explain two kinds of love: one, purely spiritual; the other, mixed. She continues here the topic of purely spiritual love.

CHAPTER 7

1. See ch. 6, nos. 6, 9.
2. See ch. 6, no. 9.
3. In no. 4.
4. See ch. 2, note 5.
5. The first redaction concludes in the following way: "Because I will treat of this elsewhere, I'll say no more about it here, except that even though your love may not be as perfect as that just mentioned, provided that it goes out toward all in general, I would rather you love one another with tenderness and delight than that there be a moment of discord. May the Lord not permit such discord because of who His Majesty is. Amen."

CHAPTER 8

1. See ch. 2, note 5.
2. Our Lord called Teresa from the monastery of the Incarnation in Avila where there were more than 180 nuns to found the little monastery of St. Joseph where the number was lowered to thirteen.

CHAPTER 9

1. In no. 2.

CHAPTER 10

1. Allusion to Ex 16; Wis 16:20.
2. The first redaction puts it more strongly: "Sometimes they feel a frenzy for doing penance without rhyme or reason, a frenzy that lasts only a couple of days, so to speak. Subsequently, the devil makes them imagine that the penances did them harm. No more penance! Not even, after some attempts, what the order commands."

CHAPTER 12

1. In ch. 11, no. 5.
2. See ch. 11, no. 4.
3. See no. 1; ch. 11, no. 5.
4. The first redaction adds: "Perform some public mortification also since they are practiced in this house. Flee these temptations of the devil as you would a plague, and don't allow him to stay with you."
5. In no. 6.
6. Jb 2:9-13.

CHAPTER 13

1. Allusion to Lk 1:48-52; 14:11.
2. The first redaction goes on at greater length and is put more strongly: "Oh, what a great act of charity and what a great service to God a nun would perform if when she sees that she cannot follow the practices of perfection and customs of this house she would recognize the fact and go, and leave the others in peace! And they shouldn't keep her in any of the monasteries — at least if they believe me — nor allow her to make profession until after many years of trial to see if she makes amends. I am not referring to failures in the penance and fasts. Even though these are faults, such failures are not things that cause so much harm. But I am speaking about persons who by temperament like to be esteemed and honored and who look at the faults of others and never at their own, and other similar things that truly arise from lack of humility. If God doesn't favor her with a great spiritual gift and if after many years you don't see her make amends, may he free you so that she doesn't remain in your company. Realize that she won't be at peace nor will she allow anyone else to be. Since you do not accept a dowry, God grants you the freedom to send a nun away. What I pity about monasteries is that often, so as not to return the money, they allow the thief to steal the treasure from them, or they do so for the sake of the relatives' honor. In this house you have risked and lost the honor of this world, for the poor receive no honor. Don't desire that others have it at such a cost to yourselves. Our honor, Sisters, must be

to serve God. If someone becomes a hindrance to your doing this, she should remain at home with her honor. For this reason our fathers ordained a one-year probation, and in our order we have the faculty to delay the profession for four years. And in this house I would like to delay it even ten years. A humble nun will not mind a delay of profession. She already knows that if she is good they will not dismiss her; if she is not good, why does she desire to do harm to this college of Christ? In saying 'not good,' I am not speaking of some vanity; for, with God's help, I hope such a thing will stay far from this house. In saying 'not good,' I mean not being mortified but being attached to worldly things or to oneself in the matters I have mentioned. And the nun who doesn't see much detachment in herself should believe me and not make profession, if she doesn't want to have a hell here below. And please God she will not have another in the next life, for there are many things in her that could cause such a misfortune; and perhaps those in the house will not understand them, nor perhaps will she, as I have understood them."

CHAPTER 14

1. In sixteenth-century Spain only the first-born male was entitled to the inheritance. Convent life, as a result, provided a secure future for many girls, and they often entered a monastery without a vocation.

CHAPTER 15

1. See ch. 11, no. 5; ch. 16, nos. 1-2.
2. The first redaction goes on in greater detail: "These false accusations, no matter how serious, did not disturb me. But in little things I followed my nature — and continue to follow it — without paying attention to what is more perfect. Hence I would like each of you to begin early to understand and reflect upon the much that is gained through all the various ways, and that no one, in my opinion, loses by following any of them. The main thing gained is that in some manner we follow the Lord. I say 'in some manner,' because, as I have mentioned, we are never blamed without our having faults."

3. Allusion to Prv 24:16; 1 Jn 1:8-10.
4. 1 Cor 14:34.
5. Lk 7:36-40; 10:38. Mary Magdalene, the repentant sinner, and Mary of Bethany were generally in Teresa's surroundings thought to be the same person.
6. Lk 23:41.

CHAPTER 16

1. The first four paragraphs constituted a separate chapter in the first redaction under the heading: "Treats of how necessary it was to mention the things above in order to begin explaining prayer." Teresa copied the four paragraphs in her second redaction but then tore them out, perhaps after having had second thoughts about the advisability of using a "vanity" like the game of chess as an example. After tearing out this short chapter she failed to revise the numbering; thus, a number is missed in the enumeration of the chapters. This chapter 16, then, of the second redaction begins with the fifth paragraph, or number 5. But all editors, from Luis de León to those of the present day, have included these delightful paragraphs in which the chess game provides Teresa with an opportunity for some profound insights and illustrations.
2. These virtues are humility and keeping silent when falsely accused. See ch. 15, nos. 2-3.
3. Allusion to Sng 4:9.
4. See L 8.4.
5. The first redaction contains some important differences: "It often happens that the Lord favors a soul that is in a very wretched state. It should be understood that it is not then in mortal sin, in my opinion. God will permit someone who is in mortal sin to see a vision even a very good one — so as to bring that person back to himself. But I cannot believe that he would place such a person in contemplation. For in that divine union the Lord delights in the soul and the soul in him. It's incongruous that the purity of heaven would delight in a soul stained with sin or that the delight of the angels would find comfort in what is not his. Now we know that by sinning mortally a soul belongs to the devil;

it can delight in him since it has satisfied him, and we already know that his delights are a continual torment even in this life. The Lord will always have devoted sons in whom he can be consoled. He has no need to go about taking those who do not belong to him, although His Majesty will do what he often does: snatch them from the devil's hands."

6. See Mt. 4:5.
7. In the first redaction Teresa wrote and then crossed out the following: "…and how well he deserved on account of his boldness that God should create a new hell for him."
8. In no. 6.
9. Allusion to Mt 21:37.
10. See Eph 6:9; Acts 10:34.
11. In no. 6.

CHAPTER 17

1. The monastery of St. Joseph in Avila.
2. In ch. 12, nos. 6-7.
3. Lk 14:10.
4. In ch. 5, no. 5.
5. The first redaction is more explicit: "I know an elderly nun — please God my life were as good as hers — who is very holy and penitential. She is a great nun and recites much vocal and very ordinary prayer."
6. See L 15.14; 17.3; 20.7, 29.
7. Lk 10:38-40.
8. Allusion to Lk 10:41-42.
9. In no. 2.

CHAPTER 18

1. Allusion to Lk 10:42, of which she spoke in ch. 17, no. 5.
2. The first redaction is more strongly worded: "And how much better is the pay than that of those who serve the king! The poor soldiers are continuously in danger of death, and then only God knows how they are paid." Some authors think this passage reveals Teresa's worries about her brothers who were among the conquistadors.

3. In ch. 30, no. 7.

4. In chapter one of her *Constitutions*, Teresa sets aside two hours daily for mental prayer in common, one in the morning and one in the evening.

5. In the first redaction the military metaphor is preserved: "You don't know when the captain will call you and give you more work, disguised in delight. If he doesn't, you should understand that you are not suited for it and that such a situation is what is fitting for you."

6. Allusion to Mt 25:1-19.

7. See no. 4 and ch. 17, no. 6.

8. Allusion to Mt 20:22.

CHAPTER 19

1. She no doubt has in mind the very popular book by Fray Luis de Granada, O.P., *Libro de Oración y Meditación,* published in Salamanca in 1554 and included in the brief list of books she recommended for the library of each of her convents. See *Constitutions,* ch. 2.

2. Jn 4:14.

3. Allusion to Sng 8:7.

4. See Ps 8:7. The censor, disagreeing with Teresa's interpretation, crossed out this section and noted in the margin: "This is not the meaning of the scriptural passage; it refers to Christ and to Adam as he was in the state of innocence."

5. In ch. 16, nos. 6-13.

6. Note that for Teresa the "living water" refers to contemplation, in contrast to the "muddy water" which refers to discursive prayer.

7. She is speaking of herself. See L 20; ST 1. The first redaction reads as follows: "So great was her thirst, so much was her desire increasing that she understood clearly it would have been possible to die of love if the raptures hadn't soothed the thirst. Blessed be he who in his Gospel invites us to drink! Thus, since in our Lord and our Good there cannot be anything imperfect, he gives us what we need; it belongs to him alone to give us this water."

8. In no. 8.

9. See Phil 1:23.

10. This account can be found in Cassian's *Conferences*. See Philip Schaff and Henry Wace, gen. eds., *The Nicene and Post-Nicene Fathers*, Series Two, 14 vols. (Grand Rapids: Eerdmans, 1964), vol. 11: *The Second Conference of Abbot Moses*, p. 310. Most probably Teresa knew of this story from the *Vida de los Santos Padres* published in Zaragosa, 1511. In the process of beatification Petronila Bautista tells of Teresa's enthusiasm for the conferences of Cassian. "She was very devoted to the *Conferences* of Cassian and of the Fathers of the Desert, and so when this witness was with her the Holy Mother asked her to read two or three accounts of those saints each day and at night tell her about them since she herself didn't have the time to do so because of her just and holy occupations" (BMC, 19:591).

11. In no. 2.

12. This quotation probably amounts to a combination of Jn 7:37 and Mt 11:28.

CHAPTER 20

1. In ch. 17, no. 2.
2. Allusion to Jn 14:2.
3. Allusion to Prv 1:20; Jn 7:37.

CHAPTER 21

1. She returns to the theme she began to deal with in ch. 19, nos. 1-2.
2. Allusion to Jn 4:14.
3. In the first redaction she refers to certain books she had read: "...and although I have read in some books, and even in several, how good it is to begin with such an attitude, nothing will be lost, in my opinion, by mentioning it here."
4. A reference to ch. 19, no. 2.
5. In the first redaction she refers to her *Life:* "I will deal only briefly with the more sublime things, for, as I say, I have already written about them." The last line of the text alludes to the prohibition in 1559 by the Inquisitor, Don Fernando Valdés,

of spiritual books written in the vernacular. See *Life*, ch. 26, no. 5; also below, note 8 and ch. 38, no. 1.

6. In the beginning she had the intention of writing about both the Our Father and the Hail Mary. See ch. 24, no. 2; ch. 42, no. 4.

7. Mt 11:12.

8. A new reference to the matter mentioned in note 5 of this chapter. One of the censors objected to the statement by commenting in the margin: "It seems here that she is reprimanding the Inquisitors who prohibited books on prayer." Teresa excluded the sentence from her second redaction and crossed it out in her first redaction.

9. In no. 5.

10. "Each of you is to remain in his cell or nearby day and night meditating on the law of the Lord and watching in prayer...." See *The Rule of Saint Albert*, eds. H. Clarke, O. Carm. and B. Edwards, O.C.D. (Aylesford: Carmelite Priory, 1973), 82-83.

CHAPTER 22

1. In her visit to Doña Luisa de La Cerda. See L 34.

2. The first redaction adds: "For, though being what I am, I would like to shout and argue with those who say mental prayer is not necessary."

3. The first redaction concludes: "Don't let anyone frighten you with these fears. Praise God, for he is all powerful and will not let them take mental prayer away from you. On the contrary, those who cannot pray vocally with this attention should realize that they aren't fulfilling their obligation. They must strive for this attention with every effort — if they want to pray with perfection — under pain of not doing what is required of the bride of so great a King. Beg him, daughters, to give me the grace to do what I am counseling you to do, for I fail very much in this matter. May His Majesty provide because of who he is."

CHAPTER 23

1. Allusion to Jn 4:14.

2. In ch. 19, no. 15.

3. Allusion to Mt 19:29.

4. Lk 11:9.

5. The first redaction concludes as follows: "This is absolutely true; I know it is so. If they don't find this is true, they shouldn't believe me in anything I say. Sisters, you already know it through experience; and, through the goodness of God, I can present you as witnesses. What has been said is good for those who are to come."

CHAPTER 24

1. She takes up once more the subject mentioned in ch. 19, no. 2 and also in ch. 21, no. 3.

2. In ch. 5, no. 5; ch. 17, no. 2; ch. 20, no. 1. See also L 13.13; 22.2; IC VI.7.12; F 5.1.

3. Mt 6:6.

4. Allusion to Lk 6:12.

5. In ch. 22, no. 8.

CHAPTER 25

1. A reference to *The Book of Her Life.* See also above, prologue, no. 4. In the *Life* she explains at length the nature of contemplation. See chs. 14-21 and chs. 22-31. See especially ch. 14, nos. 2, 6; ch. 18, no. 14.

2. In the first redaction this number reads quite differently: "It is all explained well in the book I mentioned I wrote, and thus there is no reason to deal with it here in any particular way. There, I said everything I knew. If God brings any among you to this state of contemplation — for, as I said, some of you are in it — you should strive to obtain that book after I die; it will mean a lot to you. Those of you who are not in this state will have no reason to do anything but struggle to carry out what is mentioned in this book I'm writing now, to make progress in as many ways as you can, and to use diligence; for the Lord will grant you the ability to do these things if you beg him for it and adopt the proper measures. As for the rest, the Lord himself will give it

and not deny it to anyone who reaches the end of the journey by fighting as has been said."

CHAPTER 26

1. In ch. 24, no. 2.
2. Sng 2:14.
3. Allusion to Ru 1:15.
4. The first redaction reads: "...grow accustomed to recalling that the Lord is present within you and to speaking with him often...."

CHAPTER 27

1. Mt 6:9.
2. The expressions "to enter within itself" and "to rise above itself" were current among writers of the time. As used here, the first refers to the act of interior recollection; the second to mystical prayer. In other places Teresa criticizes the theory which urges the soul to rise above itself through its own efforts. See L 22.1-7; IC IV.9.2, 6.
3. Allusion to Mt 24:35; Mk 13:31; Lk 21:33.
4. Allusion to Lk 15:11-32.
5. Allusion to Eph 3:15; 2 Pt 1:4.
6. Allusion to Jn 17:21; 10:90; 8:29.
7. One of the censors wrote in the margin: "I don't know where she got this." She could have read it in the *Flos Sanctorum* of her time. From the etymology *Bar-tholomaeus,* son of Ptolemaeus, it was deduced that the apostle Bartholemew was a descendant of the Ptolemies.
8. The first redaction reads: "And if something of this attitude is present in one of the nuns, don't consent to having her in the house; she is a Judas among the apostles. Do all you can to free yourselves from such bad company. And if you cannot do this, punish her with more severe penances than you would use for any other fault, until she recognizes that she doesn't deserve to be made from even a very wretched kind of mud. The good Jesus gives you a good Father. Let no one in this house speak

about any other father than the one your Spouse has given you."

CHAPTER 28

1. Mt 6:9.
2. A reference either to pseudo-Augustinian *Soliloquies*, ch. 31; or to the *Confessions*, X, ch. 27. See L 40.6.
3. Allusion to Ps 55:7.

CHAPTER 29

1. In ch. 28, no. 2.
2. Ps 34:19.
3. She takes up again the theme of ch. 28, nos. 2, 11-13, mentioned in the heading of this chapter.
4. Allusion to Jn 15:5.
5. She is probably alluding to *The Ascent of Mount Sion* by Bernardino de Laredo, trans. E. Allison Peers (London: Faber and Faber, 1950).

CHAPTER 30

1. Mt 26:39.
2. Mt 6:9-10.
3. In the revised manuscript of Toledo, Teresa states more specifically: "...the holy Roman Church."
4. In ch. 25, no. 1.
5. In the first redaction she adds the detail that this person was an elderly nun.

CHAPTER 31

1. In ch. 30, no. 6.
2. Lk 2:29.
3. Mt 17:4.
4. Teresa is speaking of herself. According to an annotation she made in the Toledo manuscript, the "great contemplative" she consulted was St. Francis Borgia, S.J.

5. Lk 18:19; actually "the publican would not even lift up his eyes to heaven."

6. The two faculties are the intellect and the memory. See no. 9. It is the will alone that is in the state of quiet. The intellect that is "so distracted" includes the imagination. In the ms. of Toledo above the word "intellect" Teresa wrote "or imagination." A little further on when speaking of paying no more attention to the intellect than to a madman, she wrote, in the ms. of Toledo, above the word "intellect," "or mind or imagination, for I don't know what it is." And again in no. 10 of the ms. of Toledo, to "that which torments the will is the intellect," she added "or imagination."

7. In no. 6.

8. In no. 4.

CHAPTER 32

1. In the first redaction this passage reads: "Don't be like some nuns that do nothing but promise; and since they don't keep anything, they say they didn't understand what they promised when they made profession. I believe this because it is easy to talk and difficult to act. And if they thought that words are equal to deeds, they certainly didn't understand. Make those who will profess vows here learn through a long trial period not to think their life will amount to words alone, without deeds also. So I want you to know whom you are dealing with, as they say, and what the good Jesus offers the Father through you and what you are giving when you pray that his will be done in you, for you are giving nothing else than that."

2. Mt 26:39.

3. In ch. 19.

4. In ch. 29, no. 4.

CHAPTER 33

1. In the preceding chapter.

2. In no. 1.

3. Mt 3:15.

4. In the Castilian version of the Our Father the order in the petition would literally be: "Give us our daily bread this day."

5. Mt 26:15.

CHAPTER 34

1. The first redaction contains some further thoughts: "In writing this I have felt the desire to know why, after the Lord said 'daily,' he then repeated by saying 'this day.' I want to tell you of my foolish reflections. If they are foolish, so be it because it is foolish enough of me to get involved in this explanation. But since we are learning about what we are asking for, let us think carefully about what it is so that, as I have said, we may appreciate its value and be thankful to him who with so much care is teaching us."

2. In the first redaction she went on more at length: "With regard to the unfortunate ones who will be condemned, who will not enjoy him in the next life, he did all he could for their profit and to be with them on 'this day' of this life to strengthen them. If they let themselves be conquered, it will not be his fault. And so to win consent from the Father, he reminds him that it will be for only a day."

3. Allusion to Ex 16:3-4.

4. In chs. 2 and 8.

5. Teresa is referring to herself. See L 90.14; ST 1.23.

6. Allusion to Lk 7:36-48. See *Life*, ch. 22, note 20 in *The Collected Works of St. Teresa of Avila*, 1: 296.

7. Allusion to Mt 9:20-22; Lk 8:49-44.

8. Allusion to Mt 20:22.

9. The first redaction adds: "reflect that this is a most advantageous hour for the soul, during which Jesus is very pleased if you keep him company. Take great care, daughters, not to lose it."

10. Here Teresa left out an interesting remark from the first redaction: "I don't say that you shouldn't recite vocal prayers (don't take me literally and say that I am dealing with contemplation — unless the Lord places you in it), but that if you recite the Our Father you should understand how truly you are present with him who taught it to you, kiss his feet in gratitude for it, and beg him not to leave you."

11. In the first redaction she was more explicit: "It is a wonderful comfort to see an image of our Lady or of some saint to whom we are devoted — how much more of Christ — and something that greatly awakens devotion and that I would like to see at every turn of my head and glance of my eyes."
12. In nos. 5, 10.

CHAPTER 35

1. In ch. 3, nos. 8-10.
2. Allusion to Lk 11:9.
3. The first redaction contains a further lament: "For it seems they want to cast him out of the world by tearing down sacred buildings, killing so many priests, profaning so many churches — even Christians sometimes go to church more with the intention of offending him than of worshiping him."
4. Allusion to Mt 8:25-26.

CHAPTER 36

1. Mt 6:12.
2. In the manuscript of Toledo Teresa wrote in the margin: "Blessed be God! Such a thing does not apply to this house. To say it does would be untrue because the one who has been prioress is the one who afterward humbles herself most. But I say this because it is so common in other monasteries that I fear the devil will tempt us in this way. I consider it so dangerous that, please God, no soul.... "
3. In no. 2.
4. In chs. 25 and 26.
5. In ch. 18.
6. In nos. 8-9.

CHAPTER 37

1. In the first redaction she alludes to her *Life*: "...for if I had not written about it elsewhere — and also so as not to go on at greater length, which would be a bother — a large book on prayer could be written.

2. In no. 2.

3. In the first redaction, instead of the preceding passage and the previous number, we read: "Blessed be his name forever and ever, amen! And I ask the Eternal Father through him to forgive my debts and great sins — for I have had no one nor anything to forgive, and every day I have something that needs to be forgiven — and give me grace so that one day I may have something to offer with my petition. That we might in some way appear to be sons of such a Father and brothers of such a Brother, Jesus taught us this sublime way of prayer and petitioned that we be angelic beings in this exile — provided that we strive with every effort to make our deeds conform to our words. We may thus know that if, as I mention, we do what we say, the Lord will not fail to accomplish what we ask, will give us his kingdom, and help with supernatural things (the prayer of quiet and perfect contemplation and the other favors the Lord grants us in such prayer in return for our efforts). Everything is small as far as what we can strive for and obtain on our own. But since this is what we ourselves can do, very certainly the Lord will help us because his Son asks this for us."

CHAPTER 38

1. In ch. 36, nos. 8-10.

2. Allusion to 2 Cor 11:14.

3. Allusion to 1 Cor 10:13.

4. The first redaction goes into more detail, but the Spanish of the passage is obscure and confusing. Here is an attempt at translation: "For without our realizing it, while it seems to us that we are proceeding safely, we cause ourselves to fall into a pit we cannot escape from. Although it may not always be a matter of a known mortal sin which would bring us to hell, it will weaken our legs along this road I began to tell you about — for I have not forgotten. Well you know how a person advances when he's bogged in a pit: his life ends there, and he will be doing enough if he doesn't keep from sinking lower, on into hell; he never improves. Since he doesn't improve, being there is of benefit neither to himself nor to others; rather, it does harm. For since the

pit is dug out, many others who go along the way can also fall into it. If he gets out and covers it over with dirt, he does no harm to himself or to others. But I tell you that this temptation is very dangerous; I know much about it through experience, and so I am able to tell you about it; although not as well as I should like.

The devil makes you think you are poor and makes even others who practice prayer think this of themselves. And he is somewhat right because you have promised poverty — orally, that is. I say orally, for it is impossible that, if with the heart we understand what we promise and then promise it, the devil could draw us for twenty years and even our whole lives into this temptation; 'impossible,' because we would see that we are deceiving the world and our own selves.

Well now, someone thinking he is poor or after having promised poverty will say: 'I don't want anything; I have this because I can't get along without it; the fact is I have to live in order to serve God. God wants us to care for these bodies.' The devil, like an angel, teaches a thousand different kinds of things here — for all these things are good — and so he makes the soul think it is already poor and has this virtue, that everything is accomplished. Now let us come to the test; for this deception of the devil is not recognized in any other way than by always checking carefully one's attitudes; and if care is taken a sign will be given very soon: the person has more income than he needs (I mean than he really needs, that if he can manage with one servant he not have three); someone brings a lawsuit against him for some of it, or a poor peasant fails to pay his rent, and the person becomes so disturbed and makes such a big issue of it that one would think he couldn't live without the money. He will say that he has to be a good administrator — for there is always some excuse. I don't say that he should give everything up but that he should strive to know whether what he is doing is good or not. For the truly poor person holds these things in so little esteem that, though for some reason he obtains them, they are never the cause of disturbance; he never thinks he will be in want. And if he does lack something, he doesn't care much; he considers this an accessory and not the main thing. Since he has higher thoughts, only reluctantly does he become involved with money.

If he is a religious, whether man or woman (for it is already verified that such a person is religious, at least should be), he may not have anything because sometimes nobody gives him anything. But if somebody gives him something, it's a wonder if he thinks it to be more than enough. He always likes to hold on to something. If he can have a habit made out of fine cloth he doesn't ask for one from rough cloth. He keeps some little things he can pawn or sell, even though they may be books; for if a sickness comes he will need more comfort than usual.

Sinner that I am! Here now; is that what you promised? Forget yourselves and surrender to God come what may. If you go about providing for the future, it would be better for you to have a fixed revenue. Even though this may be done without sin, it's good that we understand these imperfections so as to see that we are far from having this virtue; and we may then ask for it from God and strive for it. In thinking that we have it, we become careless and mistaken, which is worse. This also happens to us in regard to humility: it seems to us we don't want honor or that we couldn't care less about anything. The occasion arises in which a point of honor is at stake, and at once, in what you feel and do, you realize that you are not humble. For if something brings you more honor, you do not renounce it — nor do those we mentioned even who are poor in spirit — for the sake of growing more in humility. And, please God they will not go seeking out honor! And so often do some repeat that they don't want anything or care about anything that as a matter of fact they think this is so. Even the habit of saying it makes them believe it more."

5. Allusion to Mk 14:38-39; see also Mt 6:13.
6. In nos. 6-7.

CHAPTER 39

1. For Teresa's own experience in this matter see L 7.1, 11; 8.5.
2. In place of the above paragraphs the first redaction has the following: "Well be on guard, daughters, against some humble thoughts, caused by the devil, with their great disquiet over the seriousness of past sins, about whether I deserve to approach Communion or whether I have prepared myself well or about my unworthiness

to live with good people; things of this sort. When such thoughts come with quiet, calm, and delight, they should be esteemed because they bring self-knowledge. But if they come with agitation, disquiet, and oppression of soul, and if the mind cannot be quieted, believe that they are a temptation and don't consider yourselves humble; humility doesn't come in this way."

CHAPTER 40

1. In ch. 38, nos. 3-4.
2. She writes about it in ch. 41.
3. Allusion to Ps 89:50.
4. In ch. 16, nos. 6-8; ch. 25, nos. 1-5.
5. Teresa expressed herself more strongly in the first redaction: "As I say, then, this love is recognized when it is present, just as the love between a man and woman cannot be concealed; the more it is hidden the more it seems to reveal itself. However, since the love is for nothing but a worm, it doesn't even deserve the name 'love'; for it is founded on nothing — it's disgusting to make this comparison. And could one conceal a love so strong as is love of Cod, founded on such cement, having so much to love and so many reasons for loving? In sum, it is love and merits the name 'love,' for where it is present the vanities of the world must be shunned."
6. After "the bad inn lasts for only a night," the first redaction ends briefly with: "Let us praise God and always beseech him to keep us in his hands, and all sinners as well, and not lead us into these hidden temptations."

CHAPTER 41

1. The first redaction continues thus: "Now let us deal with the fear of God, although I feel badly about not speaking for a while of this love of the world, for I know it well — on account of my sins — and I should like to teach you about it so that you might free yourselves from it forever. But because I am getting off the subject I will have to let this go."
2. See ch. 40, note 2.

3. In ch. 40, no. 3; ch. 16, nos. 6-9.
4. In nos. 1,3.
5. In no. 3.
6. In nos. 5-6.
7. The first redaction has a richer conclusion: "Here you see how with these two virtues — love and fear of God — you can advance on this road with calm and not think that at every step you see a ditch you could fall into; that way you would never arrive. But since we cannot even know with certitude that we in truth have these two virtues that are necessary, the Lord, taking pity on us because we live in so uncertain a life and among so many temptations and dangers, teaching us to ask — and asking for us — says with good reason: *But deliver us from evil. Amen.*"

CHAPTER 42

1. Lk 22:15.
2. Allusion to 1 Jn 1:10.
3. In Phil 4:13.
4. Allusion to Mal 3:20.
5. She speaks at length of this fount of living water in ch. 19.
6. She is referring to *The Book of her Life.*

Glossary

The purpose of this glossary is to provide readers with help toward grasping some of the terms used in this work. Untrained in philosophy and theology, Teresa did not try to define her terms. This can prove frustrating to readers who want clear definitions. She reveals her understanding of the realities behind her words through her descriptions. When brought together under their respective entries, these descriptions help to clarify the meaning of the terms. Further nuances and developments important to the understanding of Teresa's lexicon are present in her other writings. This glossary is limited to *The Way of Perfection*. No attempt was made to be exhaustive, neither in the import of the words, nor in the references provided as mere examples. Further information may be gathered by consulting the index.

ABANDONMENT (TO GOD'S WILL). A free surrender of one's will to God (32.4). Christ is the model of abandonment; in the garden he manifested his own desire and fear, but then abandoned them to God (30.2). Great gain results from total abandonment to God's will, especially in fear of death and sickness (11.4; 32.4).

BODY. The external part of the human composite (body and soul) (31.2–3). Its senses or powers are mainly those of sight and hearing (28.5–6; 31.2; 34.12), which cannot on their own perceive the Lord, truly present in the Blessed Sacrament (34.5), or when he speaks to the heart (24.5). The more comforts the body receives, the more needs it discovers (11.2); its senses can be a source of distraction (28.5); thus it can become an enemy in the spiritual battle of this life (11.5). The body should be put to work for one's daily sustenance (34.4). In sickness it should be cared for, and compassion should be shown toward the sick (11.1). The devil tempts people toward bodily penances that can ruin their health (19.9–10). In the prayer of quiet the body experiences rest and delight (31.2–3). In rapture, awareness through the exterior senses is lost (32.12).

CHURCH. In the church, Christ walks and communes with us (1.3). Christians who do what is destructive to the church afflict Christ (1.3); it is like crucifying Christ again (1.2). The church needs preachers and the learned to defend and protect her (1.2); and those who will pray for her (1.3). The church is our Holy Mother (21.10). By believing what she holds we walk along a good path (21.10; 30.4).

CONTEMPLATION. A prayer that cannot be acquired (and is thus "supernatural") in which the Lord puts the soul at peace by his presence (31.2). It is a gift from the Lord (25.2). In it love is experienced without one's understanding how (25.2). The soul understands that without the noise of words the divine Master is teaching it by causing the faculties to stop their activity (25.2). An effort to gain the great virtues is a necessary preparation, although God may sometimes give the gift to sinners to draw them away from their sins (16.6). God will give the gift to those who prepare themselves although they should remain humble and detached regarding his gifts (17.7). Contemplation is perfect (pure) when all the faculties come to rest entirely in union with the Lord (28.7).

Vocal prayer is no obstacle to contemplation or even to perfect contemplation (30.7). Receiving the gift of perfect contemplation is like drinking directly from the fount of living water (32.9). To drink from this fount, we must give our wills to the Lord in everything (32.9–10). The effects of this perfect contemplation are humility, great love of God, detachment from being esteemed, and fortitude in the virtue of forgiving (36.8,11–13). Another effect is the acceptance of trials, temptations, persecutions, and struggles (38.1). Both the love and fear of God become very manifest (41.1). God is not content solely with bringing a soul to union; he begins to delight in it and reveal his secrets to it (32.12).

CONTEMPLATIVES. Used to designate only those whom God has brought to perfect contemplation, in whom he delights and to whom he reveals his secrets (32.12). God gives contemplatives trials that would be unendurable without the favors he gives them (18.1–2). They are courageous and determined to suffer (18.2). They must suffer as Christ did (18.5). Others should not give up trying to prepare themselves to be contemplatives, but leave the rest to the Lord (18.3,6). The deceptions and illusions the devil brings on contemplatives are not few (40.4). Being a contemplative is not necessary for salvation (17.2). Only in the next world will we know the value of delights and raptures and visions and other favors from the Lord; having them is an uncertain matter (18.7–8). What is more certain is the contemplative's readiness to drink from the chalice (18.6; 38.1).

DETACHMENT. Relinquishing what stands in the way of giving oneself to the All without reserve (8.1; 32.9); in it one embraces the Creator rather than the creature, cares not for what comes to an end but for eternal things (8.1; 32.9; 3.4). Outward detachment is necessary until one gains from the Lord a freedom in regard to the attachment (8.4; 10.1). The freedom from attachment gives one dominion over all creation (10.3). An aid to detachment is the thought of how quickly everything comes to an end (10.2). Along with humility, it is a virtue loved by Christ, who was never seen without it (10.3). Through the two virtues, one escapes from Egypt and finds the true manna (10.4). These two virtues cannot be present without love for others (16.2). The objects of detachment include ourselves, our bodies, and our honor (10.5; 12.5).

DETERMINATION. A firmness of resolve associated with perseverence (21.2). The object of it is to continue until reaching the end (21.2). The determination includes a resolve to die rather than give up the journey (20.2). The Lord highly favors those who have real determination (14.1). We must give ourselves to the Lord with the kind of determination with which he gives himself to us (16.9). It is important to begin with determination; the person who does so struggles more courageously (23.1; 23.5). The devil is afraid of determined souls, but will cause fears and never-ending obstacles to those who are changeable, unstable, and not strongly determined to persevere (23.4). The more determination we have not to commit an offense against God for any creature, the less confidence we have in ourselves and the more in God (41.4).

FAITH. Believing what the Lord says, the words coming from the mouth of Truth itself, and the truths he tells us (23.6; 28.1; 19.2). The Lord calls us to drink from the fount of living water; by faith we know of his goodness; in this respect he will not let us die of thirst (23.5). When we know this through experience, faith is awakened (30.3; 34.6; 28.1). It is a pity when faith is so unawakened that one does not understand fully the certainty of punishment and reward (30.3). Faith is strengthened by considering that in Communion the

Lord enters our house as truly as he did the house of the Pharisee, even though we don't see him with our bodily eyes and even when we don't feel devotion (34.6–7). Teresa had no doubt that miracles could be worked while the Lord was within her and that, as her guest, he would give her what she asked of him (34.8). The Lord found more faith in women than in men (3.7). You will be walking along a good path if we believe firmly what Holy Mother church holds (21.10).

FATHER (ETERNAL). A divine Person in the one God revealed by Jesus out of love for us and given to us by him as our Father also (27.1–2). Like the father of the prodigal son, the Eternal Father loves, pardons, sustains, and consoles us in our trials (27.1). He makes us his heirs with Jesus (27.2). He dwells in heaven (27.1; 28.1) and also as mighty King within the palace of our soul, where he is present in his majesty, power, and glory (27.5; 28.1). He takes his delight in Jesus (33.2). He consents to allow Jesus to remain every day with us in the Blessed Sacrament (33.2).

FIRE. A symbol for the love of God enkindled in the soul by the living water of contemplation (19.2–3). This water of contemplation makes the fire of God's love increase in the soul (19.3). This fire has its source in God, not in anything on earth, and cannot be extinguished by the water of earthly things when the fire is powerful (19.4; 40.4)). Earthly things can extinguish the fire when it is weak (19.4). There is another heavenly water given by God in prayer — the water of tears — that does not quench the heavenly fire of God's love but makes it grow (19.5). The fire of God's love cools and freezes all worldly attachments (19.5). It communicates itself to others, and wants to burn up the whole world (19.5). With contemplatives the fire shines brightly and so their love is clearly recognized (40.4).

In the prayer of recollection, the soul is well prepared for the enkindling of fire; blowing a little with the intellect can hasten the enkindling (28.8).

Fire is also a symbol for God; the soul will be warmed by approaching the fire; when one receives Communion, or makes a spiritual communion, and wants to get warm, it will stay warm for many hours afterward (35.1).

FOUNT (OF LIVING WATER). A symbol for Christ who gives living water, his own life. Drinking directly from the fount of living water is the equivalent of perfect contemplation (the prayer of union) (32.9). To drink of this fount, we must give ourselves entirely to the Lord so that in everything he may do his will in us (32.9). The road or way leading to this fount is prayer, especially the prayer of recollection (21.4; 28.5). The fount lies at the end of the way (42.4). The fount is an overflowing one; rivers stream from it, large and small, and little pools for children (beginners) (20.2). The Lord invited all to strive to come to this fount, and promised all that he would give them to drink if they do not falter on the way (19.15; 20.1).

GOD. The supreme Ruler of heaven and earth, the supreme Power, Goodness, and Wisdom, without beginning or end (22.6). As Creator of heaven and earth (6.3; 28.5), God sets forth a fathomless sea of marvels (22.6). The angels tremble before him (22.7). But God is not touchy, nor does he bother about trifles (23.3). God is everywhere, and where he is, there is heaven (28.2). In his grandeur he would fill a thousand worlds and many more, yet encloses himself in the soul; since God is love he adapts himself to our size and gradually enlarges our capacity so that we can receive what he wants to give (28.11–12). God never tires of giving (32.12). In his love for us he is faithful (15.5). We may commune with him as with a father, brother, lord, or spouse; he will teach us what to say

(28.3). In the one God is a plurality of persons, Father, Son, and Holy Spirit (27.7).

HOLY SPIRIT. He must be present between such a Son and such a Father (27.7). He enkindles the will and holds it bound with a very great love (27.7).

HOPE. Arises from a living faith concerning what God has kept in store for us in the kingdom of heaven (42.2). Those to whom God gives the kingdom here below have great hope of enjoying perpetually what is here given in sips (30.6). In the effects of the favors granted them by the Lord, they have the greatest hope that the Lord is pleased with them (37.4). The hope of being freed from the sufferings of purgatory by suffering on earth helps one to bear suffering willingly (40.10). God gives much to those who sincerely want to trust in him (29.3).

HUMILITY. It is not acquired by the intellect but by a clear perception that comprehends in a moment the truth about what a trifle we are and how very great God is (32.13; 39.15). The Lord lowered himself to give us an example of humility (12.6). One should always take the lowest place in conformity with the teaching and example of Christ (17.1). We only imitate his humility in some way, however much we may lower ourselves; on account of one's sins one always deserves less (13.3). Humility attracts the King from heaven as did that of the Blessed Virgin Mary (16.2). The more humility, the more one possesses God; there is no love without humility nor detachment without these two (16.2); the three bring inward and outward peace (4.4). Humility comprises a great readiness to be content with whatever the Lord may want to do with us and finding ourselves unworthy to be called his servants (17.6); is content with what is received (18.6); but doesn't refuse the King's favors (28.3). It is a measure of spiritual progress (12.6). A wonderful way to imitate the Lord's humility is to be silent at seeing oneself condemned without fault (15.1,2). There is more security in humility than in receiving spiritual delights (17.4). Humility does not disturb or disquiet or agitate; it comes with peace, delight, and calm (39.2).

JESUS CHRIST. The Son of God our Father, the Lord of the world, His Majesty, our Redeemer, Master, Friend, and Spouse (1.3; 27.1; 26.6). He is the Father's gift to us, has become one with us by sharing in our nature (34.2; 33.5). As risen, he wills to give to each of us his beauty, splendor, majesty, victory over evil, joy, and kingdom, but above all himself (26.4). He endured all the sufferings in his passion and death for love of us (26.5); he never fails anyone, he helps us in all trials, he may be found everywhere, he is always at our side (26.2); he dwells in the soul as in his palace, as our companion or friend, teaching us humbly and lovingly, always looking at us with love, submitting to us, providing for us (29.5,7; 26.1,3,4,10; 34.5). He has many methods of showing himself to the soul, through interior feelings and through other different ways (34.10). His words in the Gospels recollect the soul (21.3). He is present in the church (1.2,3,5). In the Blessed Sacrament he is just as truly present with us as when he walked in the world, and he may reveal himself to the eyes of the soul since our bodily eyes cannot delight in beholding him (34.2, 5, 6). No one is capable of seeing him in his glorified state; in the Blessed Sacrament he comes disguised (34.12) and gives us the manna and nourishment of his humanity (34.2). His will and the Father's were one (27.4; 33.2). The Father's will was done fully in him through trials, sorrows, injuries, persecutions, and death on a cross (32.6). He gives us light to follow his will in everything (18.10). He is the commander-in-chief of love whom we imitate through love (6.9). He is the fount of living waters (contemplation) (19.7,15). He calls all to drink from this fount (19.14–15).

LOVE:

FOR ONE ANOTHER. Three kinds are mentioned: excessive (4.6); mixed (4.12); and spiritual (4.12). The latter two are virtuous involving a friendship based on likeness (4.15). In excessive love, one is dominated by an affection based on natural graces (4.7). Virtuous love is directed toward helping one another love God more (4.6). Spiritual love is a virtuous love that does not stir our feelings of affection; mixed love is a virtuous love accompanied by feelings of affection (4.12). She decides not to discuss mixed love (7.7). Few have the purely spiritual love; it is characteristic of the highest perfection (6.1). It arises not from thinking or believing but from a clear experiential knowledge of Creator and creature (6.3). It understands that God is its origin (6.8). It entrusts to God the care of those from whom love is received (6.5). It has no self-interest, will strive to relieve others of work, rejoices and praises God for any increase of virtue it sees in the other (7.9), sets aside its own advantage for the other's sake (7.8); all it wants is to see the other rich with heavenly blessings (7.1–2). It would rather suffer a trial itself than see the other suffer it, but if it sees that the other grows spiritually through its trial it rejoices (7.3). It cannot be insincere with those who are loved (7.4). It knows how to suffer the fault of another and not be surprised and strives to practice better the opposite virtue (7.7). It helps very much to further peace in a community (7.9). It knows how to take recreation with others when needed (7.7). It becomes impassioned in its care to see the other make progress toward God and not turn back (7.1). It imitates the love that Jesus has for us (7.4). It is impossible to hide this love (40.7). We must strive to be affable, agreeable, and pleasing to those with whom we deal (41.7).

GOD'S LOVE FOR US. Since God loves us, he adapts himself to our size (28.11). In the first words of the Our Father, the Lord shows us the magnificent love he bears us (26.10; 27; 27.4). He teaches us how the love of his Father can be obtained (32.11). The Blessed Sacrament is a wonderful means given by Jesus to show the extreme of his love for us (33.1). He, seemingly, tells the Father that he is now ours and not to take him from us until the end of the world (33.4). He showed his love for us openly through many sufferings and, finally, by the shedding of his blood unto death for us (26.5; 40.7). In the love we have for God, we are certain that he loves us (40.5).

OUR LOVE FOR GOD. Out of love for God the nuns give up freedom and undergo trials, fasts, silence, enclosure, and service in choir (12.1). True love of God is completely free of earthly things and is the lord of all the elements of the world (19.4).

When the soul is enkindled in love it doesn't know how it loves (25.2). In the kingdom of heaven, everyone loves God, and the soul thinks of nothing else than loving him; it cannot cease loving him because it knows him (30.5). Whoever loves him much will be able to suffer much for him (32.7). An image of the One loved brings wonderful comfort (34.11). Those who truly love God, desire, favor, praise, and love every good; they join, favor, and defend good people (40.3). Those who love God dedicate their lives to learning how they might please him more (40.3). The genuine love of God cannot hide itself (40.3). With contemplatives, there is much love of God, or they wouldn't be contemplatives (40.4).

MEDITATION. Consists of reasoning with the intellect about the mysteries of the Lord's life and Passion, judgment, hell, our nothingness, and the many things we owe God (19.1). For those who can follow this method, it is a good path by means of which the Lord will draw them to the haven of light; when the intellect is thus bound one proceeds securely and peacefully (19.1). As with Teresa herself, many are unable to meditate without the use of a book (17.3). Others are unable to meditate, even with a book, and can only pray vocally (17.3). In contrast to contemplation, meditation may be undertaken without the virtues, as a basis for acquiring them (16.3).

MENTAL PRAYER. In mental prayer we speak to God, know and are aware that we are with him and speaking with him and understand who we are who dare speak with so great a Lord (25.3; 22.8). The time of prayer does not belong to me but is God's time (23.3). The Lord teaches many things to anyone who wants to be taught by him in prayer (6.3). It is a path, along which we journey, having a beginning, middle, and an end (19.2; 20.2–3). One must have a great determination to persevere (21.2). A great treasure is gained by traveling this road; consolation, in different ways, is never lacking along this path (20).

PERFECTION. The path to perfection is prayer (19.2; 20.2–3). Perfection has its roots in a clear experiential knowledge given by God of the nature of the Creator and of the creature, of the world that is eternal and that which is a dream (6.3). It requires the strength to be totally occupied in loving God (4.5). With this perfect love, one does not stop in the creature but praises the Creator for the creature (6.4). Persons who are perfect have trampled the good things and comforts offered by the world underfoot; they cannot tolerate having them apart from God (6.6); they are drawn by God to give up everything for him (12.5). Detachment is perfect when one embraces the Creator and cares not at all for the whole of creation; it includes all else required for perfection because the Lord then infuses the virtues (8.1). The perfect soul doesn't think of anything else but the Lord; nor, because it knows him, can it cease loving him (30.5). In what is for God's greater service, the perfect are so forgetful of self, they can't even believe that things usually felt as an affront are so in fact (36.10). Giving our wills to God and forgiving others are elements of perfection that everyone, in whatever state of life, can practice; there is a more and a less in the degree to which this is done, and so greater and less perfection; we must do what we can, the Lord receives everything (37.3). Those who have reached perfection do not ask the Lord to free them from trials or temptations or persecutions or struggles; this is a certain effect of the contemplation and favors given by the Lord (38.1).

QUIET (PRAYER OF). A form of prayer that we cannot procure through our own efforts (and thus "supernatural"); it is the beginning stage of contemplation (31.2,6; 30.7). In it the Lord puts the soul at peace by his presence (31.2). The soul understands, but not through the exterior senses, that it is now close to its God (31.2). It doesn't understand how it understands (31.2). The faculties, are in stillness, and wouldn't want to be busy with anything but this loving, but two of them are free to come and go, or even to think of who it is they are loving, while the will is held captive (31.3). Sometimes it seems that the quiet is not present in the intellect; the will should pay no more attention to it than to a madman (31.8–10). One gentle word from time to time will be enough work on the soul's part (31.8,10,13). Sometimes the will is held in that peace while the other faculties are free for acts in God's service; the active and contemplative lives are joined (31.4–5). In this prayer one is beginning to receive the kingdom (30.6; 31.3); in this rest one's strength for the journey is doubled (30.6; 31.2); in it the soul does not remember there is still more to desire (31.3).

RECOLLECTION (PRAYER OF). A method of prayer in which the soul collects its faculties and enters within to be with its God (28.4; 29.7). St. Augustine sought him in many places, but ultimately found him within himself (28.1). This recollection is not something supernatural, but something we can achieve ourselves with the help of God (29.4). All you need do is go into solitude and look at him within yourself;

or be present to the one with whom you speak in prayer (28.2; 29.5); or it can be practiced briefly in the midst of occupations (29.5,7). We must get used to saying vocal prayer with this recollection (29.6), being aware that we are with him, of what we are asking him, of his willingness to give to us, and how eagerly he remains with us (29.6). Meditation may also be carried out in this recollection (20.4). There are greater and lesser degrees of this recollection; The divine Master will come more quickly to teach the soul in this recollection and give it the prayer of quiet than he would through any other method it might use (28.4,7).

SACRAMENT (BLESSED). It is the food or manna of the Lord's humanity given for our nourishment that we might not die of hunger and might find consolation in him; we have the Person himself present (3.8; 34.2,12). Through this means we may offer the Father's Son many times in sacrifice that God may provide a remedy for us in our need, that no advance will be made in the disrespect shown in places where the Blessed Sacrament is present, that neither the sacraments be taken away nor churches destroyed (35.3–4; 3.8; 33.3). This heavenly food is a medicine even for bodily ills (34.6). In this sacrament, the Lord remains with us here in the world (just as truly as when he walked in the world) to help, encourage, and sustain us in doing the Father's will (34.1); but his presence is disguised in the accidents (appearances) of bread and wine, and one needs a strong, living faith (34.3,6–7).

SOUL. The interior part of the human composite (body and soul). It is like a rich palace of gold and precious stones in which dwells a King gracious enough to become its Father (28.9). The palace can be made beautiful through the virtues: the greater the virtues, the more resplendent the jewels (28.9). The Lord can enlarge this palace (28.12). We should empty the soul so that he may store or remove things as with his own property (28.12). In recollection the soul receives a supply of provisions to strengthen it against the body (28.6). In the prayer of quiet, satisfaction is felt in the soul (31.3). The soul is subject to many difficulties resulting from dwelling in the prison of the body (32.13). The soul has three *faculties* (or powers): intellect, memory, and will; it is wonderful when they are in accord (31.8).

INTELLECT (MIND; INTELLIGENCE). The power of understanding and reasoning. Many speak well but understand poorly (14.2). Many are unable to reason with the intellect in prayer (19.1). Some minds can concentrate and work methodically; others are scattered (19.1–2; 30.7). The prayer of recollection helps the intellect to be recollected (28.4). In contemplation, in a way very different from the way it understands through the exterior senses, the soul understands that it is close to its God (31.2).

MEMORY. The power of representing to the intellect what will occupy it; in the prayer of quiet our memories would not want to be occupied with anything else than who it is they are near (31.3).

WILL. The power of loving. The Holy Spirit enkindles the will and binds it with a very great love (27.7). In the prayer of quiet the will is held captive in this loving (31.3,9). Everything in this book is directed toward the surrender of our wills to God (32.9). Sometimes, the will may go about in the peace of the prayer of quiet for a day or two while the other two faculties are free (31.4). "Excessive" love gradually takes away the strength of will to be totally occupied in loving God (4.5). Our wills should be slaves to no one, save the One who bought us with his blood (4.8). The Lord begins to commune with the soul in so intimate a friendship that he gives it back its own will and his own besides (32.12). When the will is in the prayer of quiet it should pay no more attention to the intellect than to a madman (31.8).

EYES OF THE SOUL. The power of attending to, being aware of, or present to. Your eyes on your Spouse! (2.1). All harm comes from not keeping our eyes fixed on the Lord (16.11). The soul understands that it is close to God but not because it sees him with the eyes either of the body or soul (31.2). Let us ask the Eternal Father that we might so receive our heavenly bread that the Lord may reveal himself to the eyes of our soul and make himself thereby known since our bodily eyes cannot delight in beholding him (34.5).

IMAGINATION. The power of making a visible representations within ourselves, as when we picture to ourselves scenes from the Lord's Passion (34.8).

UNION (PRAYER OF). A "very supernatural" prayer in which the entire soul is engulfed in God; all the faculties are suspended (held bound) by God (31.10; 42.5). As one who never tires of giving, God begins to take delight in such a soul, reveal his secrets, and rejoice that it knows something of what he will give it; God even makes it lose the exterior senses in rapture so that nothing will occupy it (32.12). God takes joy in putting the soul in command and does what the soul asks since it does his will (32.12). The king of glory will not come to our soul if we do not make the effort to gain the great virtues (16.6). A refusal to forgive is a sure sign of the absence of this prayer of union; an effect of the prayer is a readiness to forgive offenders immediately and to remain on very good terms with them (36.12).

VOCAL PRAYER. Recitation of a prayer formula such as the Our Father or the Hail Mary (25.3); but we must refuse to be satisfied with merely pronouncing the words (24.2; 22.2). The mind and heart should be aware of what we are saying and to whom we are speaking (21.10; 24.5–6), centered on the one to whom the words are addressed (24.6). Vocal prayer, then, must not be separated from mental prayer (22.3). Many persons while praying vocally are raised by God to sublime contemplation (30.7; 25.1). In the liturgy, when in the Creed the words "and his kingdom will have no end," were said, it was almost always a special delight for Teresa (22.1); when we begin to recite the Hours consider whom we are going to speak with and who we are (22.3).

WATER (LIVING). Living water is a symbol for contemplation. By this living water the Lord brings us to the end of the journey without our understanding how (19.7). At the end of the journey the soul is engulfed in God and drinks abundantly from the fount (42.5). Water has three properties: it refreshes, cleanses, and satisfies (19.3.6.8). It does not let the heat from worldly things detain the soul (19.5). It leaves the soul bright and cleansed of all faults (19.6), but when the soul in meditation reasons with the intellect something from the road will stick to the soul (19.6). By means of this living water the Lord shows it in an instant more truths and gives clearer understanding of what everything is than we could have here below in many years (19.7). It takes away thirst, but there can never be too much; in giving much God increases the capacity of the soul to drink much (19.9).

Index

This index, by Regis Jordan, O.C.D., is based on the index compiled by the Discalced Carmelite nuns of Elysburg, Pennsylvania, for the second volume of the ICS Publications edition of The Collected Works of Saint Teresa of Avila. References to the text of The Way of Perfection are indicated by chapter number (in bold) and section number (in roman); thus "**26**.2" refers to section 2 of chapter 26. Other references are to page numbers.

517

Biblical Index

The Institute of Carmelite Studies promotes research and publication in the field of Carmelite spirituality. Its members are Discalced Carmelites, part of a Roman Catholic community—friars, nuns, and laity—who are heirs to the teaching and way of life of Teresa of Jesus and John of the Cross, men and women dedicated to contemplation and to ministry in the church and the world. Information concerning their way of life is available through local diocesan Vocation Offices, or from the Vocation Director's Office, 1525 Carmel Road, Hubertus, Wisconsin, 53033.